Fighting For Freedom In America

Memoir of a
"Schizophrenia"
and Mainstream
Cultural Delusions

D1291889

Clyde Dee

outskirtspress
DENVER, COLORADO

Outskirts Press, Inc.
http://www.outskirtspress.com

ISBN: 978-1-4787-5992-8

Outskirts Press and the "OP" logo are trademarks belonging to Outskirts Press, Inc.

PRINTED IN THE UNITED STATES OF AMERICA

Prologue: Point of No Return

I wake up. It's already seven o'clock. When I crawled into this bed, exhausted from lack of sleep, I must have felt a great deal safer. I stretch and my mind meanders to the subject of corruption: there's a mental flurry of familiar faces. School back east didn't prepare me for social work at the Norton Hotel in Seattle, Washington. I remember what it might mean if I'm in fact correct about the illegal conduct I've uncovered and anxiety stabs my stomach. My advocacy for the vulnerable may have put me at risk of incarceration—or worse. I remember the fear that has burned my brain for the past six weeks: that not a single guest would show up to honor me at my funeral. I pop up from the mattress.

On the road with three cylinders buzzing, I look for a branch of my bank and find one near the Washington-Oregon border. I withdraw the remaining five thousand dollars in my savings account. It might matter that I used a traceable credit card last night. From now on, I will operate on a cash-only basis. I put a small amount of cash in my wallet and hide the rest in a slit I made in the inseam of my jeans.

I stop at a mall and find an optical store where I order prescription sunglasses to disguise my face. I am relieved to see the sign that reads, "Eyeglasses ready in an hour."

After I order gold-rimmed shades, I walk down to the Kmart at the end of the mall and take a few minutes to shop for the road.

"Looks like you are going on a trip," says the clerk as she rings me up.

Her words alarm me.

I find a pay phone and call my credit card company. I inquire about the confidentiality of my records.

The person I talk to refuses to answer.

I decide I will not use my credit card again.

I collect my thoughts. The hour is nearly up. I head for the optical store with a burning feeling that I have already wasted too much time. When I find my glasses are not ready as promised, I fear the store is delaying on purpose. I am afraid cops will show up, so I cancel my order.

The clerk shrugs.

I break into a run on my way out to my car.

Adrenaline pulses as I drive. Last night I told my father I was heading for my cousin's in Colorado. In my gut, I sense going to see my cousin may be a mistake. I think my family might put me in a hospital. I can almost hear the phone activity going on between my relatives and my psychotherapist, Donna. In spite of the promise of confidentiality, I have a strong feeling Donna and my family have conspired over the past seven years to keep me submissive and sick.

I can't get away from the sense that I was somehow led into battle at the Norton through counterintelligence. It could have been my father who did this, or Big Brother Joe, my college friend who used to sell drugs. I now imagine that Big Brother Joe has all kinds of contacts. Maybe they worked in unison. My father supposedly lives off inheritance money—yet, mysteriously, he is always too busy to keep in contact. I suspect they are both supported by a lawless underworld they have concealed from me.

I head east on back roads where I will be harder to track. I pull over at a barbershop. Once inside, I tell the barber to shave my head. He shrugs as if he regrets he has no say in the matter and attacks my head with the razor.

Back on the road, patterns in the traffic convince me that I am being followed. One car turns around. It occurs to me that my bald-ass head isn't going to conceal anything when I'm driving the same car with the same license plates. Reflections of drivers on cell phones flash across the windshield and in my rearview mirrors. No matter how fast I drive, a pack of cars keeps following behind me.

I stop for an early dinner in a small Washington town and order a cheese sandwich and fries. The rural deli seems peaceful, but I don't dawdle.

At dusk I am still pushing the engine of my car, Cockyroach, to the hilt along a minor highway that shoots through the high-desert terrain of eastern Washington. I stop at a rest area, cut my engine and lights, and then watch the cars that have been following behind me pass into the distance. I sit about a minute and a half, and sure enough, a dark GMC SUV with a hunting light attached comes barreling into the rest area. It disappears down a dirt road out of the back of the parking lot.

I take my foot off the brake, roll over some dusty earth, and pump my clutch so that the engine starts. I slam on the gas.

Once I feel safe, I turn my headlights on. My pulse is pounding in my neck. I continue on at full throttle for about an hour.

When I reach Route 80, it appears I have shaken my followers. I pull over on the highway, cut my lights again, and wait. I see no one. It's close to eleven o'clock, and I am very tired. I stop for a Coke at a gas station where a man in uniform watches everybody intensely. I wonder if he is part of some rogue government agency that is conducting a manhunt.

Back on the highway I have a tail again....

The author would like to thank his parents for bearing the weight of the world for him in this manuscript; his instrumental aunt, his sister, and his ever-supportive wife; and, finally, three content editors who helped significantly.

CHAPTER **1**

WHEN I FIRST arrive in Seattle with five thousand dollars in the bank and three vague social contacts, it feels like an escape and a fresh start.

The public story I bring with me is simple: I moved out of my mom's South Jersey home my senior year of high school; I got tuition paid for me at a local commuter school and covered my own expenses; I worked my way through a graduate program in Counseling Psychology while I lived in Philadelphia; and I had planned to hike the Appalachian Trail until an injury delayed this and I decided to move to Seattle.

At twenty-eight, I have two public passions: backpacking, preferably in the mountains, and getting rejected in pursuit of an honest relationship. Since arriving in the city, I have grounded myself firmly in the Seattle Mountaineers and Quaker communities. For the first time in my life, I am surviving with just one job, a housing case manager at a large nonprofit with satellites throughout the city. In starting over again, I conceal that I come from a family where elite college experiences are the norm. I also know better than to reveal publically that I have taken a professional step downward, and that I have an off-beat history that impacts the way I experience things.

When my first birthday on the West Coast arrives, only my mother acknowledges it—with a pair of wrong-sized Teva sandals I can't return. That day, I get sick on the Mountaineers hike, repeatedly having to stop the caravan of cars to throw up. At Quaker Meeting the next day, I talk to a Thai woman named Lam. She has also recently moved to Seattle from the East Coast. She wears clothing that seems to be handed down to her from a junior high school geek. I like her mysterious beauty. I learn that she and her ex-husband have hiked the Appalachian Trail. She invites me to dinner.

Friday night, after a week of working through sickness and having my car break down in the rain, the thought of Buddhist soup motivates me to pull myself out of bed and make my way to Lam's house. She lives a short distance from me, on a road with no sidewalks and a clear outskirts feel. Lam's smile is cheerful, even though I barely have the energy to smile back.

We don't officially date; we just see a lot of each other. In contrast to Lam, who is centered and mindful, I am accustomed to spinning from activity to activity. Walking around a lake with me, she stops to experience the beauty of a leaf and discusses it in a way that doesn't bore me. Through what turns out to be a month of undiagnosed stomach pain and vomiting (just like the month that occured a year ago), spending time with someone who forces me to slow down is comforting.

After a few weeks, Lam tells me she participated in a protest in Thailand that resulted in a massacre. Although she didn't get shot, she stayed behind to nurse a monk who, amidst dead bodies, had refused to evacuate.

Not only is Lam full of compelling stories, she wants to learn from the things I've experienced. Whereas many of my friends and family don't honor the impoverished conditions I've experienced, Lam is curious. I tell her about college in Camden, New Jersey, where I made deliveries throughout the projects, coached baseball north of the Ben Franklin Bridge, and worked at the YMCA. I am able to express ways that I have been profoundly impacted by crossing the color lines in American ghettos.

Lam and I start attending free lectures in support of the upcoming November 30, 1999, WTO protest. I have always been too busy working to keep up with the news, let alone ponder the hypocrisies of the pro-business Clinton administration. Lam and I both feel we need to learn more about the issues, though we seem to share the same sociopolitical views.

Educating ourselves during that month leading up to the protest, we learn the GAP, Banana Republic, and Old Navy corporate conglomerate runs unfettered sweatshops where workers die from TB. In an unregulated world, companies avoid environmental regulations by moving production plants into poor countries where everyday people are desperate for opportunities to make money. Meanwhile, indigenous ways of life are lost as slums sprawl through cities and their residents endure horrific working conditions.

At one lecture, a professor from Argentina points out that changes to the world economy happen outside of democracy. American voters cannot choose a party or candidate who does not support the corporations. The world is run more by corporations than by nation-states as the inequality between the rich and the poor keeps expanding.

At one point, three weeks in, after I try to kiss Lam, she reports that in her culture kissing and cuddling are not the norm. I try to suspend feelings of rejection by telling myself Lam might be monk-like.

I have never been good at reading the hearts of women I date and have not yet picked up on the fact that Lam's husband was so physically abusive that she had to flee to Seattle and assume a new identity. Though deep down I selfishly struggle, I try to focus mostly on how global oppression exists to feed money-for-nothing to stockholders— all those young preppy Reaganites who mocked me in private school because I did not wear new, trendy clothing.

The Sunday before the protest, Lam asks me to take her to a lecture so we can meet a friend of hers. I feel sick but am too enamored not to drag myself across town to go with her.

I clutch my gut as we make our way to the lecture hall, an old brick building with a cramped feel. We all barely fit into the room. Next thing I know, an older man with a beard and long hair approaches us. He greets Lam with a smile and she smiles back, very warmly. He sweeps her away to a seat he has saved for her. Lam barely waves good-bye.

I feel taunted through the whole lecture. Lam only briefly touches base with me after the lecture to let me know she is leaving with her friend. We haven't even discussed meeting up on the day of the protest.

The incident does not fit with my view of mindful Lam. She seems to playing some kind of emotional game with me.

꒲꒲꒲

The next night, Monday, November 29, I stand alone on a downtown corner huddled in the rain among throngs of people, watching youth drumming on the back of plastic containers. I appreciate their energy but can't imagine mustering any of it for myself. My day visiting clients at community houses and apartment complexes has been long and hectic. My stomach pushes against my ribs as my lower back radiates pain up into my neck. I stand in darkness broken only by the streetlamp light reflecting wisps of rain. I am in a tempest of emotional hell.

The drumming continues: the escalating beat, the intensifying fervor.

We are to march through the city streets to surround the Kingdome. A little girl in yellow rubber boots, perhaps sensing the momentum of history in the making, stomps circles in the puddles while her mother cheers. Around me, the youth I observed earlier are now dancing in athletic swirls as if preparing to dive into mud puddles at soccer practice. I wish I could feel some of that energy.

Slowly the crowd starts to move.

Teams of union workers have come from all over the country. They cluster in packs with emblematic sweatshirts under their rain ponchos or trash bags. Bullhorn anthems and chants circulate through the drafty air.

I find myself next to a lone walker named Eric, and suddenly I have someone to talk to. He looks like a grown-up version of a boy who sings a flabby-chin soprano with his semi-parted brown hair, yet there is an air of real conviction in him. We stick together through the miles and chants, sharing snippets of what we've learned in preparation for this event. When he discovers I have arranged to stay in Capitol Hill at my coworker Michelle's apartment, he appears much more motivated to keep my acquaintance.

After the Kingdome has been surrounded numerous times, I have a sense this is a useless gesture. Throngs of people disperse in clusters for the night as if they agree with me. Bullhorns sound. I maneuver Eric and myself up the hill, going from cluster to cluster of protestors toward Michelle's place. En route, I look around. I see sights like hippies on homemade bicycles and tricycles. It is very festive in this manner.

I learn Eric and the multitude of the youth at the demonstration have been lucky to find a warehouse to sleep in. Many of the out-of-towners will literally be on the streets.

Up on Capitol Hill, Eric bumps into a young woman he knows. She has a certain confidence that suggests she enjoys social acceptance and has love in her life. When she reveals she and her friend are planning to sleep out on the street, I invite them to meet us in an hour to sleep at Michelle's.

Submerged for the hour in the warm world of a restaurant bar, Eric and I find the people who encircle us have questions and comments about the night's protest. While we wait for our food, Eric gets into a fairly intense discussion with the bartender, who supports us but is not fully informed. I listen, adding some talking points. I parrot things I have heard at the lectures, mixing them with my collegiate KRS-One/Marxian perspective. I am functioning much better than I usually do in a bar and cherish this.

Later, when Eric and I meet up with the two women, I hope I have met honest people who will respect Michelle's belongings. I behave in a watchful manner.

The next morning we are all up before the sun, getting the house in order with a certain adrenaline I really do not understand. The blocking of the convention center is soon to happen. I am most focused on the major protest event, a peaceful march throughout the city that starts near the space needle, but I accompany Eric downtown where he is to pick up a press pass. As we walk, a large green GMC SUV drives past with a machine gun sticking out the window. Eric and I look at each other but say nothing. It is clear we have entered new terrain.

I follow Eric to a hotel where he introduces me to a middle-class white couple who give him a video camera. They offer me some information about the green party in California, which I take, figuring my dad back east will be interested in it.

In spite of significant interpersonal distance from my father during my adulthood, I admire his solo environmental lobbying efforts. A part of me yearns to share his passion for these issues with him. Another part of me, however, is not the type to work with politically active older folk the way Eric is. I respect Eric for that, but I can still picture him as a ten-year-old singing soprano in a private-school choir.

Eric and I enter the downtown area to find floods of people. Eric disappears inside a nondescript storefront and comes back with his press pass. At the time I don't give any thought to the fact that the press pass makes him less likely to be arrested or beaten by the police.

Massive drumbeats suck me in as the crowd opens to the front of the convention center. People clad in scarves stand or kneel in lines, intent on blocking the police. I can hear rifle shots over the pounding drums and see clouds of smoke. I feel fear in my joints. I think of a younger Lam facing the bullets of repression.

A couple of hecklers walk up to the lines. One lady identifies herself as needing to get into the convention center to earn her pay. She starts screaming at a young white man.

"Why are you getting in the way of everyday working people?"

The man says something to her that I cannot hear.

The lady responds, still very loudly, "Well that may be so, but if you really believe in what you're doing, why not be a man about it and do something, instead of just standing there like a pansy and getting in my way?"

"Ma'am, I am trying to do something about it," the young man says.

The sudden sound of machine gun fire sputters in the distance. Someone comments that the bullets are rubber, but I can't help but think about the will it would take to stand there and be shot at short range. My throat burns from the challenge.

A young man shouts to those of us observing, "Come on, all of you—let's see who the real protesters are!"

I have always been taught it is right to walk away from a fight, but if others have to live and function in this fear, then why shouldn't I? If I am truly peaceful, I should be willing to take a beating without fighting back. Ideally, to me, that is the valor of peace.

Feeling like a soldier, I realize the drumming is coming from police platoons and the wafting smoke is tear gas. Running away to let others suffer for the pain of my convictions seems wrong. I step up; I step out. I join one of the lines.

As I do so, I get a memory flash of the first night at sleepaway camp watching wankers wiggle, waggle, and wave in the brisk night air. My peers had pushed me to join in a midnight skinny dip. I recall crying into my pillow that night; that senseless shame, that sadness, I could never describe to anyone.

Now inserted into a line, my decision to join in feels oddly liberating.

It doesn't take long for a brigade of police in their monstrous black riot gear to turn the corner and face us. I feel relief watching many in the crowd run, knowing I am going to stay put.

A fit and agile policeman violently kicks a man through his shield before he bends down and launches a tear-gas canister that skitters along the concrete and stops about two yards away from me.

I stay put with my fleece jacket over my nose until I can't breathe. Then I panic, lungs constricting, chemical agents overtaking my body. Suddenly, I am running. Then I drop to my knees in a dry heave.

Gasping like a fish on a hook, I am running again. I enter a courtyard in the convention center

Tactics enter my mind for the first time. If everyone gives up after witnessing one beating, the WTO conference will start on time and no one will know what these police in riot gear are doing to these struggling voices of our corrupted democracy. All that is visible to me through the smoke is the violence of repression.

When I can breathe again, such thoughts send me back to the line that has reformed in the space that the police have just cleared with tear gas. A very angry looking Asian woman stands next to me. She suddenly commands our line to turn around and sit down. A squad of police is coming straight for us. Because we have dropped to the ground, they are forced to stop and cannot beat us with their clubs. A cop pumps a white container. Another cop steps forward and sprays a powerful hose directly into my eyes while my glasses sit uselessly on my nose.

I try to stay put, but I cannot see. What is this that has just happened to me?

When I stand, the police use me to break through the line. By this time I am crying out. Some supportive protesters try to calm me.

Someone helps me lie down.

"You got sprayed with pepper spray," I hear a man say.

What is pepper spray?

"Will I be able to see again?" I yelp.

"It's okay," he says. "Lie back and try to open your eyes, and I'll flush them."

I cannot open my eyes, but I feel water on them.

"Relax," the man says.

"My eyes are still burning," I cry.

"Well," he says, "I only have so much water, but if you want me to, I'll flush them again for you."

Selfishly, I ask for more water.

"I didn't know they did stuff like that to us," I say.

"Relax," he says.

Catching only glimpses of a hazy world, I stumble back to a spot in the convention center plaza where I can be alone. After a long fifteen minutes, I can open my eyes again, but the pain continues. I don't feel I can take any more pain, so I lay low as the teargas billows like cigarette smoke just out of range.

It takes me half an hour to return to where the line has reformed. Eric is there. Masked people are now commanding the lines.

"I got some really good shots of violence over there." Eric points.

"That's where I got pepper-sprayed," I say.

Eric says nothing.

A tear gas canister lands near me again. This time I run.

Walking quickly now to the starting point of the peaceful march, I cannot settle down. Somehow, although I know I should, I cannot make sense of what has just happened. I am only able to wonder how long it will take me to get to the march. When I get to the stadium where the marchers are to collect, I am perplexed by the absence of a crowd.

I march for twenty minutes before I realize I started marching early. I turn back and march right into the middle of the crowd.

Once submerged within the mainstream, I start bumping into people I know from Quaker Meeting. I long to hear media stories; I want to be proud. Quaker friends supportively suggest that at least the meeting has been delayed by the protestors until sometime after noon. Additionally, news reports passing through the crowd suggest that leaders from African nations, via votes or speeches, are showing signs of being influenced by the demonstrators.

I bump into Walter and Nan, local friends of my father. Walter seems genuinely concerned for me. I can tell he doesn't himself believe in the confrontational protest at the convention center, but he is deeply disturbed by the police response. Having his ear and their company does quite a lot to help me center myself.

I do not see Lam. I stay with Walter and Nan. I walk and walk. Once the March snakes its way down town to the convention center, all signs of repression are gone. I am shocked. Cameras roll as we weave through the war zone, unaffected. Will anyone ever know my story? It seems like no one except Walter cares about what happened to me.

When I return home my apartment is empty. I turn on the news, which is consumed with the protest. There are no images of violent riot squads, only shots of protestors in black scarves trashing a Starbucks.

The city is under a curfew. The police are working hard to empty the streets so business can resume. As the rain pours down, images of protesters I'd seen run through my head and I can't believe they are still out there fighting.

When my roommate, Barry, comes home happy and safe, he marvels at the chaos on TV for a few moments, then calls his parents back east to assure them he is all right.

It hasn't even occurred to me to call my parents so they won't worry. I remember stopping in to see my mother before I set off to hike a 600-mile section of the Appalachian Trail. She barely even acknowledged me to say good-bye. I concluded the risks I was preparing to take on didn't matter to her.

Now, watching Barry in Seattle, I reflect on my own selfishness. Maybe my mom was too scared for me to express any emotion that day seven years ago. Maybe my parents are sitting on pins and needles waiting for my call. So I call both of them and leave messages.

They don't call back, and I never share with them what I've experienced.

The next day at work there is a buzz about the protests. I listen and laugh and try to keep my reactions limited to facial responses.

I complete the busy day with my weekly house meeting at a substance abuse house, located twenty minutes northeast from where the protest is still taking place. Stretched thin emotionally, I arrive at the meeting and head down a stairwell to fetch a woman from her room. Peering in and hearing the slur in her voice, I recall a conversation I had with one of this woman's peers who all but told me she had been using. Now the crisis is grossly apparent.

Before I can figure out how to smoothly kick a drunken woman into the street, she comes upstairs, curses out her peers in the living room, and storms out of the house toward her truck. I follow her. I tell her I have her license plate and will call the cops if she drives away. She curses me out. I run inside and call the police.

I figure with the protest raging the whole week, and the police dispatched to control the crowds, no one will respond to my tiny cry.

But my intervention works. The client comes back and sits on the porch, and within minutes, three policemen drop by.

There I am, thankful to the police for their help, when just a day ago they pepper-sprayed me.

The cops chat with me and decide the woman will go to the detox at a nearby hospital. This takes a long time, and I am extremely thankful to be in the mainstream and dry and indoors and not outside in the protest.

ﻝﻝﻝﻝ

At the rise of Quaker Meeting four sleepless nights later, I visit with Walter and Nan and their son, who invite me to a vigil for those jailed during the protest.

On our way south, Walter says he has not seen such harsh repression of a protest movement since the Civil Rights Protests in the early 1960s. This helps me feel my suffering has merit.

At the vigil, a constant stream of speakers bear witness to what they endured. One lady reports she and a group of protestors were locked in a cell and hosed down with pepper spray. Others talk about witnessing deprivations of food and health care. I have never really thought about what it means to be locked in a cell and deprived of freedom. Back east, a client had once told me gory details of his incarceration. Perhaps I had not taken him seriously because he was a paranoid schizophrenic; perhaps I just had faith in our justice system. If I had not experienced what I had at the protest, I probably wouldn't have believed the protesters or the paranoid schizophrenic. But now I am becoming a believer.

I am underdressed for the autumn chill. I tell myself I am dressed as warmly as the other protesters. I know many of them faced for days what I faced for only hours. I feel ashamed of my own fear and short-comings. I deal with this by denying myself the luxury of admitting I am cold. I shake. I am willing to shake for hours. I refuse blankets offered to me.

I talk to a woman who likewise identifies herself as a social work-er. We talk about how difficult it must be for people who have already been traumatized to endure these events. We talk through my shivers. I am, after all, a master's level clinician.

This protest movement will be hearing more from me.

CHAPTER **2**

I FIRST MEET Gail after another sleepless night, at 4:15 a.m. on a brisk post-WTO December morning. We head off in my car to a snowshoe course with the Mountaineers. The older man traveling with us brings up the WTO protest as an icebreaker. For some reason, Gail's presence reminds me to keep my radicalized emotions toned down a bit. Our traveling companion participated in the peaceful march, and we share experiences. It is well into the ride before I nervously try to get Gail to talk. She tells me she comes from Wisconsin and her father is a pharmacist. For some unexplained reason, it has taken her eight years to graduate college.

Gail is good at keeping up a conversation without letting others know too much. I don't counter with a lot of talk about myself—something I have been guilty of oh so many times in the past. We arrive at the most rustic ski resort I have ever seen. Clumps of scented pine trees mix with the cold, rolling hillsides. If not for the resort behind us, I would feel utterly astounded by the solitude.

We boot up and join the crew of approximately one hundred trainees on this, the first of numerous training courses required by the Mountaineers organization to join them on backcountry outings. I choose to remain with Gail rather than run off with more vigorous types.

I find the snow shoes versatile, and I take to climbing steep snow banks, trying not to be annoyed by the slow progression of the group as it caterpillars in and out of gullies.

By the time our leaders call for lunch, Gail and I have meandered together and are engaging in a casual conversation. She walks off a little ways and makes a seat for herself in the snow, leaving me alone. I sit and start to eat until courage grabs hold of me. I stand up, stride over, and make a seat next to her.

She seems to appreciate this.

A month later, Gail's plane gets delayed coming home from her Christmas vacation. I sit in the airport for over four hours without even the thought of abandoning her. First, the plane gets held up in Wisconsin. Then the plane has to be rerouted to Portland for some inexplicable reason. What concerns me most is the possibility that Gail might not thoroughly check the airport for me before taking a taxi home. Finally, at 1:30 a.m., I spot her walking through the lobby looking for me. We are both excited to see each other and she says, "I can't believe you waited for me."

I am barely able to sleep two hours that night before I have to get up for work, but it doesn't matter because I am in love. From this point on, Gail and I spend every night together, separating only when I work and on Sundays, when she studies and I go to Quaker Meeting.

One day, Gail gets a yeast infection and I accompany her to the ER. When she gives her information to triage, she sings my full name when asked for her emergency contact. I have always wanted to hear something like this. I am ecstatic!

꙳꙳꙳

After three months of zero conflict in our cohabitation, the day comes. She is in the other room and I pop my evening meds. We are preparing to eat the dinner we have cooked together, and she spots me from the kitchen. She excitedly asks me what I am doing. To Gail, I am almost too straight. I don't even drink.

I have feared this moment.

I sit down, put my elbow on the table and my hand over my

mouth. I tell her about going into the hospital in college, about depression, and about my medications.

She presses aggressively, wanting to know specifically what medications I take.

I explain that I take two medications for my depression, Wellbutrin and Lithium, and one for my Schizotypal Personality Disorder, Zyprexa.

She wants to know what Schizotypal Personality Disorder is. I explain I don't think the diagnosis is accurate because it involves things like magical thinking, which I really don't experience. I explain that Schizotypal Personality Disorder means I have a hard time getting along with other people although I really want to. That is true about me.

She looks at me hard and says, "Is that everything?"

I pause and gulp. I sense this isn't going well.

I tell her I had some problems in high school and had to move in with a friend, but that those were just family problems.

Gail walks into the other room and sits down. I wait about five minutes, then follow her and ask her if she is going to leave me.

"No," she says, "but I don't want you to hide this stuff from me anymore."

"Agreed," I say.

Within a week of telling Gail about the role of medication in my life, I start to struggle. When I consult her on the phone, Donna, my therapist of seven years, says she thinks I am going into another depression. This is horrible news. Past struggles run through my head. I am accustomed to family and girlfriends leaving me when I admit I am defective. It has happened to me twice before. I begin to dread Gail's inevitable departure. I start to have insomnia.

I deal with these wakeful hours by taking a walk while Gail sleeps. Sometimes I walk to a local 7-11 convenience store and talk with the lonely kid behind the counter. Other nights I stay up and talk to Gail's roommate, telling him trail stories about the months I covered a quarter of the Appalachian Trail.

One night, I leave Gail's side early and pass an open CD store on my journey. I go inside and find an old Clash CD, "Give 'Em Up Enough Rope," the CD that my oldest friend Gary used to play every morning when I first moved in with him in high school. When I play the CD, the old zing of the guitar brings me back to the familiar energy and confusion of my youth when I first lost the insulated life I had shared with my parents, my sense of home. It is part of a hard time in my life that I haven't revealed to Gail. The memories of my first recovery flood through my aching body, and I feel buoyed. The Clash helps me celebrate my losses.

When I crawl back into bed next to Gail, she awakens briefly and absently asks, "Are you all right, Clyde?"

I say, "Just fine, babe," and I mean it.

ᴊᴊᴊᴌ

At work, I get an opportunity to make a transition in employment that involves working at a housing project known throughout the city as the Norton Hotel. This is a low-income housing facility that enables people on the streets immediate access to Section 8 housing.

The massive Norton consists of two hundred apartments and takes up a whole block in the south of the city. It is attached to a well-known homeless shelter run by a different agency. The shelter takes up the second story of the building, and there are storefronts on the first level. The Norton itself occupies the top five floors of a seven story tower.

The Clinton administration particularly likes Pilgrim Housing Authority (PHA), which manages the Norton, because it represents the concept of privatizing public housing projects for profit. These facts all appeal to a sense of megalomania in me.

The day I get my orientation at the Norton, Cheryl, my manager, and two other managers from the nonprofit I work for take me out to a nearby Chinese restaurant. I am the only one of Cheryl's three employees willing to take on this project. Unlike my coworkers Charlie and Michelle, I am eager. I believe the work will fit with ghetto competencies I have gained through experience. Cheryl says going to the Norton is a step toward management. She also tells me in a sideways manner that I'll need to sleep with her in order to advance in the company. I don't know whether to take her literally, but I figure I have provided her with enough information for her to deduce that I don't give a shit about becoming a manager. In my mind, I am going down to the Norton because no one else is willing to go. I am going because I want to finally make a difference. I am going because I don't like working under Cheryl, and once free of the fetters she imposes on me I know I will be good at helping people. At the table with the teacup china and neatly folded napkins, I am careful not to exude managerial manners. I strive to keep myself fresh, authentic, and anything but a kiss-ass.

After the meal, we leave the restaurant and walk past the drug-dealing strip in front of the Norton. I feel as if some inexplicable eye is watching us. We enter the Norton, walking past a top-open Dutch door. With a managerial wave of the hand, Cheryl gets us past the security guard.

We take the elevator up one level to the mezzanine. A mechanical door opens to the right just as we get off. This door connects the Norton to the shelter, supposedly to let the handicapped into the shelter via the Norton's elevators. I will ultimately learn that this means the shelter has the ability to allow individuals to enter the building without going through the Norton's security guards.

Two men stand in the doorway on shelter turf, arms crossed like rappers, eyes glaring like owls.

We continue through a room with a pool table and a mural and into a large, open room with yellow cinderblock walls behind the elevator shaft. A few PHA employees invite us in through an open Dutch door against the back wall and we familiarize ourselves.

Darrell, the property manager, arrives. He is a friendly looking white guy who, in this context, could have been the poster child for the Gap clothing store. Along with Darrell, several PHA employees join us for our meeting. Among them is a tall and lanky man with neat braids named Jerry, the only maintenance worker. Jerry introduces himself as living in one of the many PHA housing complexes in South Seattle. He praises PHA and goes on his way.

In the meeting, Darrell takes a backseat to Tom, a very large Asian man wearing what appears to be a conservative prep-school uniform. Tom wears a Mason's medallion along with a PHA pin and introduces himself as a consultant. Despite his muscles, he is not intimidating, and he makes it clear that Contra, the company that runs the emergency shelter, is very upset about not being awarded the social services contract that is enabling me and a yet-to-be-chosen partner to start up services in the building. He suggests that the board of supervisors was just so impressed by the proposal Cheryl had written.

Five months into this position, I will hear a rumor that Tom is in fact a pimp. I will doubt that this is true.

Just two days before my first day of employment at the Norton, I go out with my coworker, Charlie, to catch a movie.

His response to Cheryl's request that he join me at the Norton is a clear "no way." We are unionized and going to the Norton is a risk. Going out with me tonight is perhaps his way of saying good-bye and wishing me well.

This outing fits in my schedule because Gail has requested some alone time with her sister, who is in town from Wisconsin.

When I call Gail from a payphone at the movie theater, she tells me we aren't going to get together later after the movie because she is breaking up with me.

I have been denying all the signs of this impending doom, though I have been seeing many for the past two months: Gail's recent move to a new community house, a house she claimed restricts visitation; missed snowshoe outings; the Saturday she didn't want to get together; her refusal to come on a Quaker retreat to meet my friends.

"But, Gail, we never fight; it's been so smooth the whole time!" I pointlessly plead.

Once I get off the phone, Charlie takes one look at me and stammers, "I'm going to give you space now." He disappears like he is a soldier who has just seen the Vietcong.

I had wanted to join Gail in the mainstream. My only sense of a safe home is now lost, yet again. All I have left is working at the Norton with all my heart and soul.

❧❧❧

My first day on the job, I catch the bus and start my ritual of listening to Rage Against the Machine and writing poetry during my morning ride to help me through my grief over Gail.

I arrive at the Norton and meet my partner, Eduardo, whose laid-back, streetwise aura I instantly like. Cheryl tells me she has had to strong-arm him into the position. I don't really think much about what that means.

This first morning, a steady stream of residents come in to meet us. We conduct interviews that are a cross between a psychosocial interview and a satisfaction survey. We interview a very intense man who has recently come off the streets. Though I have five and a half years' experience working with mentally ill adults, I am not used to someone so raw. That afternoon he attends our first community meeting with residents of the Norton. Since Eduardo isn't comfortable in front of groups and I am bigheaded about my "skills," I run the meeting.

As the meeting proceeds, the intense man, who has a tendency to rock, sits back thoughtfully in his chair. Then, with drama and urgency he pumps forward and says in a street drawl, "You've got to get back to school and get an education, son. You have no idea what you are getting into around here. Get back to school and get an education!"

I make it through the rest of the meeting, but as soon as the residents are gone I break out in tears and have to explain to Tom, Cheryl, and Eduardo that my girlfriend has just left me. Cheryl lets me go a little early as a show of support.

I will never see that intense resident again. I am too self-absorbed to even wonder why.

The rest of the week I am back at it with zest and vigor as our services to the Norton community begin to take form. As has always been my norm at any job I have ever worked, I stay at least one extra hour to make sure everything is in line. I am strong when it comes to keeping busy and this helps me get projects spinning. One thing that makes me effective is a profound respect for people in the mental health system. I feel I already know not to take people who are down on their luck for granted. I feel I have a naturally high tolerance for what emotional struggle can bring out in others.

After the second day of work Eduardo and I ride the bus home together. Though his face seems to say, "Lord, get me away from this white boy," I know not to be defensive. He is my partner in a war zone. I have to demonstrate that I am not as insulated as my skin might suggest. Stories I have from North Camden ghettos will help. I know we will bond eventually.

I soon discover I have access to a computer at the South Seattle branch of our company a few blocks from the Norton. I disappear there to write flyers. The first one I write advertises a Saturday outing with the residents. Before I can finish putting a copy on each of the Norton's seven elevator doors, I discover that all my work is being systematically removed and ripped to shreds.

There is no way to investigate. I don't give the act of hostility a thought. I respond by making multiple copies of every flyer I put up and splattering them on the walls and elevator doors of each floor. The flyers continue to disappear, but a few remain and the turnout for our meetings and events slowly grows until we have a steady follow-ing of about thirty percent of the building (sixty people).

۵۵۵

Early on, I receive an invitation from a company secretary and her husband, a company handyman, to come to dinner with Cheryl. I arrive with trepidation, barely knowing how to manage their display of pleasantries.

When Cheryl shows up, high on what I judge to be some kind of stimulant, I am shocked. She fakes niceties. Our hosts don't seem to mind.

As the evening wears on, Cheryl talks about growing up in a trailer park and eating spam. Our hosts relate similar experiences. I get the feeling Cheryl and our hosts have known each other since they were all very young.

When I get home, I call my ex-coworker, Michelle who confirms my suspicions that Cheryl has a cocaine habit. I have been aware that her ex-girlfriend, who works at the agency, has repeatedly showed up to work with black eyes, but now I have suspicions confirmed. I don't bother to talk with my therapist, Donna, or anyone else, about the fact I am working in a drug zone with a boss who has a cocaine habit. I just feel that I am right not to trust my two-faced boss who has forced me to evict people who deal substances out of their apartments.

CHAPTER 3

THE FIRST TRAUMA that hits me hard at the Norton involves a resident who identifies as a heroin addict. He has a likeable twangy street accent; he doesn't want to stay hooked on smack. He stops in frequently as we are just getting services up and running.

One day he comes to us, clearly high on heroin, and reports that two thugs are emptying his apartment. He doesn't know what to do.

Eduardo calls the police.

The man splits.

I go up to the man's room. The door is torn off its hinges, and two men I am not going to mess with are taking things out of the apartment. I go back downstairs.

Hours later, the police show up, look at the vacant apartment, and leave shortly thereafter. Their report, which I insist on seeing, reads simply that the resident is not present. They do not conduct a single interview.

I am more than willing to describe the two offenders. I am also not shy about protesting the fact that this resident has lost everything. Eduardo and Cheryl and Tom let me mouth off, but they aren't rattled.

Sure, I have heard of this type of thing happening, but I have never seen it so graphically acted out. As a social worker responsible for therapeutic healing, I feel angry at the police for abdicating their responsibility to protect the residents. How can I promote mental health and provide social services and support when incidents like this go unresolved?

I may think myself so ghetto competent; yet, I don't yet see (or respect) the true code of justice that rules the building.

Weeks later, I initiate a pool tournament in the mezzanine to encourage community members to come in and learn about us. It proceeds with little fanfare; I watch a pair of buffoonish street partners display amazing talent, sinking angular shot after angular shot. At one point, one of them breaks with his pretense of being developmentally disabled and casts a judgmental eye at me. The two of them clearly can work a good hustle. I am proud they have shared their sophisticated game with me.

Jerry, the PHA maintenance worker, also shows up to support my effort. He plays an elderly man named Mr. Smith who has recently quit his job as Jerry's part-time assistant. Mr. Smith, also is a resident of the building, and hangs out with us a great deal on the mezzanine. Cheryl and Eduardo have interpreted Mr. Smith's decision to quit as a political statement about our company's presence at the Norton. I don't see his mood swings as bearing a political message. Mr. Smith seems to just be a simple, good man

This tournament is the only time the pool table is used during my tenure at the building. In reality, in spite of my efforts, people aren't there to socialize over hobbies. The Norton is all about last resort survival!

After the game, Jerry and I discuss the state of the community bathroom on the mezzanine. At my suggestion, we call it the *Art Museum*, because it features smeared feces, puddles of piss, and spattering of waterlogged toilet paper on a daily basis.

Weeks plow forward. We visit the food bank on Tuesday, have our staff meeting with the property manager, Darrell, and the PHA staff on Wednesday, run the open community meeting with the residents on Thursday, serve dinner on Friday, and take residents on a community outing on Saturday.

During our Wednesday meetings, Darrell works to organize our efforts. He sends me out to make therapeutic contact with at-risk individuals. So, I start to see the often drunken, raging war veteran who cooks Crock-Pot slop and lets it sit for days and weeks, refusing to throw it out in spite of odorous mold. The man's existence consists of eating, walking, shopping for booze and food, and flashing back to the war.

I also meet an institutionalized old man who does an idle Parkinson's walk. I fix his toilet to gain rapport while he whistles and kisses the air to pay homage to my ass. The man reminds me of one of those odd, lonely men I encountered during adolescence, from whom I sensed erotic urgings.

Another mission involves checking in with a bald man who has a white Santa Claus beard and a hernia protruding from his gut. The first time I am alone with him, he flaps his arms and dances back and forth, clucking and exclaiming that he is a chicken. In an effort to be therapeutic, I simply smile at him and tell him, "Good job!"

Meanwhile, I come across a mainstream man who calls himself bipolar. He talks to me about having been up several nights in a row working on a book he is writing. He has a need to be heard about how unjust the system is to men accused of domestic violence. The laws do not protect men like him from false imprisonment.

I listen to him, read his writing, which is really quite good, and encourage him.

Several days later, when I go to return a packet of writing he left with me, he opens his door and a thug-like tattered male partner steps out and puts his arm around him. I turn to leave and hear a kiss puckered into the air.

I wonder what had happened to the mainstream man back in jail. I wonder if he feels trapped here. I think about how I, too, fancy myself a writer.

During our meetings with PHA staff, we report on the attendance at our community outings: trips to the park, to barbecues, to movies, to parades, to Native American powwows, and to natural sights. Some of these treks attract up to eight people.

The one community trip I lead by myself attracts all of one resident—a bearded, dark-skinned man named Mr. Wilson who looks like a street person with his bright red cotton ski cap and leather work gloves accentuating his several layers of outdated clothing. I take him across the Puget Sound on a ferry and struggle to not talk, which is what he seems to prefer. We arrive at the town of Bainbridge, far from the urban world of Seattle, and tool around. I offer to buy him lunch with our petty cash and he absolutely refuses as if this is a violation of his ethics.

The whole day, the only conversation I hear from my virtuous friend concerns his search for a fifty thousand dollar house and his claim he comes from Beverly Hills. I deem this concern and this claim to likely be the result of underlying delusions. I try hard not to see the small turnout as a sign of disrespect. I consider my time with Mr. Wilson a success, especially when he says, "Thanks, it was a nice vacation."

❧❧❧❧

At Quaker meeting, a man who lives at the Norton sometimes comes and speaks about the local "tent city," a homeless encampment, and the plight of the homeless. I have heard one or two Quakers talk condescendingly about this man. I start to feel akin to him, even though I don't live at the Norton and have never been homeless.

I think about the Quaker religion and its founder, George Fox, who wandered homeless, listening to voices for years before he found God. Fox started breaking into church services and directly challenging hypocrisy. In my mind, Fox's behavior is what the religion is based on.

I stand to speak.

"I've been thinking today about a person's right to privacy and inherent right to do what they think is in their best interest. I have a very hard time when communities of people get together and develop norms and mores that are built on excluding others. And it seems to me that an individual whose experience does not fit in with the community should not be so scrutinized. That, in my mind, is the very way that war starts. And that is what brings me to feel in conflict with the

Quaker practice of *eldering*: essentially overpowering an individual whose behavior is socially defined as inappropriate. It seems to me to be a real problem when we judge people without knowing them. I mean, we believe that there is that of God within everyone so how can we claim as a community that we can collectively judge someone as being in the wrong."

After I sit down I think about what I said. I normally speak with "uhs" and with stammering, but this speech came out the way I intended.

Another woman stands and defends the practicing of *eldering*.

I feel embarrassed, like she feels it is her duty to contain me. I try to remember she is only one member of the community.

During the social time after meeting, a man follows me and tries to tell me I am wrong. What I am seeing down at the Norton, in fact, is happening all over the community.

I listen to what he has to say without reply. I do not agree with him. Charles Bukowski's famous quote, documented in the movie Barfly, comes to mind: "No one suffers like the lower class!"

ﻌﻌﻌ

I meet a man named Will at the Seattle Mountaineers, and we start up a friendship. He is such an avid biker that he has taken off from his hometown in Maine and bike-backpacked across country. To him, Seattle is just a break on his tour of the US that will ultimately land him in Los Angeles, where he was born. He is one of the few I have met who can out-hike me. Coincidentally, we have established that we both attended the same College in some of the same years.

On the day of rock-scrambling training with the Seattle Mountaineers, Will and I buddy up.

When I complain about back pain, likely from an injury I sustained in the WTO protest, Will says, "Oh, come on, don't be a pussy!"

Late in the day, he tells me that when I went back to the car to get my sunglasses something was said about me.

I ask Will what was said.

Someone had said, "It's a shame because he is a really nice guy."

I wondered if Gail has spread rumors to others in the club about my medication or if I have just come off as crazy and disorganized that day. I really don't understand!

I don't like Will's competitiveness or the comment he had made about my back pain. In fact, my back hurts so bad I have given up on regular running and climbing at the rock gym so I can make these trips. I ice daily. But the fact that Will has not responded to the gossip makes him into something fairly rare for me: a male friend.

Over the Memorial Day weekend, the weekend before our final alpine scrambling training, I pick my friend Arthur up from back east at the airport. I met Arthur during a counseling internship during the third year of my master's program. He was Mr. Appropriate and excelled in the agency; as for me, I just barely got through the internship, battling what my therapist, Donna, helped me define as a major depression. We befriended each other after the internship was over, discovering a shared interest in hiking.

Still, Arthur is a bit peculiar. I fight a sinking suspicion he is going to be unsatisfied with my hosting skills just as I fight the fear he is interested in me only because he is closeted and gay.

In the early days of the visit, we go to a body piercing shop where I get my nose pierced. We go to the Ho Rainforest on the Olympic Peninsula and backpack. I pretend not to notice that I am exhausting him with strenuous activity. After work on Wednesday, I take him to a poetry reading at a coffee house and I recite a rap from Cool Moe Dee that I admire.

He frequently gets into long, phony conversations with women, even though he has a girlfriend, and it annoys me.

Arthur has my car to play with while I am at work and seems to make himself happy. Still, I don't trust his intentions.

When I get home one night, Arthur is still out with my car, doing some sightseeing, and my roommate, Barry, is throwing a party. I am introduced to some of Barry's reggae band members. Outside of his role as bass player in his band, Barry doesn't have a job, yet still he manages to be much more socially acceptable than I am.

The party lingers deep into the night.

When Arthur finally comes home, he gets into a chummy conversation with Barry and expresses appreciation for Barry's hosting skills.

I can't help but sense an odd agenda coming from Arthur. He is comparing me unfavorably to Barry. It is as if he has been trying to make me jealous the whole trip. It is as if he is expecting something from me I cannot provide.

The next day I take Arthur out to the San Juan Islands, but I am not very social with him. I write poetry on the ferry. I ride my rented bicycle ahead of his.

Three of my close male friends have made graphic passes at me. There are many others, like Arthur, who I simply am eternally suspicious of. When I can, I ignore the issue and maintain the relationship as if they are each just one more, flirty female supervisor.

I often wonder about why this repeatedly happens to me.

When Arthur finally leaves, I am relieved. I feel like I've gotten my life back.

I return to the Norton and learn that there has been a stabbing. I catch up with the victim, who looks like a junkie version of my friend Will with yellow hair and a red face. He wears an extremely low-quality jacket, clumpy cotton insides visible through the external maroon material.

He is grateful for my concern and says, "You're the first person who ever talked to me about this!" He continues to bleed out of his gut and fears the return of the offender, who is due back from jail any day now.

I am struck with brotherly love for him as if he is my friend Will himself.

Besides a little crack habit, is he really much different than Will?

Besides a failed marriage and an incarceration, is there any real difference between myself and the bipolar man?

CHAPTER 4

MY ACTIONS START to change as rage sets in: rage against drugs and violence, rage against my own insulated background, and rage against the lean, mean killing machine.

In the darkness after work, when I am not climbing with Will or preparing for my weekend trips with the Mountaineers, I take walks alone around the lake that I walked so often with Lam and Gail. The lake routine doesn't ground me the way it used to.

As I walk, I create vigilante rescue fantasies. I imagine coming upon a woman being raped. Maybe she is in a car being gang-banged; maybe she is a jogger being accosted. It doesn't matter. In my fantasy, I physically pump my body up and prepare to inter-vene. I beat back the boy inside who has been taught that fighting is wrong; I tell myself that doing nothing is the real evil. It doesn't matter to me if a knife or a gun is involved. It doesn't matter that I have no idea how to fight.

In early summer, I take part in planning a local International Monetary Fund protest. During the planning for the event, which happens to be near the Norton, I become vocal. I stand in opposition to two men who want to take over a bus and hold people hostage. I stop myself from suspecting that those hostage takers are undercover agents trying to infiltrate the movement. My therapist, Donna, would call that "paranoid."

At the end of the anti-IMF meeting, a hippie man asks for a ride home. He is solely responsible for artwork affiliated with the Political Penguins—a peaceful group that got a lot of publicity on the TV during the WTO Protest.

I have my car parked underneath the Norton on this select occasion and nonchalantly offer him a ride. I don't think to warn him he'll have to enter a PHA housing unit. When we walk in, I realize I am making a social faux pas. To make matters worse, we have to travel up to the fifth floor to get the keys to get down in the basement. The hippie man doesn't want to wait in the foyer, and once we are in the crowded elevator his hippie affect rapidly deteriorates.

In the elevator, a resident who has been drinking yells at me for bringing someone into the building after hours.

"What are you doing here? You guys think this is all fun and games! Do you even know what goes on here after hours? I can't believe it! You have no idea what kind of hell we're living in."

I dissolve into deep remorse for disrespecting residents and bringing in an outsider. I am in the midst of getting a street schooling I will not forget.

When I tell Eduardo about this incident the next day, he gets a kick out of it.

"Cabron muchacho," he says. "Well I guess you learned that that guy's idealism doesn't keep up with him in every neighborhood."

I smile at Eduardo's put down of the peacenik mentality. I love the conversations and camaraderie I have with Eduardo. He is comfortable enough with me to relax his fluent English. I really like his blended self. He seems to enjoy mentoring me about what it takes to survive in his culture.

One day, he explains that men in his culture don't necessarily have to fight, but they do have to stand up for themselves. He tells me of a time when someone took his soccer ball from him and he had to stand up for himself and get a handful of his amigos to come along with him.

"I used to be very passive," he tells me, "then I went through a stage when I raged about everything, enojada, man. And now I have fallen somewhere in between."

One day Eduardo tells me that, while he hasn't been sure about the job initially, he now knows he made the right choice. He is starting to feel whole again.

Eduardo spends hours talking with Andy, a Native American gangster from the Lenape tribe back east. Eduardo says Andy reminds him of an old friend.

"The thing about Andy," says Eduardo, "is that he feels mucho conflict about what he is doing. A large part of him wants to help youth live a better life, but he still engages in street shit: it no funciona, man, with his intentions."

Andy has told me, "Oh, when they came for me they had to bring an army with them; an army of *federales* just for one Red Injun." He has told me that he had been accustomed to staying in fine one-hundred-dollar-a-night-hotels.

I witness Andy on the strip right outside the Norton, feather in his long black hair as he engages in hustles with young African-American women, tooling around with strangers as though he is a poor actor in a B movie.

The Thursday before the IMF march, I go downtown to the library to get on the Internet and prepare for my speech. I do not, as many of the other event organizers boast, have access to a lot of literature. With the limited time I am allotted, I am only able to find government documents about the IMF that cast it as a philanthropic organization.

The day of the march, I skip Quaker Meeting, arrive downtown by bus an hour early, and practice the main points of my speech at a café, giving myself the liberty to freestyle with an occasional poetic rhyme. I plan to point out the linguistic links between words like, "Fiduciary Funds" (or fuck-you-ciary funds) and "Sovereign Arrears." I will hint that these linguistic coincidences seem to imply anal sex—not that there is anything wrong with anal sex, I will note, just that this alludes to a certain jailhouse mentality of the establishment.

For this protest, the SPD has assigned an escort, a begrudging policeman in a mustache and a warm coat zippered all the way up, whose motorcycle sinks a fair amount under his weight.

When the march stops in front of Niketown, the young woman who invited me to help organize the event gives a mediocre speech, pausing the march so that we block traffic for five to ten minutes. I think of the driving public's likely frustration and potential disenfranchisement and feel very embarrassed by this passive aggressive abuse of power.

When my speech comes, I start off using the government documents' positive perspective on the IMF. This pisses a fellow protester off to the point where she tries to grab the microphone away from me. I grip it tight and continue. Then I cut into government rhetoric in a way that exposes its exploitive nature of impoverishing many other nations.

My honest sense is that the majority of the crowd just tunes my punk-ass out; this is partially confirmed by one of my Quaker friends who has come to support the protest who later tells me he could not really hear what I was saying.

Not long after this, a group of our protesters get very angry with the police escorts, flailing arms, balling fists, spitting, and chanting: "pigs."

In college, the employment profile I completed suggested that I be a cop.

"Well, in a lot of ways you have a cop mentality," Big Brother Joe had said when I felt insulted by the suggestion.

❧❧❧

My favorite person at the Norton is a very sweet older African-American woman named Jane. Jane knows how to prove her points in ways that strike deep personal chords. She cannot join Norton residents on community outings because she is in great pain from Lou Gehrig's disease, but she is a leader.

The first day I meet Jane she has just finished seeing off her daughter, who is moving away. I imagine this as being incredibly painful for her, but she tells me she that she respects her daughter's decision, that she is proud, and that her daughter's freedom is what matters to her most. This is exactly what I needed to hear from my parents when I moved away. From this point on, what Jane is selling, I am buying.

When I had gone to the library to study for my IMF speech, I had taken with me a thick scrapbook of newspaper articles Jane had collected about PHA over the years. I Xeroxed the scrapbook for Jane and created a sizable binder. I put the binder on the shelf with books we were giving away in a book drive.

Two days later I had wondered minimally about who ended up removing it. I don't think much about it, though, because I don't want to be paranoid. I know what Donna would say.

I do many things to support Jane and the residents she most empathizes with. For example, Jane tells me about a secluded psychotic friend of hers who I go to visit.

"Get away from me cocksuckers!" he shrieks, as his belly bounces and rumbles from the aftershocks. When his belly finally becomes still, he shrieks the same thing again. I stand in his doorway stunned and listening for minutes until a very sweet voice emerges, "please come in, would you like some tea."

Noting the creepy décor of his room which features candles and empty bottles and cans, I call mobile services to make recommendations for how to help this man.

The expert comes, visits the man, and simply points out that the man has funny toes.

"Many *schizophrenics* have funny toes," he tells me.

He assures me nothing can be done to help this man.

I recognize Jane offers more support to the residents than the mental health experts who serve the Norton.

Jane tells me about Julie, who worked at the Norton years ago with Jewish Services before Pilgrim Housing Authority discontinued their contract. Jane speaks very highly of Julie and suggests I get together with her.

I feel attracted to Julie before I even meet her. When she shows up with a wedding band on her finger, her charm goes into hyperdrive.

Our stories spill over like Budweiser in the old commercials. Before long, Julie declares she is forming a coalition to save the Norton. When I am all ears, she suggests I attend an open meeting aimed at making providers known to each other. She also tells me she wants to send a press person in from the Seattle Times to interview me. She suggests I volunteer to speak "off the record."

The next day when I let the small female reporter in, she explains she wants to do an up-close-and-personal piece on the good residents of the Norton. She wants to move in undercover to bear witness. I look at her again and hesitate. I think of the dead bodies Jane talks about.

After my interview, I accompany her to her next interview with the war veteran. I am amused by the look of horror on her face, a look that clearly ruins any chance of an enlightened interview with the likes of him. One look at her judgmental eyes and the Veteran starts ranting in flashback.

When I get back to the office, Cheryl and Jerry are both enraged.

I am confused by the staff's instant ability to know when a reporter is in their midst. The reporter checks in with me before she leaves. In front of Eduardo, I explain the negative response on the part of my bosses as well as my shock and remorse over their reaction.

She reports her disappointment in not being able to find "the kind of people she was looking for." She isn't sure if or when the article will run.

Later in the afternoon, when I am on the computer down the street at the company office building, the site manager sees me and starts talking loudly with a colleague about what a shame it is the Norton gets bad press—a shame for the residents, really, because it takes away their dignity.

I figure it is easy to have that kind of perspective when you don't actually spend time up there. She is assuming the people I respect are pitiful, helpless objects who can't do any better. I walk away without acknowledging I heard anything.

Julie invites me to the monthly meeting of The Housing Coalition, an organization run by a well-known city activist named John Knox. Julie has a whole support network through her association with this organization for whom Pilgrim Housing Authority is one of the primary adversaries. John Knox seeks to expose the inadequacy of PHA's programs.

On the morning I plan to attend the meeting, Cheryl coincidentally brings in an unfriendly newspaper article about John Knox.

When I arrive at the meeting, a high administrator of Pilgrim Housing Authority coincidentally shows up as well. I have told only Eduardo about my intentions to attend the meeting. It appears to be a coincidence that PHA is present. If I let myself think PHA is sending someone to spy on me, I know that paranoia would apply!

John Knox's report on the Norton is primarily information I have given to Julie, including the tuberculosis scare we were told not to let residents know about.

When the concern is brought up that the night shift has an "immature-looking" security guard who carries a skateboard, I raise my hand and note there has been good progress with three hires of employees to man the front.

It bothers me that the activists are using class markers to disrespect a young man who is just trying to make it.

After the meeting, out with Julie's flock-of-females, I am the man of the hour. While Julie polishes up her young porcelain dolls to shine for me, I end up looking at her partner in the coalition, Kathy. She has a beautiful twinkle in her eye and sadness in her smile. She also has a masculine edge, but that doesn't bother me.

Kathy will be coming into the Norton to do some personal interviews. I figure I'll get a chance to pick her brain very soon.

On the ride south to the Norton the next morning, I tell Eduardo about the previous night and he laughs and states the obvious: "Yo, muchacho, you must have felt like the *man!*"

I laugh. "Yeah, I was basically like a fox in the chicken coop."

But I do not feel that a good woman like Julie, who would put her life on the line in the Norton, would purposely set me up with someone just so she could engage in a political battle with PHA. To me, that would really be a paranoid thought!

◢◢◢◢

On the day of the Gay Pride Parade, I pick up Will in my car at a local park as we plan to explore a couple of outdoor climbing walls. At the first wall, Will talks about the parade, inquiring with intensity where I sit on the issue. I present myself as nonjudgmental: I would have joined the parade just to support my friends at the Freedom Socialist party, but I'd rather climb.

"Ah, fucking faggots," says Will.

On the ride home, Will talks sadly about his adolescence growing up in Maine and presents himself as the kid who was clearly smart but just secluded. I listen intently but I do not reciprocate.

With a strange, unaccountable admiration for Will and his active lifestyle, I decide to squander a hundred dollars on a used bicycle because my back seems to tolerate this kind of exercise. I spend a full Monday biking tirelessly throughout the hills of Seattle, amazed with my newfound mobility. Between my growing familiarity with the bus system and the bike, I have no use for my car anymore except to drive to Alpine Scrambling outings.

I ride to work the next day, about fourteen miles. I use the climbing helmet that I need for my Alpine Scrambling course as my bike helmet and somehow get my hands on a bumper sticker that says "US Corporations run the Media." I also purchase a studded belt to complement used punk boots I have found at a thrift store and my nose ring. Punkish T-shirts, by this time, have replaced my ironed, button-down collar work shirts. Rage Against the Machine is going to be playing against the backdrop of the Republican Convention Protests in Los Angeles later this summer.

The news comes that Darrell is leaving his position at the Norton. A new manager named Bake will be taking over.

This is probably a good thing: Darrell just doesn't have any passion and nobody likes him. The new guy, Bake, seems young and focused, less indifferent.

During the transition of power, a Norton old-timer who speaks in loose associations comes up to me. He wants to know if I can fix the filter on his sink.

"Yes, Bake. We know that man well from Memphis Housing," he says when I arrive in his apartment. He is clear as a bell. "Bake the Snake, we call him. You can't get any more crooked than that!"

CHAPTER 5

BY MIDSUMMER, PART of me is aware that my radicalization is starting to spill out at work. Unprovoked by Donna, I seek out consultation with a Psychiatrist, whom I pay with pockets full of twenties. The Psychiatrist works for a reputable clinic even though she often forgets about appointments.

I am starting to question the battle I endure on a daily basis to get out of bed. In the seven years I've been on medication I've always struggled. Lithium, and especially Zyprexa, really knock me out. The psychiatrist and Donna suggest my trouble getting up is due to my depression. I acknowledge this.

So it is depression I notice on midsummer days. I find myself yearning for the support I had from my father in childhood. One time I call him straight from the Norton. My father, who often doesn't call me back, is beautiful in his ability to sense I am struggling. He touches me with words of encouragement as long as I am working hard.

Even Andy, the gangster Native American, notices my struggle and tries to help me. "You're having trouble getting your rhythm this morning," he says once. "Don't worry, it'll come. You just got to get your rhythm."

I feel incredibly supported by these words.

Andy is right; once I catch my rhythm, I feel better.

Mr. Wilson, the man I took to Bainbridge Island, has become a regular at my community meetings. He shows up late one night, requesting to use the phone to call his family. My bond with Mr. Wilson has grown as I demonstrate a knack of making sense of his disorganized talk. He smiles at me the way he did when he thanked me for the vacation.

Of course, if I use the phone to call home, I have to let Mr. Wilson do the same—and quite a phone call it is. I end up having to ask him three times to finish before he actually hangs up, and he is animated and clearly overjoyed by the contact with his family. When he is done, I research the area code. It really is Beverly Hills, according to Eduardo.

Later on, when I suggest to Mr. Wilson that he return to his family, he tells me he would only do this if he could do it on a US Navy ship. This is hard for me to make sense of.

The phone in our office suddenly rings. This is rare, because often the phone lines get crossed and our calls go to the resident in apartment 515. It is Julie calling to inform me Kathy is currently downstairs meeting with one of her clients at the well-known homeless café. I don't meet with Kathy long, but I do get an invite to her house-share. Saturday night, I cycle the mile and a half up to Kathy's house for the first time.

Kathy's place is large and owned by an ex-boyfriend of hers. His kid, her godson, lives there part-time. As Kathy explains these things to me, I make a note to myself that the kid is nowhere to be found.

Kathy feeds me. Everything in the house appears to be either a fruit or a vegetable. She has to dig into her godson's peanut butter to find something to fill me. I will learn that this diet is not just for show.

Kathy has returned from an afternoon run and bathed before I arrive. The toilet seat is clear plastic, revealing barbed wire inside. I love that.

We walk the household dogs. Her dog is named Lady and reportedly has a temper but has been trained to behave with a massive choke collar. I hold her roommate's younger dog, who yanks me around with his testosterone. We move through a dark and foggy night doing the regular talk about past relationships and experiences. She will be leaving to attend the University of Chicago for a master's program in sociology in three months.

Communicating with her is very easy and when I ascertain that she likes men too, I start to notice her eyes prance.

I get the invite up to her small, modest, and clean room where I learn she has a passion for reading poetry.

As evening presses into late-night hours we get increasingly comfortable. We end up in the downstairs hammock together. There is a kiss, a request to touch her boob—met with a firm "no," a response which I accept smoothly. As the hammock continues to swing, she soon mocks herself for saying "no." Things are clearly going to move very quickly.

The next morning, as I wait for her to come downstairs, I come across a newspaper clip on the wall. It is a picture of a white woman; a caption explains that this woman, a porn star, has finally achieved her sexual freedom by letting a record number of men penetrate her. I assume the clip is Kathy's and cannot begin to imagine why she would admire this woman. The porn star has such sad eyes.

Kathy's numerous tattoos and aggressiveness hadn't scared me off; now it is too late.

We separate. She has plans to go and get another tattoo and meet with a friend. She calls afterward and reports the new tattoo has been particularly painful. Then she reports the friend is John Knox, whom she admits having a bit of a crush on. She explains with some embarrassment that she has needed to confirm her friendship with John does not have the potential to become romantic. She apologizes.

Me, I am just glad to have a girlfriend who is Norton-friendly. I ignore the lump in my throat and say it is okay. When I get off the phone, I shrug it off by telling myself I cannot at all picture her with John Knox.

The next time I see her she shows me a blackbird burned into her back. I don't let myself think that the blackbird could be a sign of death, slavery, or torture as it sometimes is in literature—that would be paranoid.

Kathy's father is a mathematician and her mother is a stay-at-home mom. Though she has never actually been a homeless teenager, she has run with those who have been. Money has always been a strain.

On a movie date, she admits to having tried every drug once. She goes on to say she's lost many friends to the streets.

It is far easier to talk about my issues with Kathy than it was with Gail, especially after she tells me she was picked up running naked through the city streets during a bad acid trip. I drop pieces of my story that I wouldn't share with just anyone. I think she might be bipolar but refuse to inquire about labels. I know how it feels to be treated that way.

"Do you see the way they look at me?" she asks at one point, early on.

I haven't noticed.

"Everybody looks at me as if I am a freak!" she says.

Now I see the damage homophobia does. I can see how gender issues led her to run with street kids. Now homophobia, even my own, makes me angry.

When we go to the movies, Kathy goes right into the trash with anger to salvage wasted popcorn, and though I am a little taken aback at first, I understand where she is coming from and share it with her.

❧❧❧❧

When the next Housing Coalition Meeting rolls around, Cheryl makes it clear she does not want me going.

"Cheryl," I say, "I am very committed to my job here, but because I work here does not give you the right to tell me where I can and can't go in off hours. It also doesn't mean you can tell me who I can and can't make friends with."

Though Cheryl does not have a comeback, her concern does lead me to reveal I have been invited by Julie to a press conference that is being held by John Knox. I mention I still cannot understand the problem with pressuring PHA to invest more in our efforts. Cheryl ignores me and says she wants to come.

When we go to the press conference, Cheryl looks around, says she does not like what she sees, and ushers me away. I comply out of respect.

She takes me out to pizza. We sit at an outside table with a couple of slices. She says: "Well, Clyde, I like you, and I'd hate to lose you on this project. I hope none of your actions make us have to fire you."

"Go ahead and fire me if you can," I say. "I don't think you can!"

My words echo in my head. They are rash, tough, and I wonder a little bit about who I am becoming.

Not long after, Jane tells me Cheryl is keeping tabs on me. "You got to be careful about those women, Clyde. I'd recommend you start keeping a journal and keep track of everything they say. You know, Clyde, people end up dead in this building, four or five a year—you'll see. There will be no investigation and no explanation."

I don't take what Jane says very seriously.

But a week later, a resident ends up dead from a heroin overdose. I take it upon myself to plan a ceremony even though I have never officially met him. To me, he is a victim of the negligence of society and PHA. Cheryl supports the ceremony. Two of the man's relatives and about twenty of the residents, including Jane, show up. I lead the informal proceedings in which people can get up and express their feelings.

As the ceremony progresses, Andy, who is slender and meticulous, starts violently going after the food on the refreshment table and smacking his lips wildly. To people who don't know him, this out-of-character behavior may not seem like a big deal, but, to me, and perhaps some of the other residents, this appears to be a protest if not a threat.

♪♪♪♪

One Wednesday after work, I go to the new coffee shop I have been frequenting to read my poetry. I hear a young man who wants to be a journalist share stories he's written that champion the homeless. I approach him after the reading, and he brashly brushes me off.

Rolling with his probable dislike of my poetry, I ask him if he knows who I am. I tell him I work at the PHA Norton Hotel and have a beat on what really goes on in there. I feel like Al Pacino in *Donnie Brasco*. He softens.

I tell him about the recent death and how things like that are never investigated by the police. I tell him I have a strong sense an investigation could lead to something interesting.

That Friday, while we are serving dinner, Andy is exceedingly rude to Cheryl. I can't help but feel a little amused. She is no match for Andy. No one is.

He takes the feather out of his hair and holds it in his hand. He points it at me and says, "You have to be careful, man; some of the people you work with at that company of yours are less than honorable."

He tips his head toward Cheryl and laughs.

I make a point of going up to Andy after the encounter.

He laughs and says, "Curiosity killed the cat!"

"Doesn't the cat have nine lives, though?" I blurt.

The words have leapt from my mouth. Who is this person I am becoming?

Sleeping with Kathy that night makes me feel safer. But I wake up the next morning feeling I have done something horribly wrong. I have dreamt I slept with a Norton resident. In the dream, I did it, wondering why I was doing it. The resident has no appeal to me. I am terrified that I have broken the law and ethics of my profession. I lie in bed next to Kathy trying to convince myself this has not happened, that I am still an ethical counselor.

❧❧❧❧

When my mother comes for a visit, I offer to host her and my stepfather on my futon but they choose to stay in a hotel near the UW Campus. This makes my life significantly easier, but I never thank them. I also do not take time off time from work for their stay; I only have two weeks off a year and I am planning a week away with my sister in Mexico.

I start out enthusiastic to have them over for dinner after work, late dinner though it may be. I invite Kathy. She comes to the door while I am cooking and meets my mother and my stepfather, Dick Wigglesworth, who are seated in the living room. I can tell right away my mother does not approve of Kathy. My mom eyes Kathy's multiple piercings in her ears, her tattooed armband, the uncharacteristic housedress, and her funky thrift-store shoes. My mom looks like she is the public judging Kathy as a freak. But if Kathy sees what I see, she does not let on in anyway. She makes small talk and pleasantries with both my mom and Dick throughout the meal.

I sit mute during the evening chatter and reflect on how staying silent is always my modus operandi, not only at family gatherings, but also at bars. I am tired from my day and tired from cooking. Additionally I don't notice any questions or attention. After dinner, I start working on the dishes while Kathy sits with my mother and Dick.

Then, suddenly, *rage* is upon me. I start banging the dishes.

Kathy notices my anger, comes over, and asks if I am okay. My mother and Dick sit without concern in the other room.

I am grateful to Kathy, but admittedly fuming.

I am thinking about how when I came home for Christmas, my mother was still sleeping when I dragged myself in at 9am. I am thinking about how I always end up being the one to do the dishes for them when I visit. There are so many examples of times my efforts go unrecognized by her.

That Sunday I take my Mother and Dick Wigglesworth hiking in the Cascades. I pick a very short, six-mile round-trip hike up to an alpine lake. Without giving it much thought, I hike ahead. The trail is mostly level, but as they catch up to me at the end I can see they are struggling. On the way back, I slow up to play host. Dick Wigglesworth admits to me he has never been in so much pain.

I talk with him one on one for the first time in my life.

I imagine I know how Dick Wigglesworth feels being left behind, but he isn't complaining. This is something I can admire, really.

My mother, on the other hand, is standoffish to my efforts and walks ahead.

As I walk with Dick, I remember the bleakness of home visits I engaged in from the Eating Disorders Unit I landed in when I was hospitalized as a teen. It is true, my mother was spending a portion of the family nest egg, (I presumed it to be my college money,) to keep me locked up, but she didn't show respect for the pains of my forced, 6,000-calorie routine. On visits home, I would go to the bathroom, finger her razor, and contemplate cutting myself. There was the time she expected me to eat two hours before I was scheduled to because her boyfriend was hungry at an odd hour. When I got out of that hospital, I lived with my friend, Gary, until I couldn't take it anymore and let my weight drop, forcing another hospitalization. At that time, I'd gone so far as to sneak into the cafeteria at the school I attended and spy on my mother as she ate her lunch with the other faculty members. Her face held not a hint of emotion, concern, or remorse. I fumed. I decided that I would have no mercy. I would avoid home as much as possible.

Much as my mom does by walking ahead and refusing to forgive my rudeness, I follow suit and retaliate the rest of the trip: paddling way ahead when she rents us kayaks on the Puget Sound, taking her to a homeless restaurant to teach her and Dick Wigglesworth a lesson about the streets. I fail miserably at playing the good host on all fronts.

☽☽☽

Julie and Kathy set up an interview for me for a position at their agency. If hired, I will provide harm-reduction assistance to addicts on the streets. Julie's and Kathy's endorsements make the job seem like a surer thing than any job I've previously interviewed for.

I show up for the interview on Monday on my bicycle with my interview suit rolled up in a gentle ball in my backpack. I come in off the streets wearing my comfortable punk getup and am aware of the contrast. I figure the dichotomy of my dress fits the dichotomy of my existence.

Of course, Kathy opts out of the interview. She meets me in the lobby and wishes me luck. The others are casually dressed, seated at a table that is varnished with executive power. Julie and her coworkers are welcoming. I believe I am leaving the Norton behind.

When asked whether I feel there is any use talking to a client when the client is high, I think about the contexts I've been in at the Norton and about the job I'll be doing. It is a hard question and I am concerned about the length of my pause. I don't know what it feels like to be drunk or high. I say yes, there are some occasions when I would consider doing so in order to build rapport.

When Kathy later breaks it to me that I did not get the job, the downpour of negative thoughts leaves me stunned. I haven't considered failure possible.

When I turn to Donna with these concerns, during my weekly phone session, she doesn't offer any support. She remains mute.

I cannot understand why so many people see me as a reject.

"That's not fair, Clyde!" Kathy exclaims when I reach out to her.

I back off with my emotional need but I can't help but press her for more of an explanation. I have a strong sense there is something she isn't telling me. She offers a half-hearted explanation—her boss is a bit of an elitist and said I didn't have any hobbies, interests, or social life outside of work.

I think about my answers. Having no hobbies or interests doesn't make sense as a reason for denying me the job.

Clearly she feels she cannot tell me the real reason for my rejection.

Kathy has a way of revealing her life in tiny dots of metaphor. It is left to me to connect them.

One dot Kathy reveals to me is that an early boyfriend who ran the streets with her performed a ritual of setting a knife on the dresser every time he expected to have sex with her. I can sense how this blurred the lines of consensual sex for her and feel proud that I am a man who is safe enough to keep these issues out of our relationship.

However, I am never assertive enough to inquire about the significance of the blackbird on her back or the porn star on her wall.

Kathy does invite me to have dinner with her sister—the "normal one"— to seemingly make amends for the fact I didn't get hired. Later that night I share one of my favorite movies with Kathy: *Happiness* by Todd Solondz. I explain that I often feel like the main character in the film, a female who is constantly beat up on behind her back by her family members, teased by phonies in her stale, middle-class New Jersey world, and taken advantage of by the immigrant men she wants to help out.

Kathy asks me, "Why, Clyde? Why are you just like that woman?"

I sense she knows something about the world I do not, as though she wants to help me find the answer, but cannot spell it out for me.

♪♪♪

On our climbing exploits, Will and I find a wall we can each bike to after work. It is a round building, haphazardly bricked with smooth, semi-rectangular lava rock, leaving a plethora of footholds and handholds. The actual climbing is easy, but the wall gives us the opportunity to creatively plot our course and build our strength and stamina. Will always laps me as we make our way along the building horizontally.

One day, feeling a little enthralled with the anonymity of being with a new friend and in a new place, I, in my punk gear, make a phony comment about smoking pot to make it seem like I am experienced. Will is immediately on my back.

"Oh, don't bullshit, Clyde; I'll bet you have never even smoked a joint in your life."

It makes me wonder how visible my personality and my past are to my coworkers and the residents at the Norton.

CHAPTER 6

EARLY ONE MORNING, in spite of nagging back pain, I accompany four seasoned alpine scrambling veterans to a trailhead where we meet up with another young man. He is my age and very obviously depressed, grunting and groaning. The five of us have a mile and a half of unexpected road to walk due to a road closure, and he lags the whole way before we even start the ascent. I can see depression is holding him back as it often holds me back. Almost every day, I feel like shit, but I push through it. There is no way I am going to falter on the ascent of that mountain the way he is.

Thankfully, the young man turns back. The other men eye me when he leaves. I know I have a bit of a flat affect, and, no doubt, I, too, look depressed.

Maybe that's why I didn't get the job with the harm reduction clinic, I think.

Back at the parking lot, the group members follow each other in their cars on the way out of the maze of back roads. Then, I get a flat tire. Their taillights trail off in the distance, and I am left alone. As I change my tire, I suddenly feel extremely sick to my stomach. I run to the bushes and let go of everything I ate during the ascent.

I get home at midnight. I have the next day to recover, but I force myself to stay busy. Every day I have to stay busy. Otherwise, depression will take me over just like it took over my nemesis on the mountain.

❧❧❧❧

At the Norton, Sweet Jane is outraged by Bake the Snake, the new property manager. He shuts her out of the office and will not listen to her concerns. When I mention to Julie that PHA is keeping Jane out of the office, she dismisses this as meaningless and notes Jane can be very paranoid.

But I am starting to notice that the vulnerable mentally ill come my way for help, and that the crooked residents who pick on them go to Bake.

Bake initiates "knock and talks" with the police. The police wander through the building, knocking on doors and talking to residents. The purpose is to intervene in illegal happenings. I think it is a very good idea at first. But when the knock and talks result in vulnerable and de-lusional residents going to jail instead of criminally minded ones who actually do sell drugs, I start to question Bake.

In our weekly meeting, I point out that the people who are punished by the "knock and talks" are being threatened or lured into allowing the established drug dealers to operate out of their apartments. Residents have told me this is going on, and even Eduardo has hinted that he is aware of it.

Bake looks at me with intense eyes and says, "Well, that may be, but when they let that happen they know what they're doing is wrong and they still deserve to be punished."

I am struck with the memory of a letter I received from my oldest friend Gary dissclosing that he was dealing marijuanna down the shore. I, who was living at a sleepaway camp, wrote back and chastised him. I told him poor people in Belize end up dead in ditches over that bullshit.

Two years prior I had spent the summer in Belize. I was invited by the school principle to work on his sugar cane fields with the refugees. It was there I learned a refugee caretaker was once found dead in a ditch. I made a decision that summer I would never have anything to do with marijuana.

Gary replied to my concerns by saying that he was not trying to oppress people in Central America. He loved me, he wrote, and he was just trying to get high.

A week later, still stubborn in the meeting, I protest again about Bake's "knock and talks."

Cheryl sits there numbly, looking phony and high.

Bake tells me, "Look, some people believe that drugs are good and that people in this city have a right to do them."

I stare back as he shoots me a threatening look. Everybody in the room has heard what he said but they all are ignoring it.

Bake responds to my insolence by declaring that a number of the vulnerable residents whom I work with, many of who are Jane's friends, are now going to be targeted for eviction.

Bake glares at me again.

It is the new rule of law in the building.

I don't think this is paranoia. Even Eduardo acknowledges that it is real, but he stays cool about it in ways that I can't.

ᔥᔥᔥ

These days I cannot hold a meeting without getting what seems to be a coordinated evil eye from certain male residents. Even in my routine interactions at the Norton, I am getting more glares than I used to. Some residents, including ones I was once friendly with, halt in my presence and glare.

One morning, Jerry comes up to me.

I'd just had a slew of dirty looks.

Jerry smiles at me knowingly and said in an impressed, slightly high-pitched voice, "You're still here?"

I don't even know what Jerry knows about what I am experiencing, but I love Jerry and all his ancestors from this point forth because they validate me.

I talk to Will one night about the dirty looks I am getting from residents who I imagine to be representing the "drug dealers."

Will sounds like a mental health professional when he says, "So what's your evidence, Clyde?"

"What do you mean?"

"What's your evidence, Clyde? How can you prove to me that all this is not just a figment of your imagination?"

"You don't understand," I say, "all this stuff happens through insinuation. None of it is out in the open. It's indirect and has been like that for a long time. It is just starting to wear on me."

❧❧❧❧

The bald man with the Santa Claus beard and the hernia gut comes to the mezzanine and says he needs to speak to me urgently. Once secluded with me in the office he says, "Guess what, one time I killed a man!"

Though I feel numb and overwhelmed, I just look at him as though I hear this kind of info every day.

He looks impressed by my indifference.

I visit Andy in his room and turn my back to him at his request and suddenly my body goes numb. It is as if I can feel vibes of wild hostility coming out of him. Is Andy truly trying to scare me? If I were a fellow prisoner, would I get shanked for being so insolent?

Later, Andy comes in off the street and tells me that he likes me and has lawyers backing him up. He says if I ever need any help, he'll be there for me. Intuitively I trust him when he says this.

One day, Mr. Smith says as I am leaving, "Are you going to one of those meetings I know you go to?"

The Socialist meeting I am heading for has nothing to do with the Norton.

I doubt that he knows my personal business outside the Norton.

At some point, however, I discover Julie is friendly with Mr. Smith. She says he is like family to her. Around this time, out of the blue, while he and I are travelling together on the elevator, Mr. Smith's face fills with rage. He glares and then storms away from me in the elevator, leaving the other people in the elevator to ask me, "Clyde, what was that about?"

They ask me that question much like Kathy asked me about my

identification with the woman in the *Happiness* movie, as though they know, but they can't just connect the dots for me.

Kathy starts interviewing random people in the Norton. I marvel at her fearlessness and her ability to interview people who don't respond to me. She connects with them with the same ease that Bake does.

Kathy reports to me that everyone in the building has good things to say about me, but many residents have complaints about Eduardo.

One morning, I wake up at Kathy's house and I can't move. My back, which requires constant icing lately, has given out. Pain shoots up into my neck and down the middle of my back.

Barely able to walk, I leave work early and go to urgent care in the center of the city. I have to take the bus back to Kathy's, where my car is parked. Getting in and out of my car after the bus ride is excruciating.

Five months ago, when I last sought treatment for my back, a bearded doctor chided me, saying I didn't know what pain was. This time the doctor is female. Before I say one word to her she approaches me and says abrasively, "What's the problem here?" She takes my leg and flings it up to force me to lie down.

I yelp in as contained a manner as I can.

She says, "Oh, don't be such a baby."

The physical therapist has an astonishingly different take on who I am.

"You probably have an extremely high pain threshold," she says as she demonstrates the exercises. She gives me a pager number in case I need anything.

Being treated so well for no reason causes me to wonder: is Zyprexa, the antipsychotic listed in my chart, the cause for all the bad medical care I am receiving in recent years? It really hasn't occurred to me before this that some doctors would treat me poorly because I take psychiatric medications.

A few weeks later, when I am finally able to hike again, I take Kathy to a local park where I have found miles of decent hiking trails. Kathy talks about her fascination with what she describes as the glass eye of Nazi domination. I tough out the hike with my back pain as Kathy relates that the Nazis knew how to select people who were able to perpetrate vast evil, that humans are capable of vast atrocities, that evil is in effect used by society to exploit the vulnerable.

Kathy starts to make more and more fringe historical comments with an emphasis on evil. She tells me that Gandhi had no problem beating his wife into submission. Kathy tells me George W. Bush, who is running for president, is known to have been a cocaine addict and to have hosted known drug lords on his private jet.

She also tells me that Tom, the Asian man who consults for PHA, is known on the street to rape and beat women. She doesn't stop there. She makes comments about all the PHA staff that seem aimed at alienating me from them. Even my bond with Jerry, the maintenance worker, is referenced: "To a man like Jerry," she says, "you are nothing but a rich boy from the east. I wouldn't trust him."

Finally, late in the day, she confesses that she and Julie, with John Knox's support, are working on trying to get Contra (the company that operates the homeless shelter downstairs) to take over the Norton from PHA.

This is a shock. One of the residents has told me that the local drug kingpin works for Contra in the shelter. I think about Contra's control of the mechanical door that connects the shelter to the Norton and wonder if Contra will really change things for the better. I begin to feel betrayed.

It is all black and white to Kathy and Julie. They are fighting a mysterious war I do not understand.

☾☾☾

The very next day Mr. Smith lures me out of the office to a spot near the elevators. He slyly positions himself. I have heard rumors about a secret video camera that monitors the door between the shelter and the Norton and can't help but wonder if this is a set up.

But I don't raise this issue with Mr. Smith. I decide I don't care. I need to get to the bottom of things.

I answer a host of questions from Mr. Smith. He appears to be trying to find out what I do and don't know. When he wants to know about my relationship with John Knox, I mention the support he is giving Kathy and Julie.

"Oh, that whole issue with Contra taking over the building, that's all old news," he says.

I bluff shock. I don't know who is who in this crazy dope game anymore. Why can't the residents just be safe during their stay here?

Later that week I meet with John Knox and a colleague from his coalition. I meet with them at Kathy and Julie's workplace, stopping in on my morning bike ride to the Norton. Kathy is also present.

John Knox's crony tries to express his admiration for my work in "the trenches." He sounds naïve and presumptuous—like he just wants my approval. I no longer feel connected to their cause.

"As long as there are drugs in the Norton there will be significant trauma and risks to vulnerable individuals," I say. "And as far as I can tell, you can do just about anything you want to in there and the drugs won't be coming out of that building. They won't be coming out without dead bodies."

As I say this, I feel mine might be one of them.

After the meeting Kathy tells me, "John and his friend don't understand about what you just said in there. They don't understand, but Julie and I do."

Her comment doesn't help me feel any better.

When I next meet with my psychiatrist I try to explain to her that I am not paranoid. She has forgotten about my appointment for the third time. I am containing anger. I explain that I believe pretending my suspicions and feelings are just paranoia is starting to put me at risk in the environment in which I am working. I ramble on a bit, and then say, angrily, "Look, have you ever tried explaining to someone that you are not paranoid. It isn't very easy to do."

She laughs uncontrollably. Her eyes look glassy and unyielding, and I wonder if she has any understanding at all of what happens on the street.

"Okay, Clyde, our time is up," she says merrily.

And so I begin to feel justified in experimenting with skipping an occasional dose of medication. I find I am much more alert. I am able to bike more energetically on late night rides home. I need less sleep when I skip the medications. I am less depressed.

❦❦❦

One Sunday morning I push through the unbearable weight upon me and force myself out of bed. I drag around, following Kathy. I start the car with anger bleating like a lamb out of my pores. I drive wildly down the driveway.

Once the weekend is in motion, my torment abates. Driving has always been soothing. After a ferry ride and long drive, Kathy and I arrive at the campground on the banks of the Pacific. We find the trailhead that leads about a mile and a half to an untouched beach.

Kathy tells me my behavior in the car really scared her. I am able to observe that my rash behavior has been threatening and apologize. I am feeling significantly better.

The trail loops temporarily inland and then back out to the beach. We repeat this inland ebb and flow. I am comfortably numb. Hiking, I do feel a connection with Kathy that exists beyond the walls of the Norton. She talks about her fears over moving to Chicago to attend her master's program in Sociology. She talks about her experience with therapy. She's had a doctor she's worked with for some time, someone she can still call to check in with.

I counter with the subject of peace movements and my desire to apply them to the drug war. I state that I do not believe in any idea strongly enough to kill another person for it.

"I don't feel that way, Clyde," Kathy says. "I am willing to kill people for what I believe in."

In our tent, in the middle of an active campground, I remember

Kathy's boyfriend who put his knife on her dresser every time he expected her to have sex. As if Kathy has put a knife on the floor of the tent, I function frantically. I watch myself insecurely while Kathy's ass bounces aggressively. With her clipping of the white porn star in the periphery of my mind, I surrender to my fear. Is this freedom?

On the ride home, my thoughts turn toward my funeral and my poetry. No one except Kathy will be able to attend my funeral and know anything about who I have become. In reflecting on my legacy, I feel I have led a rich and creative life that no one has paid attention to. I have been working very hard on a long piece called "The Life and Death of Paranoia." I think about the hard work I've put into this piece and can't remember ever having felt so alone.

CHAPTER 7

I HAVE AN hour and a half layover in the Phoenix airport on my way to Mexico to meet my sister. With hopes of escaping the Norton by moving to Mexico, I have a passionate need to prove my mettle in the one-hundred-degree heat. I walk wildly along the perimeter of the airport until the dryness turn my lips into raisins and I have to return to the concourse to catch my plane.

In the plane I futz around with "The Life and Death of Paranoia." I am getting to the part where the two thugs that Paranoia has been following, believing that his girlfriend has hired them to eliminate him, actually attack the dental office where Paranoia works, not to kill Paranoia, but to steal x-rays of Marilyn Monroe's dental rot.

I am almost finished with the poem. I just need one more complex stanza in which I will conclude that Paranoia's girlfriend was, in fact, happy he got shot and that "Paranoia has a right to live in a world that's gone astray."

When I arrive in Mexico City I am intrigued by the smallness and simplicity of the airport. I feel like I am walking in a maze to get to the baggage claim. Just as I start to wonder how in hell I am going to find my sister, there she is. She has traveled by bus to the airport an hour early, because, as she notes with a chuckle, no one ever knows when planes actually arrive in Mexico City.

Though I feel mixed about the chuckle, I defer to my sister's competence. The rapid iamb of Spanish, a language I am not entirely proficient in, is overwhelming. Since I left my parents', I have never traveled outside the country. Unlike me, my sister has spent a year studying in Chile, has gone away to college at Yale for two years, and has always reported making friends who respect her. She is about to start a doctoral program in Sociology at Columbia University in New York. Four and a half years younger, she has always out-performed me.

In general, I think she acts as though I am mentally unfit to be her brother. Maybe I have been too emotional when I have sought support after being dumped. Maybe she resents my anorectic past. From my perspective, we have had almost no genuine contact for six years.

But here I am in Mexico because my sister can use her boyfriend's contacts to get me a volunteer job in Mexico so I can leave the Norton smoothly.

With my sister's social superiority on display, I have decided to go off my antipsychotic medication completely. The advice I get from Donna no longer makes sense to me. She only points to my disorders and says I need more medication. But I am now done with the hands that have been holding me down.

I tell my sister little about the Norton Hotel, as I know she will talk to my mother and I don't want my mother to worry. However, in the Taxi, she expresses curiosity about my poetry and I let her read, "The Life and Death of Paranoia." Furthermore, she gives me a compliment—not trying to rewrite it like my father would undoubtedly do.

My sister teaches me how to cut the jean seam to hide my money, a trick her fiancé, Juan, taught her. She looks at me with my boots, nose ring, studded belt, and Clash shirt and says "Wow, they are really going to love you out there on the Campo."

We meet up with her friend, Julia, who will be accompanying us. The three of us take the subway to shop for necessities. My sister points out little holes in our bags out of which half of our purchases have leaked so as to fuel the underground economy. We are all intrigued, understanding that, as gringos, we owe these little items to the poor who have to pick pockets for a living.

I spot a stylishly dressed young man who acts like he is not looking at us. I sense his very close eye and a certain opportunism and intelligence. Sure enough, when the subway reaches our stop, I see the man suddenly get off with us. Though I respect where he is coming from, I trail behind him and my sister, checking whether my paranoid senses, unfettered by medication, are correct.

Right at the moment he starts to reach for my sister's bag, she makes a nonchalant and graceful turn and he misses. I wonder if my sister, in addition to being able to navigate the complex subway, has sensed him as well as I have.

As we are thrown forward by the throngs of people, I keep my eyes on the man. He looks back at us longingly as the crowd pushes him forward out of our reach.

When I say, "Good one," to my sister, she doesn't seem to understand what I mean.

♪♪♪

Early the next morning, the three of us retrace our steps and arrive via subway at the bus depot in time to catch a bus to a small town somewhere between Mexico City and Pueblo. The depot is very modern with air conditioning and soap operas playing on monitors. I am still revising my poem and am starting to get some sense of inspiration for a new poem called "A Mexico with No History."

I don't like the way my sister, in a dominant tone, has directed me to watch the luggage while she and Julia get food. Then, they linger for an hour. I have never done well with having to wait and do nothing, and wonder how she comes to feel so entitled. I think about how she can always win points with my parents by telling them negative things about me. Somehow the world and they are on her side.

After a long ride, we have to take a local bus to complete our journey. Musicians play traditional music and everyone passes them money.

The town does not appear to be very touristy. We eat at what must be the town's fanciest restaurant where I insist on leaving a large tip, despising the cheapness my sister and her friend exhibit.

We visit a charming pharmacy and a Catholic church as we walk. Out on the zocolo (the main plaza or square), two Mexican men approach my sister and her friend and have a very nice conversation in which they particularly compliment my sister on her Mexican accent while she explains where she has gotten it from. I note the flirtation my sister and her friend use to keep these guys' attention going and can't help but feel resentment. They are eager to waste these guys' time when they are both in committed relationships. These guys seem to tolerate this behavior better than I would. Afterward, my sister and her friend talk about how nice the guys were. I wonder what these men really feel underneath. I wonder if other men might find it grueling to travel with two Gringa women who make obnoxious Gringa comments and let cabbies carry their suitcases for them.

A day or so later in Pueblo, I aggressively decide to make one contribution to our itinerary which has been repeatedly set without consulting me. When I finally find a place where the three of us can eat, I have the impression that Julia is slightly amused by my behavior, as if she thinks it is cute. Really it is both funny and absurd it has taken me so long to make a choice on behalf of the group.

My sister is outraged by my behavior and speaks with indignation. I can see the game: she is exploiting my vulnerability, trying to direct me toward feeling terrible about myself to feed her greedy ego. Finally, unstinted by medication, I can defend myself without degrading myself. Now I can see the emotional dominance and bullying that has been holding me down!

Perhaps if I still considered myself paranoid, I would beat up on myself and become depressed.

In traveling to "El Campo Verde," the tiny village where Juan (my sister's fiance) is from, my sister discloses all that she's done to make herself a welcome presence: she has brought gifts and paid previous visits. I continue to write my angry poem, but I am pulled back to the core issue that she is doing me a favor by offering me help to move to Mexico. I know I am not capable of doing so much planning. I've never had enough time to think about buying gifts for our hosts. I've barely had time to throw my shit in my backpack.

The Campo is beautiful. Juan's sister and her husband Pepe are excited to see us and make such efforts as hosts. That means proudly feeding us chicken that they serve with an intention to impress. I feel guilty that I am so used to my choice of abundance that I did not think to bring them anything. I think about how I am not capable of following social customs: I am not thoughtful to others; I don't control my emotions; my abused posture reveals depression. Before I continue in my customary line of thought as if my sister were in my head, I stop myself. I am not falling for this anymore.

The next morning I go for a walk and bump into an old man on his way to church. He invites me to walk with him and I reflexively head down the road toward a different section of town, intrigued by our conversation. Finally, the kids of our hosts come to retrieve me. Pepe explains to me that the townspeople believe Americans come to their parts only to steal babies. It is not safe for me to walk into town until everyone knows me. This sounds a little suspect to me—there might be other reasons I am not safe walking into town—but I apologize for worrying them.

We also have a visitor when I get back to the house, a man in a pickup truck. I instantly wonder what he did to be driving a pickup. Pepe's family cannot afford this, so how can he? I wonder if he might be involved in drug smuggling or some other illegal business in order to get ahead.

This rich man offers to drive us over to market and then the next day over to the school where we will have a meeting with the school principal where I might be afforded the opportunity to volunteer.

Of course, we accept. Even I know we have to. I figure we might, in effect, be under observation.

The market is a slow half hour's drive from El Campo Verde on dirt roads. Once there we spread out. I walk alone, glad to get away from my sister. Upon returning to the van to depart from the market, I see a sneaky eye exchange from one of the young boys who has come with us and the rich man and a local merchant. I eye the boy, and his eye pupils fall passive, dull, and hardened.

Returning to "El Campo," I again endeavor to test my intuition by proposing a walk with Pepe through the farm.

I tell Pepe about what I have been witnessing at the Norton. I suggest that the government is essentially promoting the drug smuggling I am witnessing and that vulnerable people suffer as a result in a community where bullying is the norm.

Pepe asks me if I want to walk further.

I say yes.

The two of us go back and forth, testing the conversational waters.

When he asks if I want to see where the drugs are grown, this seems like an important and appropriate admission on his part.

I say yes.

I tell him I am feeling stress seeing the drug war play out at the Norton. I tell him that the government-contracted companies aren't there to enforce the laws and make things safe—they just want to make money.

He again asks me if I want to walk farther.

The two of us have arrived at a large mud puddle. I look at the murk in the water and say, "No, I think we've walked far enough."

Pepe sounds relieved. We walk back to the house. He explains that out here all the men have to be "cabrones."

I remember the word from Eduardo. A cabron is a cuckold, a male goat that lets his female counterpart sleep with other males.

Pepe explains the men all have to go to whores every once in a while to be cabron.

I always knew that in Mexico I would be expected to be machismo on the outside: loyal and tough; but now I feel Pepe is schooling me on realities I cannot handle right now.

Later that day, as everyone sits around the dinner table and talks about experiences with ghosts, I struggle to follow these immensely complicated tales. My sister and her friend join in on the telling of witnessing ghosts; I do not. I do not understand nuances in the language well and feel that being honest about the fact that I do not see ghosts is more respectful. I wonder if secret Mafia actions can be explained by ghosts. I wonder if this is an acceptable way to code the cabron realities of life here. I wonder if my sister understands codes like this in what she is saying or if she is just bowing to social pressure when she says she sees ghosts.

Then, Pepe's family wants me to meet a village elder who has a cure for all back problems. I am skeptical because I am a believer in western medicine. If a physical therapist, a chiropractor, and an acupuncturist have not resolved my problems, I do not believe this elder's work will.

The "doctor" is the old man I had walked with earlier in the day. He brings with him an old stained coke bottle, a rope, and a board. He runs the coke bottle over my vertebrae; then he attaches the rope around my back, and holding and twisting the board, lifts my supine body off the ground, hoisting me to the left then to the right. He then speaks to the onlookers: Pepe's family, village children, and a stray adult or two who have come to observe his work. He tells me my pain will go away in three days. Even though I figure I will be gone in three days, I feel supported by the power of community.

The next day I change into a clean T-shirt, shed my studded belt, and we are off by truck to the school. It is the same school Pepe's children attend and the whole family spiffs up and accompanies us. We gather around the principal with formality and my sister begins speaking with him, saying she is a doctor of sociology. I recognize status and snobbery in spite of my language deficiency. I follow most of what she says and quite a bit of what he says as well. Presently, I try to engage in the conversation by telling him about some of my teaching experience.

As I do this my sister violently and angrily shushes me.

I speak up anyway, but for some reason this man does not engage with me and talks only with my sister, as though I have stepped out of line. I cannot understand what my sister is telling him.

I seethe. I do not trust my sister. It is as if this operation has suddenly become about her ego and superiority. I wonder if she says things to make me sound handicapped or disabled.

When the meeting is over, the tension between my sister and me is thicker than the humidity.

༄༄༄

Days after we leave the "Campo Verde," we take a bus away from the large town where we are staying to a Mayan ruin. I find hiking trails I can take into the jungle to escape. I feel terrible entering the jungle, and better when I come out.

To salvage my relationship with my sister, I wrap my imagination around my sister's fiancé, Juan. I feel that by respecting him I can have better tolerance for the way my sister treats me.

Juan ran away from El Campo Verde at age twelve. I think about how he had run the streets, and traveled to the US to become a landscaping foreman. One thing is for sure, he does not conflict with his compatriots the way I do with mine. Juan must be much more of an opportunist with exceptional social skills that have helped him climb up out of poverty. I appreciate that she appreciates him for this.

After seeing Julia off at the bus station, my sister suns on the beach and I walk.

I recall the year of starving: getting off an eight-hour shift at McDonalds, only to see a school peer at the drive-thru window order a midafternoon snack in her own brand new car. I recall watching her get excited as the order was passed to her when I hadn't eaten at all during my shift. I think about the three papers I had to write when I got home. But even in the hate of my hunger, I think how I managed my envy in the past. It wasn't until my father ordered me to move a woodpile for him in spite of my assignments that I really started to hate with my hunger. I think about how I obeyed my father's commandments. I think about how I completed the two-hour job, and stayed up to wee hours without eating. I think about how I have always quaked in front of my father's impractical rage, while my sister just tells him no. I think about how the result is that she gets respect. This is justice in the white America I know.

I return to do a diplomatic hang out with my sister. I see my sister ask a young Mexican waiter if he has any pineapple.

His eyes dart a moment and he says yes. In superb Spanish, she tells him she supposes they sell pineapple over at the market across the street. They each have a little laugh. Then, with a bit of flirting, she allows him to get her some.

She is not like me at all, I think; I am not into dinging bells for service. I will never take for granted the joy of ordering a McDonald's French-fry or ordering a hoagie from an inner-city deli.

I ask her indirect questions to assess her street smarts. Does she know about the drugs at the Campo Verde?

She says, "I am very quick about picking up on things like that."

Her tone implies that she feels I am not. She seems to be saying that I have wasted my time slaving a long list of shit jobs, and I am just not as smart as her.

I think to myself that if I had been greedy, she may not have had an opportunity to go to Yale and avoid low-wage work!

When my sister decides we should stay in a fancy hotel on the last night, I protest by sleeping on her floor to save money.

Mutual rage surfaces. My sister suggests that the way I am acting is not a way to treat *family*.

We accuse each other of all kinds of things.

She is mad at me for treating a young girl to a soda, assuming I was trying to pick her up when I only wanted to be nice.

I go after her with a litany of slights from the trip.

She proposes we never speak to each other again, and I agree.

On the red eye home, I get violently sick, throwing up in the bathroom. Inside, I know that no one will ever know or care about this hell I am in.

CHAPTER **8**

BACK AT THE Norton, the next day I talk to two political refugees who tool around together on the mezzanine: one from Burma and the other for El Salvador.

"We just don't want to lose our housing," says the Burmese man. He always wears a suit and waves like a politician. A permanent fixture at the Norton, state hospital records we have helped him attain say only that he had been found in Eastern Washington on the roadside lying in a ditch. The Salvadoran man tells me nervously that there was once a man who had come to work in the Norton, who had done what I've done and tried to fight for the residents. He says that that same guy had ended up losing everything and having to come back and live in the Norton himself. He just doesn't want this to happen to me.

I smile; I feel like my throat is in my gut.

I walk back to the laundry machines and find the daughter of a wealthy rancher from Montana who is known to all residents because her apartment is filled up to the waistline with maggot-ridden, compulsively collected debris. In spite of the rancid odor she emits, she manages to wear hip-hop jeans and have an occasional streetwise female friend.

This rich kid tells me Bake is evicting her despite Jane's efforts and despite her list of medical model diagnoses, which include being developmentally disabled and gay. She asks me if I think there is any hope for her out on the streets.

On occasions when she has become emotionally unraveled, I have looked into the faces of her friends and wondered how she has managed to attract them. Cynically, I have assumed it is something I, too, have benefitted from in my professional life—the potential of family money. Really, it is only my class status that has enabled me to work in places I might otherwise be enslaved to.

The rich girl's question lingers in the room, disrupting my cynicism. Hope is a concept I haven't thought about much since becoming a clinical case worker.

"Yes I think there is hope for you," I hear myself say.

But I am not sure how rich kids like she or I would do out on the streets, not really.

ﾉﾉﾉﾉ

I have decided not to continue my relationship with Kathy after she moves to Chicago. One day after work, I take a walk and talk with Kathy about this. I very consciously wear the pain on my face the whole way, a technique that seems to work on some level.

Kathy is playing the raging and jaded girlfriend.

She picks her head up in the middle of her despair and asks if I am okay.

I wonder if she is really angry or just playing a role. At the same time I am not sure if I am really distressed in the manner I am pretending to be.

A day later Kathy takes me for a raging ride in her car, the broken-down Volvo that she works on herself to keep it running. I sit calmly, conveying utter disregard for my own life—an attitude that, when she senses it in me, seems to calm her.

After work one night I bump into Walter and Nan's two children. They are out together going for a drink. I order a Coke and talk intensely about the Norton. Walter and Nan's son backs off. Perhaps he only wants to get away and have a good time. He is already familiar with me and perhaps tired of my energy.

The daughter, however, who I had never met before, works in public administration of housing in New York City, so I have her ear. She has seen corruption before, but she has never quite been caught up in it the way I am.

Above the clamor of the bar, I hear an old Clash song about Brixton Prison play. I think about the coincidence of bumping into Walter and Nan's kids and the song. Somehow it all feels connected. The beat of the song has never seemed so intense. I have never thought about what it would be like to go to prison. Still, I love the militancy of the song: bum, bum, bum, bum-bum.

On Sunday at Quaker Meeting, I see a visitor from out of town, a man I know from Philadelphia who works for the American Friends Service Committee. He is a Quaker with widely respected social skills. My group of friends from meeting is keen on taking him out to coffee afterward, so I tag along.

As we walk, I think back to the time of the recent overdose death of the Norton resident. My 28-year-old Quaker friend Sandra had also died suddenly and for no apparent reason.

Back in Philadelphia, Sandra had been unemployed and living off her parents. Her behavior, she once explained, was a grand protest against a male figure whom she accused of being sexually inappropriate with her. But he hadn't actually done anything to her, she explained, except look at her funny.

She tried for months to get me to hit on her. When I finally did, she expressed relief before pushing me away for wanting to kiss too much.

Suddenly, my guilt is unfathomable. To have squandered a friend's concerns and life feels reprehensible.

I mention something about the suspiciousness of her death to the prestigious Quaker; I imply a cover-up. I feel for her now as passionately as I felt about the drifter at the Norton.

The prestigious Quaker man comes from Sandra's bay area suburb and probably knows her parents; he reproaches me in a very gentlemanly way, as if to say, "Bad form, Chap!"

At work the next week I get a call from a woman from the Meeting

whose name I do not recognize. She understands I work with homeless people and wants advice on how to deal with some homeless men
who have started coming to the meeting and interfering with the way
"we" do things.

I ask her what her problem is with having homeless men in the
congregation. I suggest it can be a very enriching experience.

The woman becomes offended and her voice flutters dramatically.

"We feed middleclass people after meeting every week," I say a bit
provocatively. "Why can't we feed people who actually really need the
food?"

When I get off the phone, I think it is odd this woman has gotten my
number. The phone usually goes to the resident in room 515.

I recently called the resident in 515 to apologize for the unwanted
phone calls. The man there answered the phone, cool as a telephone
operator, as if he knew exactly who I was.

It occurs to me my whole existence at the building might possibly
be nothing more than a scam.

Has this man been intentionally screening our calls? Am I being
set up to take a fall?

One day, I stop in to greet a new resident and find him standing
in the nearly empty room staring into space. When I jolt him into
reality, he talks about studying computers. He pulls a book about
hacking out of a box. He says hacking information is attainable off
the Internet.

The next thing I know, this man is working with Jerry for PHA.
And then it occurs to me Jerry might be more in the know than I previously thought possible. Jerry might even have access to PHA files,
which for some reason aren't accessible to me—and therefore so too
might this hacker!

Suddenly, I think about the world of undercover those files might
be hiding. I think about the potential of a conspiracy. Speculating in
this manner makes more sense to me than not. The phone reroute to
room 515 could easily be a conspiracy.

It even seems possible that the Quaker woman who despises the homeless might not be who she says she is! Is she a counterintelligence agent being used to distance me from the support of the real Quakers I know?

I think again about Mr. Smith. Maybe he has things in common with the hacker I have just met. Both have worked for PHA at some point.

A day later, when I see Mr. Smith on the elevator, he gets mad at me again and storms away.

Have I previously failed to connect these dots?

After work I escape to a three-dollar movie at a theater north of my residence.

I have been uncertain about my desire to see the movie, *Me, Myself and Irene*, because of its widely reported mockery of the mental health establishment. But the movie offers a more hopeful view of my life to this point. Perhaps it is more than just a weird biochemical meltdown. Maybe, as is the case with Jim Carey in the movie, it is a mix of secretive abuse that society is engaging in that is causing me so much inner conflict.

After the movie ends, I reflect on how the messages of the movie fit my life and my situation in the most profound way. Am I in the process of getting set up in the Norton, just like Jim Carey is in the movie? Perhaps by an FBI that is covering up the death of an informant?

Is it the FBI rerouting phone calls to our office? Is the FBI committing atrocities against the weak and vulnerable so that the middle class can smoke their pot?

I return to see the movie again Friday night after work. I start to feel thankful that I have been off my medication for three weeks so that I still have a chance to save myself. Perhaps there is something I could still do if I think hard enough! At least I know not to shoot a cow on the highway. If I engage in such behavior, the cops will paint me as a serial killer, just like they did with Jim Carey. Moo . . . life is so bizarrely funny. Moo . . .

On Saturday, Eduardo and I take a group of residents to a fair. I study them and wonder what secrets lie behind the façade of their participation in this event.

Suddenly I have a sense that an angry African-American may be a hit man. He has a dull affect, suggestive of interpersonal weakness, but he emotionally erupts out of nowhere when his peers interact with him, as if his reactions are staged to send me a message. This makes me think he may be on some kind of suicide mission he has no control over.

The potential hit man complains that he needs to go to the bathroom. Suddenly I wonder if he has a gun hidden in the bathroom that he will use against me.

We split up and I stay far away from the potential hit man. I try to stay away from the other clients to protect them.

I start neglecting my duties in order to stay away from the potential hit man.

As a result, Eduardo has to run around and collect people when it is time to leave. I am prepared to jump underneath a car.

Back at the Norton, Andy is sitting down in the lobby wearing a jester's cap. This tells me that the joker's wild and on the loose.

When we are safe and secure in the office, Eduardo urges me to stop looking scared all the time. He seems to suggest I will put others as well as myself in danger if I look scared.

At home I get a call from my sister's fiancé, Juan. He wants me to help him out by picking up some Mexicans out in Eastern Washington, where they are working fields.

I respectfully turn him down and explain to him in broken Spanish that I am in trouble and I might not be staying in Seattle much longer.

Juan sounds respectful, as though he's gotten the information he needed. I reassure myself that Juan couldn't possibly be connected with my dealings at the Norton.

I call my mom. It is late, but I don't care. I question her about an incident that I can barely recall from when I went camping with my family in the Pine Barrens.

"Mom, this whole time I have been blaming myself for all my problems. Do you remember that time we were camping with the Woodbys down by the Lake Batsto in the Pine Barrens?"

"No," says my mom, "That was Bass River Campground."

I recall I was having a great time interacting with a very friendly man until she broke us up, making me extremely angry. She later told the Park Rangers about the strange encounter. I am intensely suspicious that she knows I have been sexually abused. I think my mind has blocked something out.

"Are you sure nothing happened to me on that trip?"

I press. I cry. I am desperate for validation. Some secret society is exploiting my vulnerability!

It is no use; my mom isn't going to support me.

When I get off the phone it is late Saturday night and I know I am not going to sleep much. I leave my room to take a walk and Barry is out in the living room sitting there with a Rastafarian friend I have never seen before. The Rastafarian says something to me in a tone of respect and compassion and I wonder if they are watching me.

It occurs to me I don't know how Barry pays rent. Sure, he has a few side jobs and minimal income from the band, but where does the rest come from?

)))))

The next morning I sit outside the Meeting House after a short and fitful sleep, waiting for Quaker Meeting.

The meeting speeds past. I am barely able to pay attention to the real things that are weighing me down. I numb out. It is peaceful. And then it is over.

After meeting, a number of my friends come to check in on me. A PhD nudist friend gives me a bigger than usual hug; I am just not exactly sure why she is giving me more boob than I am comfortable with.

"I can't talk about what is going on at the Norton anymore," I tell her.

A male acquaintance whom I have been getting close with, who could be a lifetime friend, hears me and tells me that he will hold me in the light.

When I get home, I call Will to ask if he can get me a job through his employer. Will is not all that receptive to the idea.

"Clyde, can you lift sixty pounds with your back?"

I am not thinking about my back pain since the treatment from the old man in Mexico. I have a feel for manual labor and am insulted he does not think so.

Will reads my feelings. "Now, Clyde, I have a right to ask you this question! I have worked really hard to get approval of my employer, and if I recommend you, your work reflects on me. Are you sure you can handle it?"

"Yes, I can handle it!" Nobody else believes in my back pain, why should I!

Then it occurs to me that I recognize Will from Rutgers in Camden, NJ. He was friends with Big Brother Joe!

I call my mom and tell her my plans with Will. She starts to cry.

"No, Clyde, whatever you do don't do that! Please, Clyde, don't do that!"

I wonder if lifting sixty pounds implies some form of military work. Is my mom hip to all this information?

I call Joe. I explain to him some of the details of what is going on. I talk to him about the threats I perceive.

I get the feeling he is already in the know about everything.

Before I finish my story, Joe gives me a very firm statement. "All I can say, Clyde, is that if you ever try to betray me, I think you should know that I have the power to hurt you and I will use it if I have to!"

This is my big brother figure from college, Joe. He has just threatened me!

Joe grew up in a small row house with five brothers and a sister all sharing the same bed. We met in a writing course; he was impressed by my poem, "A Vulgar Marxist Beat," and I was astounded by his, "My Hometown Sans Stelazine." Though he made personal friends with all the professors, he hated blue-blood academics. Me, I hated everyone besides Joe who didn't live in the ghetto. Joe was the most loyal friend I could have ever imagined.

I wonder what Joe meant when he told me, "I am what they call a dry drunk!"

Is there a special meaning to those words that I previously hadn't understood?

Is this his way of saying he is still making fast cash? He even told me, "I don't mean to be gauche, but I am making a lot of money."

I call my oldest friend, Gary, who has only just recently contacted me with his new cell phone number.

I recite to Gary a long list of things that have happened at the Norton. I tell him about the trip to El Campo Verde, about the possibility of turning to physical labor.

Gary is more concerned about what I am saying than anyone else.

He tells me about the deaths of two people we knew that were gunshot suicides to the head. Gary tells me he feels that in reality they were Mafia hits. He tells me he doesn't want to see this happen to me.

I inform him I had called our mutual friend and offered condolences when his father committed suicide and left a message on the machine.

"See, that right there might be how this whole thing got started," he suggests.

Now he sounds like he's running a con, I think. That's ridiculous. It's paranoid.

But what about the chemistry teacher we had in high school? I could never understand why he was so respected by Gary and the other pot-smoking kids. What about the music teacher? Gary's pick for a prom date had seemed odd. As class president, why hadn't he chosen someone more popular? Is it possible all of these unusual moves center around the smoking of pot that has always been so important to him?

"Here's what I want you to do, Clyde." Gary's voice slices into my stream of thought. "Go to work and remove those notes you wrote yesterday that you are worried about and dispose of them. Then I'll fly in and take care of you for a little while. Whatever you do, don't leave the area!"

I call my dad and keep my voice low. My dad is the king of secrets. I tell him out of the blue that my plan is to go and see my cousin in Colorado.

"I do know that wherever I go I will always take my Quaker values with me," I state. I hang up before he has a chance to say much of anything.

It will be the last time for a long while that I will be able to look at my loving father with any kind of logical perspective. I will miss my esteem for him more than anything else, because although the relationship has always had its bumps, he has taught me so much that will enable me to endure.

When I discover Barry is not home, I am relieved. I collect the most important of my belongings and throw them into the backseat of my car. I am done loading the car in five minutes. I fix a letter with a stamp and address. Inside the resignation letter I allude only to the fact that I am in danger, coding the covert reality. "All the good people at the Norton," I write, "have taught me lessons I will never forget; I will take them wherever I go."

I get into the car and I am gone. I hear "The Guns of Brixton" sound in my ear. I am done with Seattle.

CHAPTER **9**

TWO DAYS LATER, I am in Montana with my head shaved. I am quite sure that I am back to being tailed on the highway. I pay cash for a motel room and give a phony name.

I call my mother on the East Coast. She wants to know where I am.

I work my mom over a little to figure out what she knows about the gunshot "suicides" in my hometown that Gary told me about.

She holds firm to her conviction that those incidents were clearly suicides.

I think of the heroin overdose in the Norton. I think of the unexplained death of my friend, Sandra. There was a sense of cover-up in both cases, I am almost sure. Gary insinuated suicides may have been real mob hits. I am learning that a body has to read between the lines to see the truth. At this point, my death could easily be covered up.

I am brooding about how a mainstream woman like my mother—who three days ago cried because her son wanted to leave a dangerous job at the Norton Hotel to return to manual labor—could be so sure.

My mom interrupts my train of thought and asks if she can meet me somewhere, just to talk.

I say, "Sure, mom, of course I will meet you. But I will meet you only on Rooster Comb Mountain in the Adirondacks, just you and me."

My mom laughs. She is amused by my new ability to meet deceit with deceit.

My father holds swaths of inherited property around a lake in the Adirondacks. Rooster Comb was the first mountain I climbed, without assistance, at age three. I remember an old picture of me crying, my mother pointing up the trail like a drill sergeant.

The next morning I run a test before getting on the road. I devise it as a cry for help in the event I end up dead in a ditch. I walk two lights up from the motel into a semi-developed area. I start crossing the street the moment the light turns red so that the high volume of traffic will have to notice me. I do this again and again, making a square around the intersection. I can't help but emit a tinge of menace in my demeanor. I am angry about being followed. Still, I know there are a lot of good people in America who are innocent. I pray some might bear witness to my predicament.

After a few rounds, a car charges me so that I have to jump out of the way. Now I have evidence. Someone *is* trying to kill me. I call the police to file a report. The police suggest I stop walking in front of cars.

This gives me the info I've been looking for. The police *are* watching me!

I start to head back toward the motel and I see a cop who has been called to the scene. I wait, cross on green, and go over to him.

"If I need help, what would you do for me?"

He wears a pin that reads "MHP"—I know what that stands for in Washington and imagine it means the same thing here.

He tells me he can take me down the road a piece.

I laugh and tell the Montana Highway Patrolman that I know that MHP stands for Mental Health Practitioner. I apologize for my behavior and tell him I am just fine on my own. I walk calmly back to the motel.

Back in my room, I reason a hospitalization would kill my credibility. I've brought attention to the fact the police didn't do their jobs at places like the Norton Hotel. I take down the light fixtures to search for cameras or wiretaps. Though this seems futile in one sense, I leave them disassembled. I want to send the people who might be following me a message that I am onto them, that I am not going to take the fall for the lawlessness in the Norton!

As I am checking out, I leave the female clerk a fifty-dollar tip to make up for the disarray I have left in the room. I want her to remember my face. The lady refuses the tip, but I insist by walking away, leaving the money on the counter.

It occurs to me when I unlock the car that someone could easily have planted drugs amid my belongings to cover up what has happened.

My incarceration seems imminent.

I take back roads toward the Canadian border. I am being followed. I need to ditch my car and cross the Canadian border on foot to disappear, start over, and find freedom. Without a fake ID, I will have to apply for asylum.

I have no intention of getting Big Brother Joe in trouble for the threats he made last night, but I fear he has the power to track me down as he claimed. Before the Norton, I would never have thought this possible. I used to think Joe was just grandiose about his drug war stories. Now I believe the power of the Mafia is such that Joe could have me captured and imprisoned.

I imagine an isolated lake where I might submerge my car like they do in the movies. However, I am convinced some of the cars lined up behind me would follow me there.

I pull over suddenly to let followers pass, but then there is an influx of cars going the other direction. One even turns around at an intersection and joins the new cars that are lining up behind me.

My gas gauge is creeping toward empty. I start driving again, flooring Cockyroach to the point where he shakes. When the road is finally clear of traffic in both directions, I pull my car over, jump out, and run across the road, heading toward Canada. I dive into some barbed wire and rip my jeans badly. Just as I make it through, I hear a car pass behind me. I have at least a hundred miles to go to the border and realize I am exhausted. I haven't eaten breakfast or lunch and have no food or water with me. I retrace my steps to my car. I am relieved nothing has happened to me other than the rip in my jeans.

Finally, I come upon a gas station. Just as I veer in, three other cars pull in behind me. I don't stop. I drive right through and keep going.

Suddenly the back road joins a major highway. I am aware from the map that the major highway is the only way to get to the Canadian border.

I see another gas station and I stop. I am expecting gunfire from the cars that have been following me. I have the urge to jump underneath my car.

I enter the gas station hastily and grab a Coke. Two cops are standing in the aisles as if waiting for me. I walk casually toward them and they walk toward me. Before I can speak, the fatter of the two distorts his voice mockingly. *"Are your mommy and daddy looking for you? Are your brain chemicals a little distorted?"*

I am outraged. I can't believe this is real. America has turned against me. I crinkle my face in opposition. They grab me by my arms, cuff my wrists behind my back, and lead me outside.

A man in civilian clothes is outside waiting for the officers.

"The keys are in the car," he says. "I'll move her if you want me to."

He looks like your run-of-the-mill man from Montana, but he probably has a pound of weed in his jacket. As he flings open my car door, I protest.

The police officer bends my hand back. Pain shoots up my arm. I drop to my knees and stop protesting. He tightens the handcuffs 'til I am bruising. I fear I am going to jail.

When the cop sees I have easily accepted my lack of control, he loosens my cuffs.

"If you act like a good boy, this will be easier," he says. He puts me in the backseat of his car and we take off.

After we've been on the road for ten minutes, I make a calm inquiry. I find out my destination is a hospital, not jail.

"Thank you, officer. I feel so much better now," I say with a hint of menace. "I mean it, was getting like Starsky and Hutch out there for a minute, but now my mind is very clear and I feel so much better. All my work as a social worker assures me that there will be no problems at the hospital."

I note his sudden look of worry.

〉〉〉〉

The doctor in the hospital is a reasonable man. I explain my situation in Seattle—how I alerted the newspapers to corruption and how this has resulted in vague, unspecific threats.

I also tell him about my seven-year relationship with my psychotherapist, Donna. Then I intentionally lie and tell him that suddenly I remembered I had been sexually abused by a townsperson in the Adirondacks when I was a child. I tell him I feel misguided and misdiagnosed. I mention my past eating disorder.

In response to his questions, I describe the incident at the first hotel with acute accuracy, including my search for taps.

His eyebrows rise.

I emphasize I am not a danger to myself or others; I just need time to process what has happened to me, on my own, not in a hospital.

I ask if I can leave and he motions toward the electric doors that open and shut at the front of the emergency room. They are visible through the glass windows.

On the street, the setting sun spreads red shadows. It is freezing. I head toward the silhouette of what appears to be a town. An ambulance drives up with its rear door open. A young man sitting in the back stares at me. I am concerned he is following me. I turn a corner and a group of five youthful policemen in blue uniforms move toward me, giggling.

One says in a mocking voice, "Hey, are you Clyde Dee?"

I am stunned but keep my wits about me.

I shout, "Leave me alone!"

My voice echoes, and the gang of police move on like ghosts fading into the darkness.

In the chill of dusk, goose bumps erupt on my exposed skin.

I find a strip with a number of motels. I go into each and feel out the desk people to see if the joint is safe. I am concerned about whether gangsters will be able to track me down.

I choose an inexpensive motel, and I give the friendly lady in the lobby a false name. She loans me a phone book. I am relieved to be out of the cold. I make a number of calls using my parent's phone card number, which I memorized the last time I was in the hospital, seven years ago. I doubt it is traceable.

Services are fairly limited in this small city. I discover from the yellow pages that I am in Helena, which happens to be the state capital. I write down the addresses of a variety of places that I will need to visit the next day: the police station, the local Goodwill, the local university, a local lawyer, and the airport. I call out to several of these places and find many of the phone numbers disconnected. The only number that works is the police.

I call information asking for numbers of prominent law firms in New York City. At this point, it is about midnight back east, but I get a man on the line anyway, which seems peculiar.

"Oh, I don't practice that kind of law," he says, and he gives me a different phone number with the same area code. I call it; the answering machine says something about copyright law. This is peculiar as well.

I decide it is too dangerous to call using the phone card. I wonder what the people controlling the line might be trying to say to me.

The next morning, the woman at the front desk demands I leave her establishment as she knows I gave a false name. Has she been contacted?

I remember that a more expensive motel sells maps. I walk down the strip to that motel and sure enough they have a local map of Helena.

Then I direct myself to the police station, where I explain to the uniform behind the front desk that I need a ride back to my car. I accurately note it is at a gas station some eighty miles north. I looked at the mileage in the police car.

The policeman scares me with his gruffness as he fingers his club and tells me he can't help me.

I ask him for his name and badge number. Then I ask to speak with his supervisor.

He yells at me.

I run from the building.

At a nearby McDonalds, I notice a policeman standing at the door staring at me. I ask him his name and write it down for my records as I feel I am the reason he is there. I thank him and get a breakfast sandwich.

As I walk, I feel cars following me. Every which way I turn, cars are observing me. One even beeps when it passes me.

At a supermarket, I go to use a pay phone, but a man jumps in front of me and grabs the last available one. I realize that if he is an agent he could foul up my attempt to contact a New York law firm by putting a tracer on the phone. Plus, I don't have the coins for a long distance call. It seems bizarre that three pay phones would be in use at the same time when most everybody except me carries a cell phone.

I seek safety in the university library. Maybe some research will give me better insight into what is happening to me. I feel like Harrison Ford in *The Fugitive*. I want to learn about CIA technology to see if it is really possible that the phones are being tampered with. After an hour of futzing around, I am faced, however, with the fact that I have no idea how to research this. For starters, I can't even find an honest atlas. I can't even address the need I have to test out the map I have purchased. It has occurred to me that if the CIA drops counterintelligence pamphlets in Latin America, then the Feds could have placed an inaccurate map at the motel. After an hour, I come to terms with the fact that, in this state, the library is of no use to me.

❧❧❧❧

The country road I end up on runs parallel to the highway. I feel better walking and figure I can return to the highway before dusk.

A steady flow of cars passes me. Every once in a while a car beeps, reminding me I am probably being followed.

I encounter a man sitting at the foot of a driveway. He asks me where I am headed.

"Oh, I am headed up to Helena," I say.

"You're headed to Helena?" he says, pointing in the opposite direction, "Helena's that way!"

"Oh, I am headed to Helena, and it's that way," I say, pointing forward. "Everybody knows that." The man, who wears a John Deere baseball hat and has a large mustache, looks genuinely puzzled. I am relieved.

"Hey, do you want to come inside and have a beer with me?" he asks.

"Oh, no, thank you," I say merrily. "I am going to head on in to *Helena* right now. I thank you very much, though, and have a nice day."

I reflect as I walk. It's suspicious that he is just sitting out by the highway! Was he really all that innocent?

I come across a gas station and buy myself yet another fountain Coke, 44 ounces, to feed my daily addiction. Since I arrived in Seattle, I have been ingesting more Coke than food.

A little while later, I come across two young guys, each sitting in his own pickup in front of a bar, observing the highway. I sense they are *working* boys—good guys, Aryan Brothers in this locale.

I pull a fifty-dollar bill out of my wallet and give it to one of them. I tell them to go out and have themselves a very good time.

'Hey thanks, mister," says one of the boys.

I wave and walk away.

But the kid's innocence when he accepted the money makes me question the validity of my initial gut feeling. I think I have traded the money for a reality check. Maybe they weren't actually following me.

After crossing the street, I climb between some barbed wire and walk through a field heading toward the main highway. I plan to take the highway back to Helena proper rather than retrace my steps. When I am done drinking my Coke, I litter, throwing the cup on the ground—another clue to investigators in the event I am shot. Halfway to the highway, two dogs come charging at me from a nearby farmhouse.

As their barking grows closer, I turn on the dogs and erupt like a full-on madman, expressing the full content of what I am feeling. The dogs yelp and whimper. They run away from me. I am glad there was no need for physical contact. I love dogs! I continue to the highway.

Several hours later I complete the ten mile loop I have chosen and come back upon the lights of Helena. I have methodically ducked every time a car came up behind me. Now, when an ambulance comes from behind me, I see this as a bizarre sign of guidance and follow it. I come upon an intersection with a stoplight. I wait at the crossing for the light to turn green, as there is traffic. When it's my turn, I go to cross the street, but the light turns red immediately.

It is almost as if the government is trying to warn me.

At a gas station pay phone, I call Kathy in Seattle. I want to get her advice. All I get is her machine.

Then I call Mr. Alden, the father of my oldest friend Gary, even though it's two in the morning back east. Mr. Alden opened up his house for me in high school and saved me from legal problems when my car was totaled during a suspicious accident. When he gets on the phone, I say, "Mr. Alden, I am ready for your help now."

Mr. Alden sounds angry to be woken up. He shouts, "Who is this?"

I hang up. I have no one else to call. There is no one else in the world I can trust.

I am so tired I am willing to die, so I cross at the bizarre light and head back to the strip of motels.

Back at the expensive Helena motel where the sneaky man in the lobby smiles like an FBI agent, I say, "You sold me a good map, and I'll take a room as well."

When I get to the room, the TV is already on and porn is preselected. This is bizarre. At the video store where I used to work, I was known for refusing to go inside the adult curtain. Clandestine Playboys are all I can tolerate.

I allow myself to watch in spite of my morals. If the government is watching, I want them to know I am willing to cooperate!

In spite of being exhausted, my hyperalert body responds greedily four times. This has never come close to happening in the past.

Maybe I will end up being a spy. James Bond was always a horn-ball. I think of the *Point of No Return* poster that is taped to my wall back in Seattle, Bridget Fonda holding a nine millimeter. I wonder if I am being conditioned for espionage as I trail off to sleep.

CHAPTER **10**

THE NEXT MORNING I'm up early and I feel guilty for having succumbed to animalism like a hornball spy the night before. I swear to
myself I will never get seduced into working for the government. I am
not a killer.

I figure I can't walk eighty miles to my car in one day. I am afraid
of getting shot if I do head back that way. Likewise, taking a plane to
a different country could alienate a justice system that I might need
to legally protect me from Big Brother Joe's crime network. My map
shows that Butte, Montana is about fifty miles south. Hiking to Butte
would be unexpected and a middle-ground strategy. I have hiked fifty
miles in a day before. The decision feels destined, as though it is not
even my own.

The Coke machine spits out a free can for me when I walk past it,
and this reassures me my plan is appropriate.

I hit the highway walking, not ducking and hiding this time. I have
established a sense of safety walking on the road.

Before I get into my comfortable road-walking mental zone, a
slovenly man in a wrinkled suit pulls over in a Crown Victoria, gets
out of the car, and offers me a ride. His exaggerated facial expressions
appear unauthentic. He is a high level spy sending me the clear message that I should not accept a ride from *anybody*.

Three hours into the day, it starts to rain and I start to shiver.

I walk faster. A man appears from nowhere and brings me a USC Trojans football jacket. He reminds me of a bearded Vietnam vet I worked with at a carpenter's local in Camden who ripped my Bruce Springsteen shirt off my back because it was old and annoyed him. But this bearded man is friendly.

I notice right away the connection between the look of the man, who is probably a government agent, the porn the night before, and the coat that he hands me. The Trojans football jacket reminds me of Trojan condoms, reminds me of the sexualized efforts to reprogram me and keep me safe.

An hour later, I am approached by a young kid who offers me a ride. He suggests we go somewhere for a beer and talk things over a bit. I have over five thousand dollars on me and pulling me away from public visibility is likely a setup, so I refuse.

This chance encounter makes me realize that, though I want to escape and be free, leaving the protection of the rule of law behind is what really could get me killed.

❧❧❧

I think about Big Brother Joe, reviewing all the hints he laid out to me about his life. I review the long list of mobster movies he showed me. Somehow they have indoctrinated me.

Joe is a longshoreman. He heads the recoup department down at the shipyard, the department that salvages goods damaged during transport. Now I understand why he really makes physical threats to the white-collar shirts—I don't see it as his bipolar class warfare any more. It gets the law off his back so he can "recoup" drugs and illegal materials off the ships.

I recall Frank, the policeman who funded Joe in college in exchange for surveillance work. Joe often said Frank was his *Bad Lieutenant* friend. Yes, Joe had shown me that Harvey Keitel movie. Is it really just coincidence that this Frank cop had the same name as my father? Frankly, the environmental lobbying my father does seems like good cover for dealing in drugs.

I think of Keyser Soze in *The Usual Subjects*. My father looks a little like Kevin Spacey. It is as if that movie was made about him. My father also reminds me of Robert DeNiro in *Wag the Dog*. He constantly reports meeting with politicians.

I think about my last name, a "spelling mistake in immigration." My grandfather had reportedly investigated it fruitlessly. Dee was clearly not "probably Scandinavian," as I had been told. I think of names like DeNiro, DiFranco, DePaul: all Italian. I recall how the kids I grew up with always told me my last name was Irish—those twerps.

My mind skips randomly from memory to memory. I recall a Spanish-speaking black man whose case I managed. He had been talking to his Latino vocational worker at program one day while I followed along, understanding most of what they'd said in Spanish. Suddenly the Caribbean black man, who had a criminal record and had been diagnosed with antisocial personality disorder, became very interested in me when the Latino guy called me a "zapo."

"What does 'zapo' mean?" I asked the Latino man with urgency.

He smiled before reminding me the word means "frog" in Spanish.

So I now surmise they were telling me that, once kissed, I would turn into a Mafia prince. Now I am disgusted by Kermit the Frog. It is all about Mafia infiltration into the American entertainment business! It's all about black market Mafia shit! Just like when I grew up to learn that Puff the Magic Dragon ended up being about fucking marijuana.

Both Gary and my first girlfriend in Seattle, Gail, collected frogs! They are both part Italian and are probably from powerful Mafia families as well!

No wonder I have never had a sense of freedom! No wonder I have never had a sense of community!

I recall my old frog tie, how it always got laughs from the savviest of my mental health clients. They told me it was very fitting. How could I have not understood what they were hinting at? I didn't even know I was an illegal Mafia brat. I didn't understand my roots!

Now, as I am finally walking toward real freedom, I can see my dilemma: I can vengefully use the protection of the United States to get free of my family or I can become an evil monster, a feudal king, a pied piper for all the poor street children to avenge America's secret hypocrisy!

Such sensations and thoughts spin in my mind for hours on end. I lie down by the side of the road, even though I'm not tired. A policeman pulls up within five minutes, asks to see my ID, and suggests I sit in his car a little while to get out of the cold.

I tell him I believe my parents are trying to put me in the hospital.

The man gives me a terrible look, one that confirms my suspicions are true. He looks torn. I can tell he wants to do the right thing but he is stuck. I don't tell him about Joe or the Norton or anything else.

I explain I got taken away from my car and I am not crazy.

The policeman gives me a lift to the next town. He tells me it is really good that I am turning down offers for rides—he saw me do that—and I should only thumb with truckers.

I already know this, of course, but I appreciate his concern. I can tell he is not a mean cop like the one who handcuffed me.

He suggests that maybe a nice trucker will pick me up and take care of me. That is a real way to get out of this mess, I think, but where will I go after I get to Butte?

The cop drops me off at a convenience store right off the highway. I feel relief to have a friend in law enforcement; I have written down his name and badge number. I go inside and purchase a power bar and yet another fountain Coke. I am barely able to eat because my stomach is knotted from adrenaline. I figure the people who are monitoring me will probably provide water and food on the road. It is only just a bit past midday. I can always stop at another gas station along the road. I am eager to get back to walking. I won't flag down truck drivers immediately. I pray the cop is good and that truckers still communicate via CB and may even be infiltrated by FBI agents who can direct me toward what I need to do.

I reflect on Frank Dee, the Third—my crafty grandfather—poor boy off the streets of *Frank*furt, a neighborhood in Northeast Philadelphia.

I recall the story of how he'd starved during the Great Depression until he married into a moneyed English family, not for love I can now see, but to legitimize a street Mafia background. He always reported being a Yale trained "physical scientist."

"Physical scientist" is probably Mafia code for breaking bones.

No wonder his pastime in retirement was "biking" through the ghettos.

Out amid the rural poor of Tupper Lake, he would bike in his dress shoes and bikini underwear, his hairy chest bare.

This acute oddness was surely a sign of his Mafia power!

Now it makes sense why he treated his spoiled children with harshness, forcing them to clean their plates. It was all about trying to force them to respect the reality of their black market background.

I realize now how the mixing of classes in my family bears all the signs of Mafia infiltration.

My grandfather on my mom's side was the poor son of an Irish preacher in Montana.

Is it really so much of a coincidence that Montana is where I find myself now?

Grandpa McCain went east to attend college at Wesleyan University and married into English royalty and then gained fame in his field, advancing until he ran the Yale Psychology Department. At Yale, he befriended Timothy Leary, or should I say O'Leary—Irish Mafia.

I find myself reflecting on my adolescence. I recall the Deweys, the welfare family who rented the bottom of the enormous lodge my father owned up in Tupper Lake, New York.

My father admired the work of Freddie, who was two years older than I. My father often said that, in spite of my best efforts, Freddie was much more talented than I was. I recall that, after he eventually had to kick the Dewey's out for failing to pay rent, he gave me a hammer for my thirteenth birthday.

"I bought the hammer for Freddie," he said. "I just couldn't bring myself to give it to him. His mother owed me so much money. I just couldn't do it."

My father's attitude hurt me, and my efforts to communicate this always ended up blowing in the wind. I so feared triggering his earth-shaking rage.

I worked with Freddie and my father the summer prior to getting that hammer. Freddie and I had been on the roof removing the shingles on a porch we were taking down when my dad took a sledgehammer to the base of the frame.

"Dad, we're swaying up here," I complained.

My dad growled and continued with the sledgehammer.

"Okay, dad, but if I fall off the roof and die, I want to be cremated," I said.

My dad didn't respond. I looked up at Freddie to see if he shared my frustration.

Freddie looked at me and said, "If I die, I will be cremated."

I felt a bond with Freddie at that moment.

I had wild fun with the Dewey's. We did wheelies on their dirt bikes, ran for weeks on end without bathing, and turned berry-picking outings into raucous blackberry-smearing brawls. Freddie's younger brother insisted on buying me candy with his only birthday gift, a five-dollar bill.

My father was right. There was really no difference between me and them. We had been brothers. Why was it they had to end up running drugs, holding up stores, and going to jail?

𝄌𝄌𝄌

I have thrown my empty water bottle on the shoulder of the highway and am waiting for someone to offer me more water. I am tired, and my feet are sore. I have walked about thirty-five miles and I am hungry. It's going to be a long way to Butte. The last fifteen miles are always long. I start to think I would have been better off heading back to my car. For an hour, I have been trying to thumb down trucks like the copper suggested, but none stop.

I enter a very small town. In the hills I see a billboard that reads: "Dead Man Hanging." While it appears to be a tourist attraction, I am very concerned. The sign could have been erected to send me a clear message that it is not safe to get off the highway.

Sure enough, as I round the bend, a lone police officer is standing near the ramp into town, as though he is directing traffic. But there are no cars around.

As I walk toward the cop, he directs me to keep walking. From a safe distance, I get his information off his pin in case I need it for court. I stop and write on the paper I am keeping in my pocket. There is no one else around and I am not going to defy him. If I go into town to obtain food and water, he could capture and incarcerate me. I leave, waving and exaggerating a wink. I walk with renewed vigor.

♪♪♪

Perhaps my role as a whistle blower began when I was an inpatient at age seventeen at Philadelphia Child Guidance Center. They videotaped my family's sessions and the tapes may have been illegally leaked to law enforcement.

I presented myself four years later at a psychiatric hospital as a twenty-one-year-old, with slicked back hair, black Converse shoes, and an urban drawl. I filled out the Rorschach using Marxist interpretations and denounced the AMA. It didn't occur to me then that Marxist concepts in an American Hospital were sure to attract attention from the government.

I agreed to take a daily dose of antipsychotic rather than question my psychiatrist's ethics. I believed there was something wrong with me and that he wanted to help me. Now I think that psychiatrist was just trying to change my politics for his own profit.

As a kid, I was never scared when I should have been and always scared when I shouldn't have been.

I recall training for a fifty-mile day hike in the South Jersey Pine Barrens. Most likely my two hiking friends were government spies! They told me how Holocaust survivors walked fifty miles without shoes and food.

The pain increases, and the sun sets.

Once, I took a week-long backpacking trip along the Appalachian Trail in Pennsylvania. A ranger came out and interviewed some thru-hikers I had met in town toward the end of the trip, telling them a serial killer wearing a backpack had been seen approaching the trail. I hadn't realized law enforcement might have been referring to me.

The two thru-hikers suspected me: one thru-hiker, who must have been frightened by my behavior, came up behind me in the woods when I got lost on a side trail. He was breathing down my neck where we came up on the main trail where the other thru-hiker had been waiting. We all shared a tense two-against-one moment. I just smiled and waved at them, not even realizing how badly I'd scared them.

Maybe I would have understood if I had realized I was the son of a don.

Memories stream on.

I know my father is not all bad. I remember how he permitted me to drink chocolate milk in the hospital instead of continuing to force pointless fruits and vegetables on me. In spite of all the pressure, he tried.

I close my eyes and imagine that Andy, the Lenape "street hustler," will be there for me and protect me when I arrive in Butte. I now think he is probably a Fed.

༄ ༄ ༄

I start climbing; the highway goes higher and higher toward what I believe to be a mountain pass. The temperature drops to the point where I can see my breath, and I am just walking and walking. Finally, when it gets to be 11 p.m. and I am still climbing, I give up and lie down on the side of the road. I haven't really rested since the run-in with the first cop some twelve hours before. I lie there in a ditch on the side of the road, wondering whether I should get up or let the sweat freeze on my body and kill me.

Within five minutes, a cop car with a spotlight shining from the side arrives and two friendly cops get out. I think about my father; I think I ought to refuse their help and keep going, but then they might capture me.

I say, "I'll go with you if you give me a Coke."

The cheerful police officer says, "Mr. Dee says he'll come with us if we give him a Coke. Sure, that's no problem, Mr. Dee."

ʓʓʓ

The hospital ER in Butte is a lot like the one in Helena except the night casts dark shadows through the glass. The police leave me in locked quarters and do not buy me a Coke. I request to eat before I am evaluated but am not granted any food. While I am questioned, I remain calm and collected. I repeat the phony story about the remembrance of sexual abuse that happened in the Adirondacks. Besides that, I am very careful to be absolutely honest. When asked if I have had an increase in sexual interest, I figure I was likely watched by law enforcement at the motel with the porn so I specify: more potent but not more interested.

Because the psychiatrist is savvy and therefore knows not to offer me a position as a spy, I am particularly careful to detail the police involvement in distancing me from my car, telling me to thumb down truckers, and directing me to keep walking when I would have otherwise refueled in the town. I drop the names of the cops I have collected. I add that, by the way, I am not at all a danger to myself and I am capable of walking another ten miles.

"Oh, you're going to get admitted," he says.

I run for the electric doors, which are locked. I calmly walk back and again request a meal. I am still very hungry.

A half hour later, I am given a single sandwich—an English muffin with a piece of ham and no condiments—which I scarf. I am handcuffed and led to the backseat of a station wagon. I am too distressed to sleep.

I am mindless during the car ride.

An hour later, I am being interviewed. I have surrendered the four-thousand seven-hundred plus dollars remaining from my savings which I had secreted in the inseam of my jeans. The clean-cut man who takes the money looks at me with disgust. I don't know if this is because I own all this money and he is jealous or because he just doesn't like his job, but now I am sure I don't want him to know anything more about me than he already does. I still haven't gotten my Coke, and I continue to complain about that. Two nurses are conducting the interview, and they are nice enough, but I don't tell them anything. It's about two in the morning, and I stink. I wipe sweat off my forehead. I started my walk with a Coke twenty hours ago.

I am led through a maze of corridors that appear fairly new. They are constructed with square block with box crevasses where the mortar should be. They are light brown in color and the only trim is a dark brown rubber band along the floor. The floors gleam white where they are not covered with brown rug. I walk past some Coke machines, but all my money has been taken away from me.

Then a unit is unlocked. I walk in. It is cold. I am shivering in my wet Trojans jacket. It occurs to me it's made of cotton, not latex. The clean-cut guy who is accompanying me says some things to some staff behind a desk and then opens a door. For some reason, there is a tub in the middle of the dark room. He tells me I have to take a bath before I go to bed.

He's got to be kidding me.

He smugly apologizes for there being no hot water or heat and gives me some special soap that he says removes indigent diseases like lice or scabies. He emphasizes I need to use it carefully on all patches of hair that might exist on my body.

When I ask for privacy he rolls his eyes, as if no one would want to be enclosed in a room with a naked lunatic like me.

As if I have just read his mind, he says that nobody would want to look.

I fill the tub a very little and then use a washcloth to soap up my crotch and armpits. Sure enough, the water is freezing and painful to sit in. I am shivering wildly as I drain the tub and refill it.

Through the half open door, the clean-cut guy reminds me to thoroughly soap all my hair. I ignore him and get the funky lotion off my pubic hairs.

When this is over, I am led to a room with a bed. I am given two sheets and a blanket and told to be sure to make the bed before I sleep. I check some paper in my pockets where I have written the names of four different policemen who dealt with me in Helena and on the road. I want to make sure I hold on to this evidence when I have a hearing about my competency.

꜊꜊꜊꜊

I wake up and check my watch—it's four in the afternoon. The evidence I have collected on the police is missing from my pocket. The walls in the room are yellow. The cot I am sleeping on is shitty. I still want my Coke, but I know I won't be getting it. I go out the door and into the unit.

A suspicious-looking woman sits at the front desk. She is short with very straight, graying hair and twisted, conniving eyes. FBI, I figure.

"Oh, you're up," she says and gets on the phone.

I ask a different person behind the desk for food. She says I will have to wait because I have to do an interview first.

I walk around the main room. Two other inmates sit on chairs that are plastic-institutional so they can be easily cleaned in the event of diarrhea, piss, or vomit. In the far corner, a square room with glass walls protrudes and I see a number of people in there watching MTV.

I make use of the space. I pace in a triangle until someone at the desk calls me over and introduces me to a ponytailed man in jeans and boots with a patsy decorative leather strip. Maybe he thinks that strip of leather will help him be down with the folks.

He takes me to a room and asks me typical questions that I recognize and respect as ones I might ask a client I am assessing. No one has told me who this man is or what his job is, but he seems more mental health or rodeo than FBI or Mafia.

I effectively evade all questions.

He refuses my request for food and glares.

His glare scares me, reminding me of the meeting table in the Norton. I can't stand the lump I feel in my throat and I am so damn hungry.

Finally, I tell him a brief, edited version of my story. I omit things like the threat Joe made against me, my conversation with Gary, and the fact that my Grandfather Dee wears Mafia bikini shorts. I need him to believe me.

After the ponytailed man is done taking notes, I ask him what he thinks.

He tells me he believes I have an illness called: Schizophrenia I will have it the rest of my life and will always have to be on medication.

I use my education and work experience to challenge this assessment. He has not asked me about the role of childhood trauma. He hasn't assessed for earlier hospitalizations to find out about anorexia.

He doesn't care the least about these points.

Next, I meet my admitting psychiatrist. I recognize him; he is the slovenly, wrinkle-suited agent who offered to give me a ride in his Crown Victoria on the roadside outside Helena.

This shit is all a crazy racket!

He does not even bother to interview me. He appears to be acting like a total idiot on purpose.

I tell him the ponytailed man's diagnosis of schizophrenia is ridiculous. Then his face becomes comically overly expressive.

The man tells me my parents will be arriving to help me get my affairs in order so I can have some clean clothes for my hearing, which will be the day after tomorrow. He tells me the average lock up time is three months.

I tell him this is ridiculous, that I am being starved before each of my evaluations.

He just makes another exaggerated cuckoo look that tells me he doesn't care at all.

Once the interviews are over, I find a measly cold meal waiting for me in the unit. Dinnertime was five, and it is now well past six-thirty. The staff members behind the desk have all changed, and I see judgment in their faces when I complain. They don't understand how hungry I am.

I try to cool off. I know I will only get abused if they think I feel "entitled."

I wander into the TV room where MTV is playing. Two young twenty-something females are sitting on a blanket. They seem to be the social center of the unit. One of them cries out, "Oh, he's so cute," as if she knows everything about me and has been waiting for my arrival. She invites me to sit next to her. I refuse.

CHAPTER **11**

AS PAPA ROACH punk pop hammers from the TV, I think of a poem I wrote years ago, "Ode to a Cockroach," modeled after John Keats. It had been my effort to cope with all the cockroaches that filled my Camden apartment. I leave the glass room and again circle the triangular day room. With all the drama at the Norton circulating in the back of my mind, I can't believe this is happening to me again. I think about the irony that my fascination with cockroaches goes back to the early nineties, when I wrote the poem to welcome myself back home from my stay at a private mental health hospital. A part of that poem follows me wherever I go. Now for the third time in my life, the walls of the institution are closing in on me, leaving me with the same old angry, victimized thoughts in my head.

"Cockroaches will inherit the earth," I used to say to people I was trying to impress in my past life. Gail and I used to banter about my roach fetish—that all seems a lifetime away. I am no longer interested in impressing anyone by being creative and thought provoking. I can hardly believe what is happening is real.

Still, as MTV drones on, all I can think about is how I will go through hell for an opportunity to testify. I will *testify* no matter the cost.

It is all I live for.

An hour later, I move in with a Native American roommate named Marley who introduces himself as a "hillbilly." He has a brown felt hat on his bald head that looks like it belongs on a scarecrow. He strikes me as extremely intelligent and announces he has schizophrenia and a 130 IQ. My IQ is also around 130, I think. I wonder if he is there to teach me about myself.

"I am here to tell you that the Mafia is out to get you," he clarifies.

I am wearing my best numbed-out con face. Hearing him say this almost makes me doubt that it's true.

He cracks a smile and then says in a very dry manner, "I can tell by the way your face looks that the Mafia's out to get you."

Suddenly a person outside shows up at the window and passes Marley a note through a screen he has sliced open. Marley reads the note. Then he says he'll be right back, he has a "mission."

When Marley returns, I, impressed by his power, try to pick his brain cautiously for much-needed information. He tells me that the woman who thought I was cute was Cindy Diaz, daughter of the local Mexican Mafia boss. We talk but he is elusive and reveals only that he used to work on ranches.

When he reports that Robert Kennedy killed Marilyn Monroe by sticking cyanide up her ass, I don't know whether or not to take him seriously. Until recently, I would have just thought he was a schizophrenic in a hospital. Now I wonder if he has special information from the underworld, like Kathy.

He asks me one question that he seems to feel is very important: do I know how the Mafia got involved in my life?

I think of Joe, I think of the Norton, I think of El Campo Verde.

I tell him in a false, reflective, Alan-Alda manner that I believe I was born into a Mafia family and they have been trying to keep me in the dark for years.

I note Marley's doubtful look and this I store as evidence that I am right about my family. He seems like the kind of guy who would intentionally throw me off.

When it's nine o'clock and time for evening meds, I have been prescribed five milligrams of Zyprexa, which I am willing to take.

Even I have to admit things have been different since I stopped taking five milligrams.

But the Zyprexa hits me like a ton of bricks. I feel profoundly drugged.

I lie on my bed, fighting off sleep, and I notice Marley is not in the room. By now, it is ten o'clock. I peep out of the doorway and I can see Marley at the medication room window, where the lights are on. He is standing at the door chatting it up with the staff member. The medication room should have shut an hour ago. I remember the note that was passed and the Mafia. The Zyprexa could have had anything in it. I fear that if the court gives me a drug test and I am positive, it will deplete any ounce of credibility I might have during my upcoming competency hearing.

I recall a client I worked with years earlier who had one positive test for heroin. She had not seemed like the type to me, and she adamantly denied ever using drugs or alcohol. Because of that one positive, my social worker peers treated her insensitively from that point on, like she was a lying drug addict. This kind of craziness could happen to me now.

♪♪♪♪

I pace in the ward. Cindy Diaz undresses me with her Mafia eyes. Her spoiled little friend flaunts all her soda and snacks. A mute young man acts like a child while the staff surrounds him to force a shot on him, and a round young man talks to himself and laughs hysterically at his own jokes.

I continue to circle.

Sure as shit, I get told my parents are flying into town.

I get on the pay phone and call my stepfather, Dick Wigglesworth, to get a feel for what to expect. Dick Wigglesworth sounds like he wants to give me inside information. He tells me my mom and father and my uncle *Ham* will be there. I ask him to repeat himself and he clearly emphasizes the word *Ham*. He sounds a pinch more goofy than his regular old phony, nudist self.

Then, he tells me a little more seriously that my parents are going to be there for my day in court tomorrow. They are worried and want to help.

I hang up the phone. My uncle's name is Sam, not Ham. He is one of my favorite uncles, in spite of his academic elitism. But this reference seems to be a hint. He is definitely the one to watch out for from Dick Wigglesworth's perspective.

Uncle Sam is Jewish, but perhaps my stepfather thinks he is like the pigs in *Animal Farm*, known for his intellectual power in his ruling elite world of academia. Uncle Sam from Yale could therefore easily be connected to my therapist, Donna, who is also Jewish, and from Columbia, the same university that my sister is set up to attend for her doctorate, and then there are the police who trapped me in this ward, who are also often referred to as pigs.

On the other hand, Dick Wigglesworth, with his slicked-back hair, had lived in South Philly amid the Italian Mafia and could just be being anti-Semitic, an Italian's view of a Jew, linked to World War II.

And there I am with my head shaved bald looking like a skinhead. Suddenly, I am so ashamed to be bald, and angry with my Jewish therapist. I love my Uncle Sam.

Then I am led out of the unit with a host of burly men who are dressed like cowboys.

A door is flung open and I feel like *Ham* Solo in *The Empire Strikes Back,* staring down the rectangular table at Darth Vader.

A nurse from the unit is there to officiate. I use her presence to talk up Dick Wigglesworth's use of the word Ham to refer to my uncle.

My mom defends Dick Wigglesworth, saying he probably just got confused.

My father ignores this and speaks with power and disapproval, explaining they have to go pick up money I left at the motel in Missoula.

I tell him I only left the lady a fifty-dollar tip.

My father raises his voice. It quakes with the rage I recognize well. In fact, he tells me, I left quite a bit more money than that!

This is nothing but a twisted ploy, but I am not sure if it is my father's.

My parents say they have already consulted with the admitting psychiatrist.

I interrupt and criticize the man's hygiene, his crooked eyes and wrinkled clothes, and tell them about how he had tried to pick me up on the road outside Helena.

They ignore me. The admitting psychiatrist has said that what is happening to me, though it may subside, is likely to return again and again throughout my life.

I am taken back to the unit with the laundry basket of clothes my parents have retrieved from my abandoned car. They are going to store my car at a Quaker contact of my father's in Butte. I never realized my father's Quaker influence over the nation stretched to Butte, Montana. I sense my father has lost all hope that I will end up anywhere but permanent lockup.

I buy a Coke from the machine with a dollar my mom gives me but I must wait until dinner is served to drink it. Before I get my dinner and Coke, I must meet with my psychiatrist, a lady with frizzy, graying brown hair and an aura of superiority evident in the way she holds her flabby chin. She doesn't look like she belongs in Montana—she looks like a teacher at a Quaker school who rides to work on a bike with a wicker basket hanging off the front. She does, however, appear to be better than the FBI quack who is supposed to be her boss.

As a result, I talk.

"I don't think your parents are drug dealers," she says.

I get very angry and ask her what evidence she has that has made her come to this conclusion.

"Your parents just don't seem like drug dealers," she says.

I tell her that is not good enough evidence to lock someone up. I tell her when I end up dead in the back of the van she'll have my blood on her hands.

I spend the evening pacing to keep myself out of the pit of hungry misery I feel in my stomach. I still won't join the others and watch MTV.

I think, I plot; I am going to get my day in court. When it comes down to it, I will *testify*.

）〉〉）

I am escorted with another man to the back of a large white work van with no windows. I eye the man I am traveling with. He is short and thin and crafty and seems capable of pulling a trigger.

Once at the courthouse, I am whisked out to the breezy cold air and into an old building. The staircase has a metal handrail that has been painted a shiny, institutional gray. On the second floor, I am told to take a seat on a bench in a hallway. I focus on a few men in law enforcement uniforms. One is very skinny with graying combed-back hair. He is eating a Snickers bar and acts busy doing nothing.

My father appears and joins me on the bench.

I make some comment under my breath about how odd it is to see a cop who is so skinny eating a Snickers bar.

My father leans over and whispers to me as though he is trying to befriend and impress. He says that that cop is probably skinny because he is *working* so hard.

I don't understand this sudden collegial behavior; things haven't been like this since I was a child. It doesn't match his quivering rage from yesterday.

A few moments later, the cop comes over and states he is eating a Snickers bar because he's *working* so hard.

It occurs to me the cops may have a bug on my father and may be trying to send me a message before they use me to slam him. I feel conflicted.

The next thought is they in fact are paid to work for him; they may be letting me know that he is the man with the master plan.

The open courtroom is full of people, and I am led into a backroom. Here I meet my lawyer, to whom I instantly pour out my needs like I am a dog at a water spigot, just out of the desert.

I make clear I was set up and I am not in any way a danger to others or myself. I coach him. I make a "you have to" statement.

My lawyer, from his seated position, looks up at me.

"You can't tell me that I have to do anything. You can't be sure of anything. *I could walk out this courtroom and be shot dead the next day.* You can't tell me to do anything."

This bewilders me. I wonder if it is really possible my hospitalization is above the law. Is really possible that a Mafia death threat has been made against my lawyer? It is still possible that this man is just being a jackass.

When I am led out into the courtroom, the ponytailed man I trusted the day before is now there, testifying against me. He gives me a diagnosis of schizophrenia, but comments that, interestingly, my behavior is very goal directed.

When it is finally my turn to tell my story, I feel myself unraveling in front of the judge's glaring eyes.

My lawyer offers me no help.

Briefly I am above myself, listening to what I am saying about the cops setting me up to walk up the mountain pass.

It doesn't sound good. This makes me unravel more.

When I finish talking, the judge looks even angrier. The verdict is given and the lawyer hears me and repeats clearly to the judge something I told him in the backroom: "My client says he would like to be represented by a large New York City law firm."

When the verdict is over, I return to the backroom with my lawyer. Now that I have my wits about me and I think of the three months I will be spending on that tiny ward, I begin yelling at him.

The ponytailed man opens up the door so the court can hear me and stands there with an angular, threatening glare. I am sure that, from the court's perspective, he is just dutifully making sure I don't get violent.

I am humiliated and contain myself.

When I walk past my parents, I loudly tell them I never want to see them again. I am led back to the white van. The short man is in the back waiting. I turn my head away from him.

I close my eyes and wait to feel a gun barrel against the back of my head.

I remember Joe's story about how his brothers had fought to keep him out of Ancora, the State Hospital of New Jersey. I think he was lucky to come from a family that cared for him.

ふ

I am restricted to the ward for two weeks. I vow not to converse with others. The nurse with the twisted eyes writes my treatment plan and makes sure I see it in spite of my obvious efforts to evade her. Under my personal strengths, the only thing she has written is that I have good family support.

"I know you don't see it that way," she says.

I just stare at her, miffed.

I think of all the bullshit notes I have written about schizophrenics over the years and how, in doing my job, I never realized I was engaging in such propaganda against a person.

I have nothing left to do but go internal, deep into my senses, feeding upon the remains of my psyche. I circle the ward like a cockroach making a testimony as details of my life unfold in my brain, as they had on the road, in ways that do not foster forgiveness.

I remember being left with George McKinley, the lumberjack, in the Adirondacks when I was four years old. A goat came up to me in his barn, backing me into a corner, thrusting angry horns in my direction.

The symbolism and vividness of this memory builds.

Maybe my parents rescued me from this lumberjack who had raised me locked in the barn. Is it possible that mom had an affair with the lumberjack? Maybe I am just a case of mama's baby, papa's maybe.

I remember how Joe had remarked that my dad and I looked so different—had he been hinting to me about this covert reality?

I resemble the males in my mother's family. Really it is just as likely that I was secretly a product of incest. I think about how one particular uncle with an alcohol problem tends to always look shamed and awkward whenever he's in my presence.

Either this, or it's true—I am really am a Mafia brat!

I continue to circle like a Camden cockroach, preying upon the good fortunes of others.

When I can't take it anymore, I talk to a woman who Cindy Diaz is scared of, who looks like she might be related to Big Brother Joe's family. I make reference to my internal struggle, assuming that she is informed about the details of my life like the townspeople in *Me, Myself and Irene*. I am careful to only insinuate that she looks like my friend Joe. The twinkle in her eye tells me she does understand.

Sometimes she tries to help. Much of the time she takes it in and responds with wild assumptions.

"Oh, Clyde, your self-esteem is in the toilet!" she says.

"How do you know that?" I remark.

"You put your dirty clothes in a laundry basket that is shaped like a trashcan. Anyone who does this has got to have bad self-esteem."

I had never realized that I was judged like this before. I figure she has a point.

At one point she gets frustrated and says, "Clyde, I can't help you out any more, you just have too many problems!"

All the staff people behind the desk cheer and congratulate her. They want me to know that I am being annoying. They want her to use boundaries against me the same way they do.

What solid community support they have here in Montana!

I call people. I investigate.

I call my friend Maria from Trinidad. I've never bothered her about the three hundred dollars she borrowed from me in the past, but now that I am facing excommunication and being on the street, things are different.

She tells me she doesn't have it.

I know she makes sixty thousand dollars a year and I can't imagine she couldn't spare three hundred to honor her debt. My suspicion that she might have been a spy for the US government against my family is hence confirmed. I am starting to wonder if all my gay and lesbian friends are government spies. When I confront her she says, "Clyde, it's me, Maria."

I tell my friend Will back in Seattle some bogus story about how I had biked down to LA and am staying at 4682 (coded from numbers to letters to read IMAT) Warm Springs Avenue, (Warm Springs is the town of the State Hospital) if he wants to come visit.

He responds by sounding really motivated to figure out where I am and I feel comforted by the anonymity.

I mention remembering him from college. He had brought in the movie *Roger and Me* to my sociology Class. Big Brother Joe used to know him and tell me he was a *good guy*.

He responds by stating, "Clyde, I only know you from hiking in the Mountaineers. If you think anything else about me I'd have to say I think you are a paranoid schizophrenic, like they say you are!"

I hadn't even said anything about the diagnosis of schizophrenia that I could remember.

I slam the phone down.

As I continue circling, I notice a quiet heavy-metal man with long lumberjack hair in whom I sense a violent streak. He wears Van sneakers, as does the mute kid that I have seen get shot up the ass.

The mute kid goes through some drama one day with the staff during which he breaks his silence by saying, "I love you." The whole unit except for me is extremely impressed by this. I am more impressed by the Van shoes, which appear to be very popular in Montana. They almost represent some kind of cult membership or affiliation.

So, when the mute kid wants to trade his Van shoes for the Teva Sandals my father has given me, I ignore the Van sneaker fixation and oblige him just to defy my father.

After I make the swap, the only staff member that ever actually takes the time to come out from behind the counter and talk with clients asks if I really know what I am getting myself into.

I am not sure what he's talking about and I tell him this.

With my cult fixation theory now confirmed, I start to distance myself from the man with lumberjack hair and the mute kid to send the caring staff person a thank you message.

The unit manager, Jeff, is assigned to be my point person. Jeff tells me he is a former naval officer and wears memorabilia from his time in the service. Judging from his age, he just missed Vietnam, but his memorabilia reminds me of Joe almost immediately. Joe wore his father's WWII memorabilia daily.

Jeff seems energetic and sincere and responds to my concern about the slit in Marley's window screen by repairing it and moving Marley, so I tell him about my daily struggles in the unit.

He informs me I have the right to make complaints about my treatment and provides me with forms. This gives me something to do. I use carbon paper so I can keep my own records about abuses against me.

I don't get to meet with my psychiatrist or social worker in spite of frequent requests.

My records are extremely specific and insinuate details of a severe, larger plot. This gives me something to do beside write poetry, which I continue to do regularly on occasions when I am not pacing.

Jeff accepts some complaints and rejects other, but the time he gives me is the only thing that keeps me going through my captivity.

I am interrupted from my torments only to eat small portions of food slop that they bring me from the cafeteria. Every time I eat a meal, I feel profoundly drugged and sleepy.

By this time I have started refusing all my meds to protest my captivity, but I believe I am being drugged through the food. My helplessness and vulnerability in the face of this arrangement puts me in a panic most evenings.

One night this gets to me so bad, I threaten to call the cops on the hospital. One of the other patients gets very alarmed by what I am saying and he tells me firmly, "Stop!" The staff seems to appreciate his intervention as I put down the phone.

I can tell many people's Mafia livelihoods might depend on my being locked up and drugged. I am angry with them, but also respectful.

ﮮﮮﮮ

In some reflective moments I see myself as having lived the life of a superego in denial that the capitalistic world I live in operates on the impulses of the cockroach id. Now I can feel my id and it is all that I feel.

One day I think that I am just going through what Eduardo reported going through with his anger when he first talked with me at the Norton.

For the first time, I understand why people who have hurt me with their ids have done so. Now I find myself brave enough to shoot from the hip with my id.

Oddly, people seem to like me better. I feel respected. And Cindy Diaz even treats me like I am a celebrity.

Acting more like an id is my primary route to being more acceptable to American society. I continue with the poetry of subtle id shit.

An Irish psychology intern starts her work on the unit and my id sees right through her embroidered lace to her anxiety and vulnerability.

When I find out she went to the University of the Pacific, I instantly connect her to my first Italian supervisor who hired me into a master's level position because I helped her get a paper published. She moved out west to a teaching position at the University of the Pacific. I can now tell this PhD supervisor had clearly been on the take from my father. Why else would she have helped me so monumentally launch my career?

When I explain this to the psychology intern, she tells me there are many different campuses of the University of the Pacific. Therefore, I can trust her.

I laugh at her, even though I know it will wound her. School has not taught her about places like the Norton or political prisoners like me. It never taught me about such things.

I don't believe she will see past the medical model to the fact that I really am not much different than her. She thinks her phony embroidery is all she needs to be above me.

CHAPTER **12**

FINALLY, AFTER THE longest few weeks of my life have passed as slow-ly as I can possibly imagine, I am permitted to go out of the unit. I can go down the hall to the dining room. When I return from breakfast, I am preparing to go to an art room where I have been told there is a com-puter on which I can type up the notebooks full of poems I have been rewriting during breaks from my tormented circling. A feeling of free-dom surges through my joints as I prepare to fully escape the confines of the day room. The nurse with the twisted eyes notices I am eager to get out of the unit and calls me over. She tells me I can't leave the day room because I have to do some lab work. The lab people will be arriv-ing any hour now.

I am exasperated, and then she hands me my grounds pass with a smile.

I hate this woman's sadistic ways, but I figure she is making a point. She wants to say I should trust the people who are locking me up because it will benefit me. It is a typical staff mentality. Jeff always responds to my anger toward being held captive by reminding me he wants to make me the captain of my own ship. But another part of me knows I will never forgive the nurse for pulling a jest like this. I will never be thankful for incarceration. I don't believe incarceration is treatment.

After I have filled my hour in the art room with typing, I take off to scope out the grounds.

The hospital is surrounded by a barbed-wire fence, cows, and miles and miles of barren plains that stretch into the horizon. I walk up a gravel road and pass the building where my ward is located. To my right, I see what appears to be a jail facility—a small building with a barbed-wire enclosed yard in back. In the not-so-far-off distance, I can see the horns on grazing cattle. I hang a mandatory left and see a group of people sitting under a canopy. Then a car comes up behind me. I look at the horns in the field and am afraid the driver in the car is going to kidnap and sodomize me. I scuttle away from the car and toward the men under the canopy. One of them introduces himself as Elvis and suggests I get back to my unit now. This Elvis appears to be Native American. He looks like he knows what he's talking about. I respond with an immediate sprint back to my building, running through the grass. I wonder whether I am averting a kidnapping or just being a fool.

Back at the unit, I gasp in efforts to slow my heartbeat.

I hadn't been so scared before incarceration, I think. I am only being further damaged here.

That night, I finally enter the glass room and accept the invitation to join Cindy Diaz on the blanket she lays out. It is the first time I have ever seen reality TV. Spoiled-girl Cindy brags she was almost selected to be a character on the show. I am not impressed. I figure all TV is probably controlled by the Mafia.

A new man, who is less than four feet tall and resembles Quasimodo from *The Hunchback of Notre Dame*, joins us in the unit. He writes Navy Seals over and over again on his piece of paper. I talk to him because I feel bad he has to be locked up for a few weeks the way I was. He tells me he is a very important man. He says he can make me famous if I join the Navy Seals with him.

I do not take this guy too seriously, but I think that if spies do exist then he would make a great one. I remember the sense I had on the road that becoming a government spy might be the only ticket I have to get away from my family.

Shortly after the Quasimodo man comes onto the unit, I notice my CDs start to go missing. He has been visiting me in my room, probably to decide what to steal. Others in the unit claim to have caught him red-handed.

A week later, he is sporting a black eye. When I ask him who did this, he points to a round man I noticed when I first got into the unit. He looks sad, like he was hurt in the line of duty.

When the Quasimodo man says I have what it takes to really do something with myself, I am relieved someone sees potential in me. I watch him shave his face, without forgetting to shave between his eyebrows, a piece of hygiene I often neglect.

Spies are something I am definitely concerned about.

One day, a staff person suggests I talk to Diamond, another person preoccupied with spies. She is the only other vegetarian on the unit and I am very concerned we are both being fed drugs in our food because she sleeps twenty hours a day. She says if she is getting drugged she is really glad about it. She is maybe twenty-three and fiercely attractive beneath her bizarreness. She admits she engages in a little spying herself. I wonder who she works for. She also says she's married to a Chinese man, but he never comes with the rest of her family to visit her. I suspect this is just a story to keep men away.

Every once in a while she makes a sexualized comment that she doesn't seem to mean; then, she drops whatever she is doing in shame and runs back to her room. I don't know what to make of this, but I do know I am not going to be seen following her. Conversations with Diamond make me decide to quit vegetarianism. I am fairly sure my food can't be drugged if I eat what everybody else does. Diamond may be willing to be tortured for her lifestyle, but I sure as hell am not going to follow suit.

Additionally, I am not ever going to engage in spying on others the way she does. That's bullshit!

❧❧❧❧

Somehow, I can't avoid association with Cindy Diaz. She lays claim to me as if it is her sole purpose in life. Her mom works at the hospital, and occasionally she gives me a piece of information that seems pertinent to my survival. For example, she tells me Marley's main concern is land. I figure she's hinting that Marley would use land to grow drugs. That is how he's tied to her father's empire. Cindy also tells me the dirt on all the staff who are friendly with her mother. I see how deeply Mafia networks have infiltrated the hospital.

Everybody in the unit acts as though I belong to Cindy.

One night I stay up with a recent arrival, playing cards. When doted upon, he plays the weak victim; however, when he lifts his eyes to meet mine, it is all shark business. He isn't really invested in the card game, either. He's trying to convince me to hook up with Cindy. "It's not a Mafia thing, man. She just likes you. It's okay. You're way too hard on her for her drinking and drugging. I just want to see you happy, man."

Another new arrival is thug-like and hyperalert. He tells me in a loud voice, "Yeah I work for the Diaz's." When we are all asked to step out into the encaged patio for an emergency drill, I am concerned this man could get at me. After the drill I return to a sense of safety, though the thought a Diaz associate might get me in my sleep lingers.

The unit is becoming a respite for people in the Mafia. New arrivals are people often transferred from jail for crimes unknown to me. Some say they are depressed; others bang their heads on the wall in efforts at self-mutilation.

One day, we are all in the TV room watching a Clint Eastwood movie about three fugitives set in Montana. They plan a robbery, but in the execution of their plan one of them gets hurt. The remaining robbers throw the hurt man out of the car and continue on.

"Oh come on!" I say, "That wouldn't happen in real life. They wouldn't do that to a partner in real life!"

"No, Clyde, that's what it is really like!" says the man who played cards with me a few nights before.

When I turn to look at him, I see two-thirds of the room is solemnly nodding as if in agreement.

"That's what it is really like," another new arrival agrees. When this new arrival showed up in the unit a few days ago, I shared a snippet of my history and he had whispered very frankly, "Yes, Clyde, I have heard of the Norton Hotel before."

I have pegged him as an undercover reporter for the newspaper. Now he is chewing tobacco and fitting in with this crowd and being an asshole toward the staff as if his life depends on it.

What an idiot!

I respond to this incident by telling people I have done drugs in the past. Maybe it will help me get released from the hospital sooner. I also feel the Mafia might back off if I soil my reputation a bit.

First, I figure out who actually has experience with doing heavy drugs. A prostitute who is all beaten up and has no teeth fesses up. I get her in private and she describes the experience, agreeing to tell no one of our conversation.

I tell Cindy that although I never drank or smoked marijuana, I did smoke crack and sniff heroin when I was completing my studies in Camden.

Cindy is delighted, "Oh, you are so sneaky," she says, enthralled.

I talk to Jeff about my history of drugs and he accepts this confession and suggests that AA and NA groups can be a very positive experience.

My heart sinks. If Jeff is so ready to believe I would actually do drugs, it confirms my suspicion that he doesn't understand me.

❦❦❦

One day, Brian, who has been in the unit the whole time I have been, responds to a conflict I am having with a staff member by backing into the corner of the day room and deftly performing martial arts moves. Brian is a small, crafty, and cultured young man with long, brown hair that is always groomed.

"Brian comes from the Rainbow People," says Cindy. She explains the Rainbow People are like hippies who travel around camping out in campgrounds.

Brian initially caught my eye when I first arrived. When I was confined to the unit, we played poker with eight cohorts. He repeatedly dealt me winning hands. I sensed right away that he was counting cards and started trading in my good hands in objection to his talent. He couldn't hide a perplexed eyebrow when I consistently produced hideous losing hands. It took him three hands to figure out I am not the type to let him play me. But by remaining cool so that nobody knew about his talent except me, I figure I have established something.

Brian's martial arts moves seem to be another message directed my way.

I invite myself into his room and we have a marvelous conversation. He is earnest, genuine, intelligent, and clearly on my side. He agrees with me that I just might be one of the most abused people on this earth. He talks about how his own mother doesn't respect the choices he's made in his life.

I tell him he is precocious.

He acknowledges he has gotten "training" in the past for the kind of stuff we are going through.

When I leave, he gives me a classical music CD to listen to and tells me to listen to track number five. I tell him I don't like classical music but he insists.

Brian is the first person I've met in this dump I can truly trust. I figure he is an FBI mole with an exceptional cover who's got my back.

When I listen to track number five it is all scratches, and I tell him so when I give the CD back.

"Exactly!" he says.

Now I am perplexed.

That night, FBI Brian starts requesting access to his guitar. His demeanor is anxious and elevated. It seems like a staged emergency.

I want to send the message back to him that I support him. I don't know what's in that guitar, but it might be some form of FBI communication device. Having made contact with me, perhaps he is ready to evacuate. I'm still willing to testify to get out of this hellhole.

At the same time I want to protect his status to the three staff members who refuse him. I suspect *they* are all *connected* to the Diaz family based on my read on what Cindy has told me.

I tell them I will communicate with my *family* and pull any strings I have to get that boy his guitar. I figure real Mafia people will like to hear me talk like this. Cindy certainly seems to like this, as she, idiot that she is, gets filled with emotion in support of Brian and his guitar. The staff continues to refuse his requests and tell him he must stop his disruption.

The three staff members call for backup. I reason that if my family really isn't Mafia and if my incarceration is in fact just, the staff cannot possibly see what I am saying as a threat. What I am doing is really a win-win. This way I can find out the truth about my family. I am finding smarter ways to make everyone happy. Only Brian and I really understand my true, justice-oriented intention.

Next thing I know, the Cowboy Security Squad is coming into the unit. Cindy bows out of the fight. The staff, who has congregated, congratulates her for doing the right thing. Instead of going after Brian, they surround me. One of them sticks a knee in my back and forces me to the floor. Pain spasms up and down my back. Fists and elbows pound me.

I do not resist as I am lifted. I start kicking my legs. The thought of the resumption of nagging pain is overwhelming. My back has not hurt since the treatment I received in the Campo Verde.

I expect that what just happened will be covered up in the notes, and my veins pulse with resistance. When my feet touch back on the ground, I knock my glasses off and stomp on them.

One of the Cowboys cries out to the others, "Oh no!" He seems worried his gang will get in trouble for this unauthorized beating.

Brian, who goes with the security people in a compliant manner, is put into one of the restraint rooms and I start screaming out his name as if I am never going to see him again. It doesn't occur to me this behavior might blow his cover.

The security squad throws me into the seclusion room. In the cold darkness, I keep screaming Brian's name. Finally, there is nothing to do but sleep, shivering beneath a sheet on a cot in the corner.

The next morning, I wait and wait and hear nothing from the staff. I pace as loudly as I can.

Finally, the nurse with the twisted eyes comes in. She mockingly presents my lunch. She has brought a hamburger on a bun that has been purposely soaked in water.

"Oh, are you too good to eat this?" the nurse says. She pauses. "I think you, Mr. Clyde, know exactly what you are doing. Anyone who would go and research the history of the Norton Hotel and publish thirty articles in a book knows exactly what he is doing."

I find myself laughing as though I really do know what I am doing. Then, it hits me that I cannot report this deprivation and abuse to anyone. I stop.

"Leave me alone," I say in a rueful, political-prisoner tone. "I will not allow you to treat me this way."

"Have it your way, Mr. Clyde," the twisted nurse says.

She returns a half hour later with my favorite staff member, Lilly. I have sensed nothing except unconditional positive regard from Lilly and now the voice of the nurse with twisted eyes sounds sweet and innocent. She explains that what I did was not appropriate but I am free to go.

When I learn Brian was released from isolation long before me, I figure I misjudged him. His desire to play the guitar now seems to be just what it was. I now doubt that he is a genuine agent.

A few days later, I see a bunch of staff running down the hall and a few minutes later Brian is escorted out of the unit. Cindy tells me Brian has been transferred to the forensic unit. I don't see Brian for the longest time, as he is on lockdown.

Using carbon paper, I document my complaint about the incident, stating I broke my own glasses so the Cowboy security squad will not get in trouble. I respect working people and know they are just doing their jobs. My honest words are the only weapon I have left.

Three weeks later, I see Brian at the Halloween dance. He has lost all his craftiness and culture. He dances like a crazy person with his new friends from forensics as though he is just grateful for the freedom to dance at this bullshit festivity.

He comes over to my wallflower space and explains he was caught getting his dick sucked by one of the female patients on the unit.

He says, "I tried to help you, it's just that there is so much corruption."

He tries to persuade me to move in with him in some cheap subsidy housing when we have both been released. I resist the urge to tell him that, based on my experience, subsidized housing is a scam, a trap he may never get out of. I no longer trust him enough to issue him fair warning.

❧❧❧

Now that my damaged back hurts, I do exercises in the weight room. I also spend time in the library researching towns where I can start my life over again. I send requests to the chambers of commerce of places such as Fresno, Sacramento, Denver, Albuquerque, and Bend. I distance myself from others. I write and write. I walk around the grounds. I am not quite as distressed now.

Cindy plots to run away from her father, begging me to come along. This seems like another ruse to test me.

I try to be nice when I reject Cindy, though.

Meanwhile, an attractive older woman has come into the unit and I take to walking with her. This makes Cindy intensely jealous. I see this older woman as a safe resource, someone much more mature about being crazy in the world.

I have written a poem called "My Fellow Warrior," and since the older woman reads a lot I share it with her as well as with Jeff. I am pleased by their responses, as they are intelligent and complimentary.

Of course, neither of them likes it when I change the title and mood of the piece to "You Punk-Ass Warriors."

The older woman explains the first piece sounds more idealistic and reminds her of the sixties. She has a fixation on Pocahontas and frequently flips into telling me the history of the woman, as if she believes she herself is Pocahontas. She is a bit hard to understand when she does this, but I keep hanging out with her because every once in a while she throws me a pearl.

For example, one day, knowing I am a little fixated on the Mafia, she tells me, "You know the only way to get away from the Mafia is to go toward religion."

Soon, Cindy is moved to "B" ward. Now to visit her I must use my grounds pass to get out of the unit and make a date. We walk around the grounds and she tells me in detail about how her father and mother met here on these same grounds some twenty-five years ago. I am still not attracted to her but I feel bad because I think she has a genuine crush on me.

One day, I decide to test to see if she is really Mafia. Maybe Cindy and Big Brother Joe really are delusional.

I start to act like I am in love with Cindy, but only when I am in public. When I am alone with her I act uninterested. With this behavior I hope to get some form of clarifying feedback from someone.

Cindy tells me that her father has sent some of his goons to talk to Jeff, my counselor. This seems unlikely.

I ask her if her father would like to use my Social Security number for some of his Mexican immigrants. I figure if there are a few of me out there walking around, I will be harder for the government to track.

She says "yes," but I never actually get around to telling her my number.

A day or so later, I'm in a meeting with Jeff and he stops what he's doing and says in a very firm voice, "Hey, don't fuck with the Mexican Mafia!"

He continues with the only helpful comment he will ever make to me: "Hey, this Mafia stuff, it's all really kid's stuff."

Had the goons told him to say this, as Cindy implied? In any case, I stop leading Cindy on. I have my confirmation that the Mexican Mafia is real. I know Jeff well enough to know he wouldn't lie to me about something so intense.

ƸƸƸ

I talk to my friend Big Brother Joe numerous times during this period. I tell him many of the things I am learning about the Mafia in message innuendo. I try to feel out whether certain ethnicities insinuate Mafia connections. As I talk to Joe, his voice glows through the phone like he is a proud big brother in support of my conclusions. He says I am finally starting to understand.

I also talk to my mother.

She will not tell me anything about her underlying scheme to get me put into this hospital, but unlike my father, she accepts some level of responsibility. She clearly wants me to stay here! I wonder if they just called the cops on me or if they were plotting the whole time. She says she is just so relieved I am off the streets and safe in the hospital. I tell her it is ridiculous for her to say such things when I am surrounded by violent Mafia pimps who could easily get at me during my sleep! I go on to tell her what I learned about El Campo Verde, the way my sister treated me like property, and my testing of my sister's fiancé's brother-in-law, Pepe.

My mother says my behavior on the trip was very troublesome. I was rude to my sister. My sister's fiancé says there are no drugs being grown on the farm.

I ask her for the ten thousand dollars my grandfather left me to help me start over again. Initially, I had not wanted any inheritance when he died, but she had said she would hold it for me.

She refuses. I will be on my own when I hit the streets. Additionally, she tells me I will have to stop using her credit card to use the phone as I've charged nearly two thousand dollars in calls.

Finally, in frustration, I tell her Joe has threatened my life.

She says she doubts that very much and I shouldn't say such things because Joe really seems to care.

Then she adds that, by the way, she had to put my dog to sleep.

One afternoon not long after this conversation, I yell at Joe on the phone, telling him that real friends don't threaten each other.

Joe says in a menacing manner that it is time he pays my mother a visit.

I call my mother to warn her, but she only yells.

Meanwhile, my father sends a letter. It is well written and thoughtful and would have been a nice gesture, but at the end it concludes: "I love you, Clyde, more than life itself."

I think about this statement carefully and consider my father's likely Mafia reality. Although this statement might sound loving to an outsider, I read into it as he probably intends me to. If I don't start validating him by accepting my role in his family, he will use his Mafia power to kill. The feeling that he controls me creeps through my body like a hand that grips me by the neck and chokes. Will I really have to start listening to classical music just to keep him from killing others?

The day before my birthday I have another bad conversation with my mother. I have told her the staff smashed my glasses and that I can't see anything. She says the staff have told her I was violent and had to be restrained, and it is a relief to her I am locked up.

I respond by telling her in a menacing way that I have a great memory. "And don't bother calling me on my birthday!" I add.

When my birthday comes in a few days, I receive no call from anyone in my family.

Cindy also does not come around and I am left totally alone. I do not believe this is a coincidence.

〰〰

Around this time, the psychology team is finally starting to become involved in my case. I meet with a macho meathead of a psychologist who wears cowboy boots. He doesn't even seem to believe me when I tell him I was anorexic in high school. He wants to give me a personality test, one I've both taken and studied before. I don't know what use it is to take the test; I have taken it three times before and know he won't even bother to share the results with me.

When I ask the meathead what colleges he attended, the only

thing he will tell me is that he was in the Navy. This I find very interesting, but he discourages the positive response. The meathead psychologist, I've determined, is probably having a relationship with the insecure Irish-lace intern from the Bay Area I had previously refused to meet with. I see them together at lunch in the dining hall and there is sexual tension between them.

Pushing these thoughts aside, I remember that the last mental health professional I had trusted got me locked up in this hellhole where, still, in spite of all my written complaints, I have yet to meet with my psychiatrist.

I start to explain to the meathead psychologist how I unintentionally ended up being a link between my private school friends and the inner-city drug gangs.

I tell him about Ray G, my friend and coworker at the deli back in Camden. I tell him how I worked with Ray for about two years, fifty hours a week in the summer, and had been there for him, through all his girlfriends. I tell him about the time when Ray had got caught in a gang fight and had to hide out in an abandoned building all night long. I tell the meathead I drove him to the hospital when he cut his hand in the meat slicer and even went with him to an amusement park without ever understanding his rock-star status.

Then I tell him I suspect that, when gangsters in the ghetto are calling themselves "G" and "B" and "C," it is really all about drug affiliations. I tell him I had never before realized this. Thus, Ray was the connection to my best friend Gary and Gary's friends, and perhaps even to Big Brother Joe. I provide details.

Now that I understand Ray G. and the secret connections a little better, I explain this was how he had "coincidentally" ended up at my friend Gary's beach house two years later with a third-party friend from my high school.

I look up to see if the meathead is still listening. I am vaguely aware I have gone into complex detail.

"This is all interesting," says the meathead psychologist, "But if all this is true, why didn't they just kill you on the road?"

"I thought about that," I say, "and I am not sure. There's still a lot that I don't understand."

I am given the stupid test to tote around on the unit and complete on my own time, A charming patient who I recognize as a likely transfer from jail urges me to lie on the test. "If you don't," he says, "they will probably just brand you a schizophrenic the rest of your life."

I have observed this very likeable guy for a long time. He is always alone and never in need of companionship. He seems to have studied me carefully in order to make this recommendation to me.

I say, "If I understand you correctly, you could be a man's best friend or his worst enemy.

The man laughs and says in a charming way, "Well I have to say, Clyde, you are right what you say about me; I can be a man's best friend or his worst enemy."

♪♪♪♪

A week later, the psychologist invites me into his office and says, while he cannot share the results of my personality test with him, he was impressed by my honesty. He says he will recommend me for therapy with the insecure psychology intern if I am willing to attend.

I know this is a stupid sales pitch, but I agree. It's nice he is willing to share his girlfriend with me.

The next thing I know I am in a room with the insecure woman.

When she discovers I trust Jeff, she asks me: "Why, Clyde, what do you trust about Jeff?" I am struck with this sense that she doesn't think it is a good idea to trust Jeff. I imagine she has been on the other side of the door with him and has heard the things he has said about me.

I don't answer her question; I interrupt. I've noticed one of the few books she has on her bookshelf is called *Trauma and Recovery* and I read it in graduate school. Like most of the few books I have actually read in my lifetime, I remember it pretty well.

I start in. "I found that author a little hard to take when she says something along the lines of all men pose an ever-present risk to all women of sexual abuse, but for the most part, I really valued that book. I liked how she emphasized that first, safety must be established during the first third of the therapy experience, and then the full details of the trauma must be relived within the trusting relationship, and then how the last third of the therapeutic experience should be about helping the victim rejoin the dangerous world with a new sense of safety.

"Trauma, that's what I've been through; recovery, that's what I need. I wish there was someone around who could go through these stages with me. All I've got is people invalidating me and justifying their bitter, mean behavior toward me by calling my experience Schizophrenia."

I leave her office having no idea whether my straightforward words will have any impact on my treatment, but I feel better.

⁀⁀⁀

That night, the Quasimodo man tells me he is going to break out of the unit. If I want to come with him, I have to be ready for the really dangerous work ahead. But, as a test, in order to prove my loyalty to his cause, he wants me to tell him that Ronald Reagan was a really great man. For all the suffering I've been through in captivity, for all my desire to escape from the hold that the Mafia seems to have on me, I cannot pledge allegiance to Ronald Reagan.

I ask the staff to sleep in the isolation room that night. They oblige me.

About five days after my birthday, I get some packages from my parents. My father has sent me two work shirts that actually are marvelously my style and desperately needed in the frigid autumn air. My mother has also sent me exactly what I asked for—a red fleece.

On the same day, Cindy Diaz, who has been released from the hospital, comes to visit me with a gift, a backpack tote. I appreciate her support. I walk and talk with her, and she tells me her mother feels very bad for me. This validates me.

I tell her I called my cousin in Colorado to feel him out for any warmth he might feel about my resettling close to him and how he towed the Dee line and discouraged the move.

I also have established some contact with my black sheep aunt in California, who is very receptive to helping me out, but I don't reveal this to Cindy.

Even my sister responds to my birthday. A few days after Cindy's visit, a couple of used Bruce Springsteen CDs arrive. The CDs are badly scratched. My sister, like Brian, is using advanced spy techniques on me. She thinks she is so fancy and precocious. I send the CDs back to her with a letter that simply reads they are too scratched.

꒦꒦꒦

By this time, I have a job working for the local mechanic, a coveted position on the hospital grounds. It helps me keep busy for a measly four hours a day. I help the mechanic change oil and vacuum out the interior of vehicles. Under the mechanic's tutelage I learn to change brakes and tighten tail pipes. I get a kick out of watching his genuine excitement every time Johnny Cash comes on the radio. Time passes and the mechanic takes a liking to me.

The other men who work at the shop, though, I don't trust very much. One is Elvis, the Native American man who helped me avoid capture the first day I was released from the ward. Elvis, like the Quasimodo man, is a reputed thief, which means he very well could be a spy.

My other coworker wears sweats, is unshaven, and tends to talk about the fact that he is Jewish. He sits down with me a few days after he meets me and tells me he has friends in the FBI. He laughs at me, saying, "Wow, you're really fucked up. But why don't you love your family? I love my family." He, like Elvis, is in the forensic unit so I have no idea what his shtick is.

But still, I love getting out of the unit early, throwing on a shirt or sweatshirt, buying a Dr. Pepper for a change, and walking through the freezing wind to the mechanic's shop for part of the day. After work, I fill my afternoons with walks and working out. The pain of confinement is starting to lift.

I go to the hospital advocate, who only shows up to work for a half a day every other week and who additionally calls out sick regularly. I show up with copies of all my complaints and ask for help contesting my confinement, a task she is far too busy to even consider. When I finally get five minutes with her, she informs me that, instead, if I get the necessary letters from the administration building and mail them on time, I can gain permission to vote. I can't believe this is all the law can do for me. Though time moves very slowly, I start to focus on accepting incarceration.

CHAPTER **13**

JUST AS THINGS are starting to look up, I am moved to Unit C, the unit for the most chronically ill on the compound. I walk through the door, my belongings divided between my torn hamper and a garbage bag thrown over my back. The level of hygiene seems to sharply decline in Unit C. I recognize a few familiar faces mixed in with a host of lifers who haven't seen the light of day for twenty or thirty years.

I am led almost immediately to a clothes closet because even the staff acknowledges I am not equipped for the unit's temperature, which never exceeds forty degrees Fahrenheit. I make use of beige work pants that say "forensics" on them, as wearing this label will fit in with my punk rock boots and belt. I also take numerous warm shirts and hats that, unlike the pressed pants, are old and raggedy.

At night, as the temperature drops, I watch the ice collect on the inside of the window under which I sleep. I pile the ancient wool blankets I have been provided over my face and shiver.

I grow accustomed to a constant buzz about the lifers who are responsible for famous killings. I watch my roommate's lifeless eyes. He has been locked up twenty years. I note the way he is grateful to staff for the slightest of acknowledgements and wonder what crime he committed to get him permanently warehoused as such.

In this unit I am sure to take a shower every day, watching cum run along the slimy tiles that very clearly don't get cleaned on a regular basis. I would love to clean up after myself in the shower, but I know I will not be granted that privilege so I don't bother to ask. I have become too dangerous to society to manage cleaning agents.

I count the warts that appear on my hands as if they are natural punishments that accompany the fungus growing on my now schizophrenic toes.

I spend as much of my time out of the unit as I possibly can. I take to squandering a dollar a day on classic movies like *Cool Hand Luke* to fill the empty eves. Mostly, I can't view the movies because I still can't see anything without glasses, but stationing myself on the dirty floor beneath the TV, I listen to old favorite lines as seated staff and an occasional peer laugh above me. Gone are the days of cable TV and MTV videos. I miss watching Papa Roach, Rage against the Machine, and spoofy Green Day videos. I particularly miss the video with Green Day's Billy Joe, and his missing tooth characterization of Mister Whirly from the song, Misery.

Now I wonder if I am destined to be Mister Whirly himself! Am I that very character destined to become homeless in the Bay Area, in Haight-Asbury?

ﭢﭢﭢ

Within these confines, I circulate with those still struggling to tolerate their distress. People who still have hope for freedom stay active in the below-freezing Montana temperatures.

Mafia Marley is clearly one of them; he continues his telling of hilarious hillbilly jokes at the canteen. Every time Marley walks past me, he lets out a gurgling, horrific fart. He appears to be able to fart on command. I recall how my father and grandfather always used to fart at the dinner table. My grandfather farted through his bikini bathing suit at his island on Tupper Lake, as he gnawed through meat gristle. This ability to fart on command must have been a form of Mafia communication I hadn't picked up on. I understand farting now as an angry technique employed to threaten whistleblowers. Flatulent messages trail back into the furthest recesses of my mind every time I pass Marley.

In other respects, Marley is a good man trying to support those less fortunate. I often see him trying to support this incredibly sad and defeated young woman, whom I too befriend, not out of sexual interest, but just because of my amazement with how broken she is.

It is people like Marley and me who are left to take care of people like this woman who isn't reachable any other way.

Then, one day while I am walking with her, she lets out a horrific fart and gives me an angry look. I realize the Mafia has even gotten to her.

An older veteran has established a healthy hatred for me. Every time I walk past him he resentfully mutters, "One thing you can do is write."

I figure his contempt is partly because I have been selected ahead of him to work at the mechanic shop. The staff has been holding the carrot of work over his head for a long time, trying to control him.

Whenever anyone talks to him, he breaks into stories of such graphic violence that every ambushed listener has to tune them out to maintain sanity.

One day in the bathroom by the library, he is standing back looking at himself in the mirror when I have just finished taking a leak. I walk in front of him to wash my hands and he screams and pushes me. He says he'll finish me if I ever do that to him again. The librarian runs in, looking petrified.

I stare straight back at the veteran. The indifference in my stare seems to make him think about the consequences of hurting me. The wind seems to sink out of his sails. Finally, the librarian, who accepts my power, moves me away. It's the same technique I used with Kathy when she tried to scare me in her Volvo.

Later, the veteran joins me in working at the mechanic shop, and I have never seen someone so desperate for work. It makes me sad.

The librarian is a man I have dealt with quite a bit. He is naturally industrious, unlike the rest of the staff. Even though I am convinced he has crossed me, using his computer skills to spy on my personal writing, he doesn't hold it against me when I sneer at him. In fact, he continues to make efforts toward communication.

He endeavors, one day, to introduce me to his son. It appears to me to be like an apology for all the things he is doing to me, an explanation that he is doing this to support his son. For some reason, I feel respected and human.

๑๑๑๑

The major snow starts. I am bored and the weight room is locked. I take a basketball and start to circle the court, dribbling. It is after lunch and the staff and some of the townspeople take over the gym and play basketball. Before I get very far with my dribble one of the bonehead players I don't recognize shouts at me like I am a dog and tells me to put the ball away. This stuns me into compliance, much as my father's raised voice did when I was a child.

Jeff, who is in the game, says, "Clyde, what has happened to you?"

I am too stunned to assertively tell Jeff that I am getting abused by a bonehead for no good reason. Instead, I look at my raggedy clothes. I, like FBI Brian, now look like a crazy person.

And suddenly Jeff has offended me to the core. I look the way I do so that he can get his salary. And I am supposed to learn a lesson from his insult that is in support of an abusive bonehead?

In early November, all the clients are pulled into the gym where cake is available and October birthdays are acknowledged. My name is read from a list in a ritual that makes me feel at a new low. I cannot even remember the gifts that had arrived late just a few days before. All I remember is that I am living in filth in Unit C, that life is a blur without my glasses, and that I will soon be released to the streets.

At work on a Friday shortly thereafter, I am working with my Jewish coworker.

Then, out of the corner of my eye, I see him holding my Dr. Pepper bottle in his hands.

When I am finished with the task at my hand, I politely ask him if he wants some of my drink.

He smiles very smugly and says that he doesn't want to get my germs.

I wonder why a germ-sensitive dude would think it is okay to pick up someone else's soda-water.

A moment later, as I am drinking the soda under his eyes' tutelage, I have this gut feeling that he knows I am destined to get sick.

That night I am stuffed up. My head and throat hurt, and I have no energy. When I ask the staff for some aspirin or Tylenol, they refuse, explaining the doctor hasn't ordered anything.

Since it is Friday and my doctor doesn't work on the weekend, I have no hope of relief. I take my heap of blankets and lie down in the hall. I suffer on the floor for hours, waiting to get punished for this behavior, which will probably be seen as attention-seeking.

When staff finally comes, I get yelled at.

I point out the undisputable fact that there is ice on the window right over top of my bed.

"Well, why don't you move your bed!" says a staff member.

"I didn't realize I was allowed to," I am barely able to whisper.

The staff person walks angrily behind me. I start to move my bed; he interrupts me with a roll of the eyes and a jerking nod of his head and moves my bed for me.

When night falls, I cannot sleep. I cannot breathe through my nose and the cold air in my mouth is uncomfortable. I tolerate until I can tolerate no more. I go down to the staff desk, although I know it is futile. Through all my pain, I beg the nurse on duty for some aspirin.

I listen as she gives me the standard refusal, but then, midway through, she shrieks, "Get your hand out of your pants!"

Suddenly, I am jolted out of sickness and realize I have let my hand slip under the elastic waistband of my sweats so it rests on my hip.

I jump backward and yank my hand off my hip bone.

For a moment, the pain stops and I am floating in embarrassment. When the woman calms down, I realize the full ridiculousness of the situation. I am locked up because I am paranoid and yet I am here with a "normal" person whose fear of me amounts to paranoia.

By Monday morning, I am well enough to move around. I am hungry enough to brave the bitter cold to walk the cafeteria and eat for the first time in three days. A staff person who once brought me home-cooked spaghetti warns me that the woman who freaked out because I had my hand in my pants a few nights earlier has written me up as being sexually inappropriate.

I request to speak with my doctor who still has yet to meet with me in spite of my complaints. I am a nervous wreck as I wait under the damp blankets.

When the doctor comes, I, empowered by food and receding fever, explain specifically what happened.

"Clyde," says the doctor, "I have never known you to be sexually inappropriate."

The relief I feel is astounding.

She asks me for the first time about my willingness to take medication and I am more than happy to agree.

The doctor, at my suggestion, puts me on a mild dose of Trilafon—six milligrams. I feel most primary care doctors won't recognize the medication.

She sees the gratitude in my face and says, "You know, Clyde, one time we had a gentleman come in here who said the FBI was after him and it turned out that he was right—the FBI was after him. He had done some things that had gotten him attention, but he really didn't do anything wrong."

Is this a coded confirmation that the FBI is in fact involved? I am too afraid to ask for clarification.

The psychiatrist continues, "But, Clyde, I need you to know that you act like you are entitled—very entitled. Everybody around here says so."

It is as if I have been patted on the back before being walloped.

But it makes me think.

Back in the Observation Unit, I had witnessed a staff person use ᵗ

her power to bash patient after patient for no reason. Instead of recalling how my own mentors in mental health had encouraged this mentality, I confronted her.

"Angie," I had said, in a purposely mature tone, "When you insult us like that it makes me feel hurt and I feel it damages all of us."

Her eyes had filled with rage.

I need to stop this behavior if I want to be released. State Hospitals aren't about truth and reality. I should know better.

At the psychiatrist's request, I begin to meet with the male intern who is assigned to Unit C. When I arrive for my meeting, I note the intern is getting very angry with the client ahead of me, a woman I know vaguely from the Observation Unit. She walks around in Lion King Pajamas and carries stuffed animals. I cannot imagine that any conscientious therapist would believe it is helpful to shout at her so. In contrast, when I come in for our meeting, he is overwhelmingly pleasant to me. I am uncertain how to proceed. Unless the woman was giving him Mafia instructions, I see the split in his behavior as something that makes him fundamentally untrustworthy.

He asks me if I have read any of the books on his shelf. He seems upper class and might respect the fact that I am too, deep down, upper class as well. Chances are, he is the epitome of all I don't like in the field: an insulated therapist gaining professional experience on the backs of the poor and doing a shitty job of it just to get into a private practice.

◢◢◢

In calling my father to complain about the fact that I was not permitted to cast a Ralph Nader vote in spite of heaps of effort, I expect at least a moment of empathy. But he ignores me, and pleads with me not to leave the hospital.

He tells me he would rather I stay where I am for at least nine more months. He says if I go back out on the streets he is afraid the same thing is going to happen to me all over again.

I haven't been so mad at him since he told me in the Observation

Unit that he, too, had put his dog to sleep. Both dogs had been put to sleep within a week of each other.

I do the only thing I can do: I hang up the phone.

I vow this will be the last time I talk to him!

The temperature is falling. It is usually between zero to ten degrees Fahrenheit outside and several feet of snow has stacked up in the fields outside. Each day I seem to end up stuck underdressed outside the unit in the cold waiting for the staff to let me in.

In the cold, I feel like one of the cows that sit on the other side of the barbed wire that surrounds the compound. I am there to provide income but left to suffer without so much as a gesture of remorse.

I continue to fight worthlessness by thinking up lines for poems, but even my poems have started to lose insight and inspiration.

Work is sometimes cancelled due to the weather and because there isn't enough work. The boss sets me to work restoring an old Model T Ford, something that is of no interest to me; and even he seems to get annoyed by my constant need to be busy.

All the fight, all the urgency: for what?

CHAPTER **14**

ONE EVENING, I am out circling the perimeter of the compound, as I do every night. I bump into the Irish lace intern, who is out walking her dog. I get the feeling she is going through her own strong emotions, so I give her space. Life is probably hard when you have a meathead as a boyfriend. She ignores my body language. She comes over to me, looking beautiful with the heavy wind blowing her hair.

"You see, Clyde," she says, "We are both trapped here on this compound. There's not all that much difference between us."

I tell her thanks and ignore the sexual tension.

I notice the slight feeling of tears in my throat.

I don't get so caught up in the moment that I forget that she has a home to go to and a dog to keep her company. At least she isn't sleeping in a barracks with lifers.

But this is a powerful moment for me. And this is the point when it hits me: all I want is a dog and a simple life. If I can get these things back I can be happy again.

Weeks later, I am meeting regularly with my social worker, who is supporting me in preparations for discharge. Talks with my aunt are going well. I have decided to move to Fresno, three hours away from her home in the Bay Area, three hours away from Mister Whirly and his fate. I get an overwhelming sense that she is Mafia, but I also know she is the black sheep. She has an easy time criticizing my father for letting me rot in the hospital.

Like the rest of my family, I haven't always had much respect for her because she doesn't work and likes to lavish money in expensive restaurants. But the deprivation I've experienced has shifted my worldview. Now, the fact that she is the only one who doesn't toe the deadly family line makes her an asset. I have a sense her Mafia rule will be kinder, gentler.

She seems to encourage and promote this line of thinking.

By this time, I am not averse to my mom visiting me. She gets a week off work, something that is not very easy to do mid-school year, and rents a car and a room within the compound. And then she is there in front of me, and I am forcing myself to greet her.

My mother and I end up outside the young intern shrink's office, waiting for an appointment.

The intern enters.

My mother pulls out a list of questions that she and my father have written.

"What is Clyde's diagnosis and what does it mean?"

I answer her question like a competent social worker to demonstrate my knowledge and then add my perspective.

After a few more questions I notice the furrow over the shrink's brow. I know he cannot improve on the quality of my clinical answers, but neither he nor my mother acknowledge my competence. They seem to feel I am menacing.

When my mom asks if there is any chance that what I am going through is "organic," he responds by suggesting that my mother come with him.

I throw my hands up. My shrink ignores my body language. They leave the room and are gone for forty-five minutes.

When my mother gets back I ask her if she feels better.

She says, "Yes, I feel better because he says you are the kind of person he wants to work with."

This helps confirms to me that the young shrink is just completing this psychology internship to get his credentials because he wants to work with rich people. He does not feel for the people who are helping him get ahead.

When my mother offers to take me off the hospital grounds, the urges I've had over the last three months to run away flash through my mind. I feel oddly proud of myself that I stuck out the incarceration. Here I am, getting to leave the grounds legally.

We head down the highway toward Butte and come out on a visitor center where we stop to inquire about places to hike.

The snow is so frozen that we can hike through it without snowshoes. There is nice countryside everywhere we look. We start walking down a path leading along the highway from the visitor's center and freedom feels so good. I just don't know what to do with myself.

We walk about forty minutes and I am just talking and talking.

I ask her questions like: "Is dad really my father?"

At one point as I am getting heated and making some good points, she just disconnects from me and starts running back toward the car, stating that she is cold.

I walk back alone and I think she is right—she is cold.

I am thinking of all I've dealt with that she can't even begin to handle. I believe she is only here to feel better about me being locked up.

By the time I get back to the car I have settled down and I ask in a concerned way whether she was able to warm up.

〰〰

Back in the unit, this guy I have been avoiding since I first met him in the Observation Unit talks to me. I have avoided him because he has a gang brand on his back, as if he were a cow. Though he is clearly depressed, I haven't wanted him spying on me.

"Clyde," he says, "What happened out there? Do you owe some people some money?"

"Nothing happened," I say, although I am curious about what he's heard.

"I only say that because my boys and I can help protect you if you need us," he says.

"No, I am fine," I say. "I was just getting nervous for a time back in the observation unit when we had a large number of gang bangers coming from jail with supposed mental health problems."

He is contained in his response to me. "You mean guys from jail with depression like me." He has understood my intended disrespect and shouldered it. He sits with a slight angle to his back for a minute and then says, "Well, I do have depression."

I can't help but respect him. He can handle my contempt so much better than my family can. I feel bad for him, bad that he is branded for life.

ﻌﻌﻌ

During the next three to four days, I struggle to see my mom as an angel.

I drive with her, following signs downhill away from the mountainous plains to a park that appears to be in a heavily wooded gully. It is dark and ominous with snow falling off the branches of the trees. The freedom to explore this area gives me outrageous energy. When my mom says this place scares her, I hold my tongue.

We find a small town that is carved into a hillside, park, and start ascending a mildly graded jeep trail that takes off from the edge of town.

To test my mom, I talk as though my father is not Mafia.

She talks about my father with compassion, as though he is a broken man.

Houses and children's sledding hills thin as we make our way up the hillside.

I continue to talk outside the Mafia lingo about my father's rigid support of incarceration.

"You know, Clyde, you are probably going to have to take care of your father, because he doesn't take very good care of himself."

In my education, I have read that Irish parents follow an

unconscious cultural norm in which youngest sons are left behind in the old country to care for parents and become schizophrenic as a result. It is somehow easier for me to think what is going on is part of our covert, Italian heritage.

As the two of us climb higher, I leave the talking behind and take the lead. I walk angrily, yet am mindful not to leave my mom too far behind. After walking out to the crest I initiate the switchback descent and follow along behind her, letting her set the pace. While she does this, I educate her about the Norton.

By the time we are down in the town again, I am having a good time and my mom is listening. She even validates me, saying, "You know I was so worried about you, but now I can see that you are not too bad; you make some sense."

Gee, thanks, mom.

We go to the mall in Butte and she buys me a much-needed jacket. I choose one that is uniquely Montana yet veers toward punk. I get a duffel bag that I can use when traveling to Fresno; she buys me glasses that I can be proud of, that fit my new look. The hospital had taken me to a budget glasses shack some weeks before, but I'd arrogantly refused to waste my money. Having my sight restored and looking less like a mental patient makes me feel spoiled.

Several days later, when driving toward Glacier Peak, my mother validates me again by acknowledging for the first time that I may have undergone some emotional abuse by my father.

I think of the time I requested more than twenty-five cents per pulled tooth from the tooth fairy; my father ended up flinging me down the stairs in a rage.

But I also remember all the things he'd done for me over the years. My father always repaid me with love and time. I think about how this kindness was sometimes so important to me. Kids at private school were always so mean to me.

My mother interrupts the prolonged silence, "And I feel bad about a lot of things I did after your father and I broke up; it was just such a confusing time for me and I was really out of control."

Never before have I received an apology and I am amazed by its power. I am actually elated.

❧❧❧❧

And then my mom is gone and I am left to do the things I need to do to get ready for my move. I sell my car to a peer at the hospital who talks me down from three hundred dollars to two hundred and cries when I accept.

I am confident about my decision to sell. Two hundred dollars can keep me eating for two extra months if things go really bad; I don't ever want to be followed in a car ever again. Everybody in the hospital believes I am being foolish. Cindy Diaz, on a farewell visit, says sympathetically that it is hard to move to a new town without a car.

Hospital staff members take me to Butte to purchase my tickets and set up a bank account.

On a Saturday morning I am taken to the bus depot with everything I own in a duffel bag, including a month of medication. As soon as the hospital staff has left, I slip into the bathroom and shave my face, something I haven't done since I arrived in Montana. My hair has grown significantly in three months and I cover it up in my hat. I look very different than I did before I entered the hospital. I check my bag and the next thing I know I am boarding the bus.

CHAPTER **15**

MY JOURNEY TAKES twenty hours. I watch each and every passenger, looking for signs of Mafia infiltration. I transfer buses in the wee hours of the Salt Lake City morning, spotting drug dealers in the depot who do not take unusual notice of me. I board an anonymous Sacramento-bound bus at 3 a.m. The sun rises as we ascend the Sierras. I feel reborn as the snow melts and we descend into Sacramento. I pray I have what it takes to recreate myself. When the bus pulls in, I see my aunt dressed in sunglasses and a scarf. I feel safe. I feel free. I have left Montana behind.

The car barrels down the highway and I appreciate my aunt's optimism and hopes for me; they are refreshing.

As we head to Fresno, I have a sense that, moving forward, I will need to adapt to new worldviews. I'm worried about seedy, roach-infested motels, vengeful drug runners, pimps, and other signs of poverty. I fear the cheapness of the motel I selected, noting that things that once attracted me have now become my worst enemy. I believe that kings of the ghetto, who don't necessarily live there, are responsible for my hospitalization. I won't mess with them anymore; I just don't want to be powerless and enslaved anymore.

The car cuts through miles of the flat, fertile Central Valley terrain. No one except my aunt and I know where I am headed.

Once in town, I direct my aunt to the street where the motel is located; I'm relieved to see it is in a commercial area of the city, close to Costco, Wal-Mart, supermarkets, and other foundations of the modern world. I check in and drop my bag off in the small, clean efficiency apartment. I use the Yellow Pages that are sitting by the phone to locate the nearest bike store. I am in control here. My aunt has no idea where the store is located.

At the bike store, my aunt embarrasses me, making a minor scene in front of the salesperson. She explains to him that I am new in town and starting over with a bike. I am too pleased with my freedom to worry about the fracas. The salesperson, a husky white man, appreciates my situation. My aunt makes her departure and I remain grateful for her help. The salesperson gives me a discount on some of the accessories I buy. The next thing I know, I am flying free down the street, noticing that I am underdressed for the encroaching cold and darkness.

Back at the efficiency, I lock my bike up inside and head across the street to the supermarket to purchase just enough for a dinner: a pot, some silverware, Kraft macaroni and cheese, and some cookies for desert. Once I return to my new home, I prepare dinner and find my aunt has called and left a message. I continue to feel touched by an angel.

I wrestle with installing special tubing into my tires and when I'm done, I turn in for the night.

ɔ.ɔ.ɔ.

I delve into the daunting task of looking for work. During captivity, I toyed around with different career decisions. No longer willing to be a mere cog in the social-work machine, I recalled things I was good at when I was at the Norton: the planning of events, the making of flyers, the leading of meetings, and the building of communities. I have decided the safest people to save from Mafia circumstances are children.

As a kindergarten teacher, I can help society's innocents grow healthy and drug free.

An ad in the paper leads me to a Head Start that is far south in what I learn is an expansive slum. I realize that I am going to have to dig up old references and old job supervisors. I know better than to rely on Cheryl for a reference.

I head to Fresno University to research getting a teaching certificate so I can be prepared during an interview. Other days pass in like manner. I fill out applications at movie rental joints, Kinkos, and Target for part-time supplemental work.

In a long employee questionnaire at Target, questions like, "Are you street smart?" stand out. I remember how I would have written "no" in my younger years, feeling that anyone who answered "yes" would have to be stupid. Now that I am older, wiser, and actually "street smart," I feel conflicted. All the complex navigating I did in the hospital to survive matters to me. I answer "yes."

I go to an employment agency and fill out applications for both manual labor and desk work. Most of the questionnaires ask about use of drugs and alcohol and tendencies to fight. I am too honest to lie about being a drinker and a fighter. When I don't get a call back in spite of my follow-up phone calls, I figure I am too clean-cut to get help from an organization like them.

By Thanksgiving, I give myself a break. I only have four thousand dollars to burn through until I have to hit the streets, but I buy a book about the local mountains and head out on my bike, through briar greenery and dust, up the barren highway that heads east. I ride toward the mountains where there is a dam and a reservoir. I use climbing shoes, which I have brought with me, and devise climbing routes. When I tire of this lone endeavor, I bike a little farther to a casino, where I get a flat and have to change tires before biking miles and miles back into town.

꒱꒱꒱ᕼ

I move forward, structuring every last moment with more errands and applications. On a Saturday night, I ask the manager of the motel I am staying in out on a date. The familiar Latino twang in her voice soothes my loneliness. I can tell she is nice by the way she says "no." I wonder who in the world would feel safe with a drifter just released from a mental institution!

The next week, I have an interview with the KiddieKare Center and am offered the job a day or so later, after my references check out. I will be making seven dollars an hour. That is like a hundred ninety-five dollars a week after taxes; that times four will cover the rents I have been seeing in the classifieds and give me enough left-over income for food. Later the same day, I get an on-call catering position where I can make extra money.

Before work starts, I visit three to four apartments a day. I have never before been picky about where I live, but now I want to avoid associations with crime. One landlord pulls up for our appointment in a truck. He is dressed in spackled shorts and a worn T-shirt, and his long, curly hair is tucked underneath a nondescript cap. The man lifts his dog down from the cab, and the dog immediately puts its rear on the grass and shimmies along about twelve feet. The man follows and pets it, saying, "You itching?"

The place he shows me is semi-furnished and more than adequate at only three hundred a month. When I tell him a little about my story the guy gets really interested in me, though he is not very thrilled that I want to get a dog. To my questions, he talks in detail about the crime in the neighborhood, revealing he allows a few of his tenants to smoke medical marijuana.

I wonder how he would handle phone calls from Mafia agents like Marley or Joe or Cindy, who could extort him based on his pot policy. I decide to increase the rent I am willing to pay.

Just west of where I am currently staying, I find an apartment for five hundred and five a month and it seems like a much better decision. Moving into such a legitimate complex will involve my uncle cosigning the lease. My aunt and uncle agree without question. I am amazed.

My first day of work, I ride away from all the development and through a tree orchard. In this rural wonderland I feel like I've zapped back fourteen years when I explored the sugar cane fields of Belize. I contemplate the privilege of my past as it sits in contrast to what lies before me. In spite of all my rage against my parents I can't help but be grateful for the things they gave me that have enabled me to overcome the confines of Montana State Hospital. I have contacted my mother with the address of my PMB (Personalized Mail Box), but not my father.

Then, with a right turn, I am back in town, arriving at a very clean-looking building with modern play equipment outside. The houses in this area of the city are large and well-manicured. The last time I worked with kids was at the Camden YMCA. I can tell already I will be walking into uncharted territory.

Once I am inside, a woman ushers me into a playroom where a few of the older children are gathering. She is the site manager and she introduces me to my supervisor, a full-bodied blonde woman named Michelle who is about my age and grew up raising horses. I start interacting with the kids, who attend area elementary schools with split sessions and have working mothers who are able to pay top dollar to keep their children occupied while they are on the job. Many of these kids will go to school and then later return to the facility where they will stay until their parents pick them up at five or six.

A young woman flashes past me and says I should move to the Bay Area; I don't belong in a place like this. She disappears into the nursery, which is on the other side of the building. I wonder who the hell she is and what she actually knows about me. The wealthy Bay Area is the last place I want to move. I do not want to end up like Green Day's Mister Whirly.

Moving forward, I do my job with a little play-therapy flair. I have a lot of energy stored up from incarceration and it spews out in creative efforts to connect.

By the time snacks appear, more kids arrive, as does a coworker—an angry looking Latina woman with freckles. When we take our group, which has now grown to number approximately fifteen, out to the play yard, I get a chance to talk with her. She instantly takes a hostile stance toward me, asking why a man with a master's degree is taking a job like this. Sitting back while the kids play quickly gets boring. I leave my coworker behind and interact with the kids. I find this prevents problems before they start.

When I get back from a short lunch break, I read the kids a book. Then within an hour I am joined by throngs of kids and two young girls from Fresno State University: one is a live-at-home Caucasian, a makeup and nails champion; the other, Lashawn, is an African-American from LA, who is culturally proficient and vigilantly professional. The crowd grows, and we are busy interceding and solving problems.

Late in the day, Michelle bursts into the chaos and calls the room to order. She demands compliance, putting troublemakers into lengthy, unmonitored time outs.

I really dislike this, as I can feel the agony in whole room.

Afterward, the multitude of little bodies thins, and each of us gets freed up to do a chore, such as vacuuming or cleaning the bathrooms. And then it is time to go and I bike back to the motel and prepare for my move.

〽〽〽〳

By the end of my first week of work, I have scheduled myself to take the California Teacher's Examination to prepare for entrance into Fresno State. By coincidence, Michelle, who has been doing this work for years, is scheduled to take the exam on the same day. When she offers to drive me to the exam, I agree to meet her at the job site because I don't want her to see I am still living at a motel. Michelle seems nice enough away from the job and the ride to the examination is uneventful.

Taking the test, I am able to remember that I hold measurable strengths. When I was locked up, I had no gifts; I was just subhuman and substandard. Driving home with Michelle and looking at her affect, I remember that even though Michelle may have been raised with horses, I too was born with gifts.

After the test, I hit the streets searching for places to get cheap used furniture. I ride down to the south Fresno ghetto.

A couple Latino kids on dirt bikes suddenly barrel toward me like cops. One gets in front and one behind me. My heart had freezes the same way it did back in Camden when I got my baseball glove copped. I remember it wouldn't have happened if I hadn't stopped to talk to the teens who'd done it.

I weave through traffic as though I deal with situations like this every day. As soon as I get on the other side of the road, I coolly weave back.

I complete this pattern twice until the kids give up. Then, I hightail it out of there, adrenaline dissolving throughout my body.

Instead of harping on this incident, I buy everything I need for the apartment for just four hundred and fifty dollars. I stop on the way home and shop because I know I will get some good deals in the ghetto. I find a clothing warehouse where I pick up some thickly corded brown pants—a new ghetto style—and some shirts that fit this emerging image. I find a very cheap cross I wear around my neck. I opt not to get a tattoo of a Pac-Man because of the cost.

♪♪♪

The next Saturday morning, after a successful move, I use my trusty map to navigate the outskirts of the city to the animal shelter. When I tell the lady at the shelter that I am limited to a twenty-five pound dog at my residence, she guides me to a squat dog that I walk around but don't feel any connection with. Feeling guilty, I return the poor thing to its cage. Left to my own devices, I stumble upon a tan and white dog, who has the same coloring as the dog I loved as an adolescent—the one my mom recently put to sleep. Like Tootsie, this new dog has a blue eye and a brown eye, but her demeanor tells me she, unlike my lost love, is capable of spending hours alone at the house. I get this dog on a leash and walk her around. She is sensitive and patient, with fluttering eyes. I can't imagine a more perfect angel.

I am so lonely back at the apartment with my angel scheduled for spaying, that I break down and call Joe back east from my unlisted number.

Joe is dismissive of my worried-well concerns. I figure he is just in one of his bipolar moods.

Then, he tells me, "Cheer up! I mean, it's not every day that you get two jobs in one day!"

My mind jumps. I have not let Joe know that I got two jobs in one day.

Joe's little message indicates that the Mafia is watching.

When I get off the phone, I am so angry that everyone just assumes that I am a schizophrenic.

❧❧❧

The next few days at work, I continue sharpening my style with the kids. One young African-American child named Kyle often gets in trouble because he touches his private parts in response to being viciously picked on by an angry mob of mostly white kids. Other kids torment him and then report to the instructor when he touches himself. This causes every instructor to punish the young Kyle.

I interfere with this pattern. I visualize Kyle as being homeless, psychotic, and alone on the streets of Seattle. I go into the mobs of white kids and punish aggressive provocateurs. In my assessment, the child may be getting picked on because he has been sexually abused. Additionally, being so racially isolated seems exceedingly unjust.

The provocateurs are shocked by my intervention and complain, but I am mild in my punishments, the pattern is interrupted, and Kyle's behavior improves.

After work on Wednesday, energy surges in my appendages. I scarf up food and set out on the eight-mile bike to the animal shelter. I make it there before closing, hand over my paperwork, and am led to the lucky room where my sweet girl is waiting. She wags her tail just slightly when she sees me. I solemnly secure the purple and blue collar I have selected around her neck. She wags her tail just a little more when she gets this attention. The two of us are led back to the front desk, where I pay and receive all pertinent paperwork and a dog license. Again her tail wags as I hook the license on her collar.

The woman at the counter asks for the dog's name.

I tell her "Maxine."

I get the necessary instructions about affordable shots and then the two of us are free.

We hit the vacant streets, where it is good and dark. When we finally reach a sidewalk we come upon a convenience store. I tie Maxine up outside, lock my bike, and run in. When I return, I empty the contents of an Alpo can on the sidewalk and she eats ravenously.

It takes a long time to get home, but it doesn't matter. By the time we get there, Maxine has peed and pooped. I give her a thorough flea bath and feed her again. Finally, at about two o'clock, I settle into sleep. She is scared and comes up to cuddle with me. I feel incredible relief. I have been so lonely for so long. She cries on my shoulder and I cry with her. Again, I have found an angel.

At work the next morning, I relate what I had been up to the night before to the site manager, and she smiles at me and asks me questions about my dog and the support feels great. At lunchtime I speed home to take Maxine out to pee and poop and she seems to be trained already.

Back at the job, one of the kids overhears me talk about my dog.

"Maybe you should feed her just a little bit at lunchtime," he says

The kid's gesture is not only cute; he has a good idea. Growing up, we always fed our dog just once per day. Now I am free to make my own rules and I know that three small meals is better than one big one.

"I will take your advice," I say to the kid.

When I get home after work, Maxine has pooped on the newspaper and opened up the sliding closet where I store her food. She's gorged; her stomach is bloated. I point at the poop and tell her no, and she responds very guiltily by rolling on her back and lifting up her leg. I point at the food, and she repeats the gesture and wags her tail.

I was taught by a family friend to aggressively stick the dog's face near the mess and yell at her. I ignore this. In this way I celebrate my freedom. I sculpt the kind of relationship I want to have with Maxine, paying attention not only to my needs, but also to hers.

Saturday, I walk with my girl down the street to the Wal-Mart and buy a rubber toy that fast becomes her favorite. She enjoys the challenge of capturing it as it bounces around haphazardly in the open field behind the apartment complex.

I also take Maxine to the dog park, where she can run free with a pack of dogs that chase her all over. She gets excellent exercise and never stops smiling.

꜒꜒꜒

Christmas break will be hectic at work, with kids needing to be herded during their school vacation. The potluck Christmas party is planned for the Friday before. I bring Maxine, who is particularly well behaved. She walks freely around, getting attention without being tempted by the various dishes that sit at her eye level atop little-kid tables. The site manager makes a point of warming up to me and adoring my dog—it is the best Christmas party I have ever been to.

When I get home I hug Maxine and thank all my angels.

CHAPTER **16**

THE VERY NEXT morning, I am out of my medication. I ride to work. A man on a black mountain bicycle comes up from behind me at a red light. When the light turns, he rides left, turns around, and then rides off to the right. He is wearing black, like a SWAT team member. His facial features are hidden beneath a black baseball cap and sunglasses. He could be bearing arms.

By this time I have devised a number of shortcuts to get to work; I take one and contain my distress. Before I know it, I am at work and focusing on being good to the kids. Work is easy. The site manager even takes some time to talk to me in private about how much she appreciates that nobody has to tell me what to do. It is Friday and I have that sense of TGIF as I vacuum the floor and prepare to see Maxine.

Mindful of the incident that morning, I take a different route home. As I am riding through the Wal-Mart parking lot, a Latino man follows behind me, running. He is not dressed as a runner, and I note that, as I swerve on my bicycle, so does he. I slow down and start to talk to him.

"Wow, it's just great to see you running this way," I say to him as if I am talking to a child.

"Yeah," he says, "I want to stay in shape." He smirks a little.

"Well keep on running and you'll be *the strongest man in the universe*," I tell him.

I stop at the video store. When I come out of the store, he is nowhere in sight.

That night, after I have played with Maxine and her rubber toy in the vacant lot, I hear a rap on the door. It is a cable salesman. He wears a hard hat, has a vacant stare, and displays a bizarre intensity. My heart is in my throat.

The next day, a new sign in the dog park indicates that surveillance cameras have been installed. I see no obvious signs of them when I look around. A gentleman comes up to me and tells me he used to train attack dogs for the military. He talks about how they used to encourage the dogs to be vicious fighters. "But," he says, "Those fighters have *got* to listen to their master."

Also at the dog park, a woman I have talked with before tells me she is a waitress at the Spaghetti Factory. I wonder if her boss is connected to the Mafia, as she seems to be digging for information.

Under the surveillance of cameras, I ignore a woman who looks extraordinarily like Kathy. She may be some kind of plant, or perhaps is Kathy herself. I can't even tell.

I go to the animal shelter. Heading out to the animal shelter is an unexpected move. Perhaps the trackers have been unable to anticipate it. At the animal shelter I do the paperwork on a very young kitten.

I head home, drop the dog off, and prepare to buy the necessary materials to bring the cat home.

As I approach the PetSmart, a fire engine pulls up beside me and flashes its lights. Though I acknowledge it could be a coincidence, I can't get the experience out of my head.

I know that it would be a good idea to go back on medication. However, I am not willing to talk to some quack psychiatrist who would only want to put me back in a hospital.

꙳꙳꙳꙳

At work, I immediately sense the difference. The place is mobbed with excited kids living out Christmas fantasies. Quiet mornings are now replaced with vicious competition: winners, losers, tears, anger-flashings.

Michelle, with the help of the boss, has arranged day trips on a rented bus. None of the trips are very exciting: we stop at parks, we monitor kids; we look at light shows, we monitor kids.

Michelle starts to use the fact that she is in charge to attack me.

One day she screams at the kids to get off the rocks when not a single kid is on the rocks that surround the play area. I am alone standing on the rocks so I can better intercede if something goes on. I get off the rocks.

The next day Michelle sends kids over to use the bathroom when there are prisoners cleaning up the park and then calls me over, yells at me for her decision, and tells me to get over there and monitor the kids. Michelle is doing everything in her power to kill me professionally!

A few days later, Michelle arranges for a police officer to come and talk with the children. He talks about citizenship and following laws before launching into a lecture about good touch and bad touch. When he finishes this, he shoots a glance at me, and mentions how perpetrators are usually single, white, bizarre men, "like this guy," and he points toward me.

One of the little kids shouts, "No, that's Mister Clyde," and the entire room erupts into cheers.

I manage to find my smile.

The cop goes on with his presentation and the boisterous African-American boy I am always defending acts up. The cop gets right on him and asks him his name. Then, he asks if he knows what kind of little boys perpetrators tend to go after.

Kyle acts ashamed.

"Little boys who are weird and who stick out in the crowd, like you, Kyle," says the cop. "Kids whose parents don't treat them well and aren't loved at home like the rest of us."

I maintain my smile. After Montana, even un-medicated, I would never publicly question cop authority.

Later in the day, Michelle makes a point of correcting my efforts to reduce the targeting of Kyle. The boy makes another inappropriate sexual gesture while being taunted and she punishes him harshly. I take my concerns to the site manager.

I tell the boss woman about my suspicions regarding the young child's sexualized behavior. I ask her what she's going to do about it.

Apparently shocked by my tone, she says, "You are a mandated reporter," she says. "If you suspect abuse, you have to report it."

I can see the game immediately! If KiddieKare reports, they lose a customer. If I do and the child's Mafia family is in communication with mine, it could result in Mafia revenge.

I make a grounded professional explanation: I don't actually have the evidence to make a report. I would need to work with the child in one-on-one play therapy to elicit a detailed admission before I can report. That is why I'd like to be able to refer my concerns to the agency. The boss woman looks puzzled. I do not realize it at this moment, but this is the last time I will ever talk to her.

❧❧❧

The weekend cast of characters at the dog park submits to hidden camera surveillance. A man with a rough beard and pompous attitude establishes rapport with a young yuppie couple by handing them a card, earning him an involved conversation.

The man is probably a government plant.

The Kathy look-alike is there and flirts out loud, "Oh, I guess you are not going to talk with me?" I give her a respectful, flirtatious smile and escape. Not in front of the government, I am not!

I bring Buddy home from the shelter in the plastic cat box that I strap to the back of my bicycle.

At home, Buddy goes wild, trying to capture a cloth mouse on a stick. He takes to curling up with Maxine and sucking on her nipples. Maxine looks proud and bonded to her brother. It is very cute, and it helps.

When I learn my credit is cut off, I believe my father is paying big money to try to force me back into the hospital. I have only been trying to send some tokens home for Christmas, which is just a week away, anyway.

As I check out at the Food Max with the last of my remaining cash, the cashier tells me, "Hey, man, you have very expensive tastes!" I look at the powdered Gatorade and the fruits and vegetables and it occurs to me the cashier is right. This is the last time I will drop fifty bucks on a week's worth of food.

ﾉﾉﾉﾑ

When I call the police to ask what might be going on, the detective I talk to sounds exactly like the man who came to the day care center.

"The man on the bicycle might have been one of us," the detective admits. "The fire truck may have been a coincidence; sometimes they flash their lights right before they enter an intersection—they shouldn't have, though." The detective sounds slightly concerned. "As for people running up behind you, the best thing to do is travel different routes on your way to and from work."

Then the detective's voice changes a bit. "Now you say you came from a drug area in a different state, are you sure you haven't done anything to piss people off?"

"I never touched a drug and would never do anything to bring this attention on me," I say. "I just want to start over."

"You mean to tell me that you've never smoked pot in your life before?" he says with a lack of professionalism.

"No, I've never smoked pot!"

"Well, then, I'd say you should be okay, if you're telling me the truth."

"Yes, I am telling you the truth."

I get off the phone and start crying.

I have used my phone call well. I haven't ratted anybody out, in case the phones were tapped.

Now what should I do?

﹥﹥﹥

I get an invite for Christmas from Lashawn, the African-American student at Fresno State who grew up in LA. She supports the way I operate, particularly the way I try to change the community dynamics with regard to the way poor Kyle gets victimized. The student drives me home after work and I have every intention of taking her up on her invite.

The day after, I notice real oranges line the route as I ride to work. They are just sitting there in the street! There are also some remnants of a porn magazine interspersed among the oranges in the gutters on my way to work.

The next day, as we are loading up the bus, I act out against Michelle, who has been exceedingly rude to me, criticizing me for being the last one on the bus as if I am a dog.

I take a back seat, and thinking that it will distress her I read some articles on the Norton that I am toting around with that my aunt has sent me. As I read the articles, I start laughing in a slightly maniacal manner. I am sending Michelle a secret message I figure she will understand.

A couple of the prepubescent girls who are used to my sense of humor respond to my bizarre laughter, saying it must be really inter-esting, the reading that I am doing. I acknowledge them but continue leafing through the articles.

That evening, I start to stress over the bathroom detail. The little girls come in and use the toilet while I am cleaning. I am afraid of being accused of something, and, of course, if Michelle sees my fear, she will exploit it.

She is a killer. She drinks Pepsi like all the hospital workers in Montana. I do not. This makes her potentially FBI!

﹥﹥﹥

On Christmas I wake up to a whole lot of nothing and take Maxine for a long walk, figuring the streets will be clear. For a short while, I am correct, but as we walk and the streets fill with cars, people honk when they pass. It's like walking along that highway from Helena to Butte.

The signs I am being followed mount like oranges. A few hours later, when a man parks his car and waits to get out until I pass, he bumps into me. Then he walks up to a closed shop. I see him stop, turn around, and return to his car.

I cannot believe that he would give up his Christmas morning just to send me this menacing message!

We continue the walk, even if it means I will ruin the Christmas of others. If they are paid to follow me, let them work! We pass an open restaurant, but I have no cash remaining and no credit card so I will just have to wait to eat a crappy, processed turkey lunch at home.

I could have spent Christmas with Lashawn if not for the oranges.

When I get home and have no message on the machine, I am furious. I think about how my parents are home celebrating. This confirms to me they are responsible for all the public harassment, paying local Mafia.

I get on the phone and share my rage with my mom. I yell at her for having me followed. I hang up and have no one else to talk to.

A few days later, mom will send me one thousand dollars along with some fast-food gift certificates. I know deep in my gut I am being unfair to her. She is just a cog in the Mafia machine.

᭝᭝᭝

The atmosphere at work the day after Christmas is the same as it was before the Christmas rush. At lunchtime, I go home to care for Maxine.

When I return, an Indian woman that I have worked with tells me I am to go home; I am no longer needed at the facility. Michelle and the site manager are on break and not available to discuss it with me. The whole place seems empty.

The Indian woman, who has been friendly to me in the past, appears unaffected by my dismay. She responds with a short statement of sympathy but points out I am back from lunch ten minutes late.

I apologize and point out that no one has communicated to me that this was a problem—I was following the advice of a police detective that I had talked to on the phone and varying my route to avoid harassment. The Indian woman furrows her brow and says it doesn't matter and wishes me well.

I figure I have been on probation. I figure the fact that I didn't want to replace Michelle enables the company to do this. I figure this whole hire was a plot and it doesn't even occur to me to contact HR.

Once home, I call my mom, who forgives me for my last call and seems likewise scared at my situation. With her gift, I am about two thousand five-hundred dollars away from being on the streets.

CHAPTER **17**

THE NEWSPAPER IS loaded with advertisements for master's level counselors, as if there is a grand scheme of recruitment. I am aware job opportunities could be used by Mafia to obtain information, but can no longer afford to let this influence me. I am all about survival.

I touch up my resume, write cover letters, and take breaks to apply for jobs in person. I stay busy.

The first job that catches my eye involves a long trip down to a county office. The job is open and waiting for qualified applicants. The application involves presenting an overview of every job I have had in the past ten years. This involves digging up old addresses and references from past minimum-wage employers. I am grateful my mom is willing to help.

Working on this application I learn I have to register with the California Board of Behavioral Sciences. I go to a library and print out the application. Becoming registered is a lengthy process that involves getting university transcripts and being fingerprinted. I am concerned the FBI has amassed false documents about me. Perhaps the report by that paranoid staff person in Montana that I was sexually inappropriate will result in me being monitored as a sex offender.

I go to Kinko's and print out resumes, leaving a fake name at the counter. Of course, when I apply to work at the same Kinkos for the third time, I am forced to use my proper name.

When I deposit the Christmas check my mother has sent me at the bank, the young woman processing it says, "Wow, that's a generous gift!" I feel guilty for my own ingratitude. I am also upset that the girl is jealous and nosy. I fear she is on my parents' payroll.

When I stop at a pet store to fill out an application, the kid behind the counter smiles. "You have to be able to work with reptiles," he says. I glance around the store. I see no reptiles. I figure the adolescent punk is referring to reptilian Mafia figures. The application goes in the first trashcan I can find.

The next time I shop at the Food Max, I fill out an application for employment.

In the checkout line, one of the women I worked with at the day care is behind me with her son. "We're not following you around, Clyde," she says.

I wonder why she would make such a statement. I wonder what they are saying about me back at the old job.

"Have you tried applying at Costco?" the woman asks supportively. "I hear they're hiring and they pay thirteen dollars an hour."

I like the idea. There is a part of me that now trusts this woman whose kid I had a good relationship with.

I bike down to Costco following the lead, but the man at the entrance won't let me in, assuring me Costco is not hiring. Having passed three oranges en route, I figure the man at the entrance is a Mafia plant. A large company like Costco would not pay a man to stand out and greet customers for no reason! No longer can I trust references from the people at KiddieCare.

To obtain copies of my transcripts, I contact the Counseling Psychology department at Villanova University, where I got my graduate degree. With one transfer, I am talking to a professor I loved: "Registering for an MFT internship, now does that possibly mean that you are living in California at this point?" I had never realized how savvy and in-the-know he was.

To help me with the procedure for requesting my transcripts, the professor transfers me to the "gatekeeper" professor, as she likes to consider herself. I recognize her voice.

The minute she hears it's me on the line she starts to tell me how to slip around the Villanova bureaucracy and then stops. "Clyde, are you possibly taping this phone call?" she says.

"*I* wouldn't do that," I reply.

She changes her advice midsentence and I can sense anger in her voice. I thank her and follow her directions and feel validated at least by her acknowledgment of all the clicks on my telephone line. My mother denies that she hears the frequent clicks.

ﭏﭏﭏﭏ

The first interview I get is at a medical office called Kaiser Permanente. This feels like a very professional opportunity and I think I better have a suit. I have been making persistent requests to my father through my mother to have my belongings shipped down to me from Seattle. My mom tells me my father has not responded favorably to those requests.

I break down and call my father from my unlisted phone for the first time since the hospital. In an angry voice, I request my interview suit and other belongings urgently.

My father's response only suggests I am being selfish. Walter and Nan will have to volunteer their time and they are busy. The fact he is only angry and has no remorse or desire to support me doesn't fit his love letter to me in the hospital. This reinforces my hunch that the letter really was pure Darth Vader shit!

I match his irritation with calmness and explain that I have a job interview.

My father sounds indignant. He will not give me an answer.

I am clearly not going to get my suit. I hang up on him.

I stay professional and call Big Brother Joe. Joe responds to my predicament by advising me to use him as a reference—he will tell my future employer that we did side jobs together back east during the three months when I was in the hospital. He says this is how things work, that friends look out for each other.

If the CIA *is* listening in on my conversations, I wouldn't want to demonstrate dishonesty.

Joe, who can detect my hesitance, says, "Come on, you mean to tell me that there is not a car wash or something close to where you're living where you could use me as a reference?"

I think about the car wash on the corner.

Joe says, "Clyde, if you come back east I can get you an apartment and make sure no one comes by to bother you. Come back east, Clyde." I recall Joe talking about the days when a friend rented him an apartment where he had laid low and didn't let anyone come around.

Later in the day, I return home from one of my many errands and a worker from the corner car wash runs behind me in a bizarre, distinguished manner.

Still, I am not ready to corrupt myself and apply for work under Joe's tutelage. Though clearly not responding to this job opportunity would send an unfavorable message to the Mafia, I still believe in an America that can protect me from all crooks. I will find a real job that will set me free!

❧❧❧❧

The next day it rains. I am on my way to the mall to pick up an interview suit.

I stop, soaking wet, at a thrift store. I buy a ten-cent plastic hat and am given a trash bag for free. I poke holes in the bag and wear it to deflect the rain.

At the mall, I lock my bike at the empty rack and get myself into Macy's.

Once inside, my sweat socks are so wet that I take off my shoes. Even in my garb, the salesman respects me enough to suit me up. I make a painful decision and drop one hundred eighty bucks on an interview suit, which will be altered in time for my interview.

When I leave the mall, my bike is no longer at the rack.

On the phone with the police, I feed plenty of details to the dispatcher. She tells me it is unlikely I will ever get my bike back.

The bus ride home through the pouring rain is miserable.

I feel like I will not be permitted to work, eat, sleep, or shit until I start to obey Joe and my family!

The next day I take the bus to the Goodwill to pick up a used bicycle.

On my way to the bus stop, I notice a suspicious looking man with a backpack follow behind me. He is carrying a paper bag. He sits in front of me on the bus.

He gets off at the same stop by the mall that I do and opens the door of a free newspaper box and drops his paper bag inside and moves on toward the mall.

The coincidence of our connection is uncanny! I hightail it out of there in the chance that there is a bomb in the paper bag.

A person who is passing by has taken notice of me and is *laughing*.

I head north toward the Goodwill.

The Goodwill has only two crappy over-priced brown bicycles for sale. I choose the better of them and drop an additional sixty dollars at the door.

On my ride home, I see a homeless man begging for change near the mall and get a lump in my throat. Once again, oranges line the route of my ride. The people who put them there know my every move.

I rent a car so I can look settled when I arrive at my interview. I use the car to pick up my interview suit. I have done everything humanly possible to set myself up for a good interview at the nice square institute called Kaiser Permanente.

The morning of the interview I get a call that my interview has been canceled.

My father must have gotten to them.

I don't even bother to follow up and inquire about rescheduling.

A day or two later, my interview suit arrives.

So grossly have I underestimated my father's power!

Weeks of failed interviews and hundreds of completed applications pass. During an interview at Food Max I am asked to wait at island thirteen and I know then I will not be hired because of the unlucky number. I am led up the iron industrial staircase into a large office that belongs to the manager. He is a fat man who asks to see my resume. On the wall behind his desk I see a picture of his face implanted on a surreal comic background: a caption underneath reads, "Rush Limbaugh." I know his face looks nothing like Rush Limbaugh's face; the picture is just bizarre.

All the man's workers are of African-American and Latino descent. I wonder how they feel about having to look at this picture in order to work for this fat conservative man.

He asks me why, with my resume, I want to work at his store.

I tell him I want to supplement my income.

It's just another interview that seems like it's staged by government agents who are trying to attack my way of thinking with counterintelligence tactics.

On the way home, I pass a man parked in a white truck just a half block from my apartment. I know what he is doing. There will be crushed oranges lining my route, so I give him the finger as I pass by. He gets out of the truck. He is young with meatball biceps and he chases after me as I speed away. I can see by the rage in him that he hates me. He will do anything to hold me down.

The meaning of the oranges becomes clear when I watch a movie in which Robert Downey Jr. plays a man dying from AIDS whose bisexual ex-boyfriend, Wesley Snipes, is currently mixing with the homophobic heterosexual world. They have an exchange in the movie when they talk about the *orange* as representing the significance of life.

I can see now that the oranges are meant to be death threats.

In addition, flocks of blackbirds have started to surround my apartment. Clearly, someone is purposefully leaving out dead meat to attract them. I recall the tattoo of the blackbird on Kathy's back and I can see now, as I did back at the Norton, that death is all around. I rent a movie called *Down Came a Blackbird,* and it is about torture!

In the landscape of my life, buzzards, vultures, and Mafia dirt bags abound!

I have a number of bicycle accidents because the used bike's frame is built for someone larger than I am. The semi functional brakes are coupled with narrow fraying tires. On one of my spills, I aggravate my back. On another I hit my balls.

My aunt suggests I let her send me the bike I had in Seattle. I speak positively about Corporate America so the people tapping my phone might appreciate this as a clear shift in my thinking. I will affiliate with anything that is honest and doesn't involve killing. I still object, though, to Ronald Reagan.

My aunt says it is good to hear me talk in this manner.

I talk to my aunt about how I have been receiving special information about the CIA from the TV show *Nightline*.

She seems unthreatened and very interested.

Comforted by this response, I confide in her about how all the dogs at the park dominate poor Maxine. In my eyes, Maxine is so gentle and good compared to them. I go on to explain that I have taken her up the other side of a fence of fierce guard dogs and stood by her as they barked at her, to try to help her remedy this.

"Maybe Maxine is just a runt," my aunt says.

I feel profoundly insulted. My relatives have always treated me as the runt since my eating disorder. Even my aunt doesn't understand the injustice of this epigenetic presumption.

Recently, I've taken notice of tiny businesses that have cropped up in the industrial structures across the street from my apartment. They could easily be fronting for surveillance operations.

A PG+E truck is always parked in the unpaved lot where I like to play with Maxine. There is an electricity crisis going on across the state: roving blackouts are rampant, proving that government jobs are full of corruption.

I see blackouts in effect at the Kinkos and other corporate businesses. Meanwhile, there are always plenty of PG+E workers across the street that could be working on the blackout problems, but instead they are clumped together in the lot across from *my* apartment complex.

I sense the same corruption that causes these blackouts is involved with repressing me. At times I worry my situation is the cause of these roving blackouts.

One rainy day between errands, I walk up to the PG+E truck with Maxine. I encounter a man in a hard hat, PG+E vest, and jeans. He is kicked back, doing nothing underneath a tarp. He sees me and sits up and turns up his radio.

♪♪♪

On my way to an interview at the pound, I come across a police checkpoint. After I pass through, I don't see any more oranges on the roadside. This emboldens me and I believe I have a shot at getting the job.

At the animal shelter, I wait next to a beautiful young woman who is apparently being interviewed for job as well. I can't help but strike up a conversation.

She has just moved to Fresno and is living out of a truck. She says she has a job working at the Spaghetti Factory, which instantly connects her to that woman I know at the dog park.

I tell her about the experience of getting my bike stolen.

She tells me that she is having her parents ship her bike to her personal mailbox.

I ask questions about her bike and she almost perfectly describes the bike my aunt will be sending me.

I ask her how much the bike costs.

The young woman looks stumped for a minute, "Uh, I guess like *a thousand, five hundred dollars.*"

During the interview, I am not swayed by my run-in with the young woman. My interviewer seems to be simple and accepting, but, as always, I focus on honesty. I present my genuine love for animals as evidenced by my recent adoptions, and my desire to get away from my chosen profession for a while, perhaps forever.

But then the man asks me how I feel about something that does happen at the shelter—euthanasia.

Though I don't believe in social Darwinism, I remember that I could be homeless in a month if I am not working. I give him an intense message of acceptance and submission in the name of survival. He makes a bit of a surprised "Huh!" It's as if he appreciates my elegance.

I wonder if he is crafty enough to pick up on the defiant allusion to Islam.

He suggests that pounds in the *Bay Area* don't practice euthanasia.

᠉᠉᠉

When I pick up the bike my aunt has sent me at my personal mailbox, the man at the counter mentions my parents and gets alarmed when he notices the intense scowl on my face.

I am angry that this man's business has been infiltrated!

"Don't you think your parents did a good job?" he says. "After all, how else would you have turned out to be such a good person?"

I begin to cry when he says this. I can tell I am wearing down.

A week later, I have an interview at a foster care agency. Sure enough, when I pull up to the agency to double lock my bike at the rack, there is a shitty brown bike locked to the rack that I recognize as the other bike at the Goodwill that I rejected when I purchased my bike. Of course, it is likely that my bike will be stolen during the interview, but I defiantly step inside anyway.

I am met by a cute African-American female supervisor who gives me her card. I definitely get a positive vibe from her. She makes a phone call and before I can settle myself down in a chair in the waiting room, an upper-class white woman appears to chaperone the interview.

During the interview, the upper-class white woman asks if I have seen the movie *Finding Forrester,* which is still out in the theaters. This is a clear sign that she has some inside information about my private life. I remember how the drinking, socially isolated Sean Connery character seemed to be a representation of my father and how this resulted in my having mixed feelings about the movie.

When awkward feelings show on my face, I hear the upper-class white woman say, "Well, I thought it was a great movie."

I remember my impending homelessness enough to weather her clear message that she approves of my father.

The interview lasts a good hour and a half. On my way out I see a police officer in a phony, security guard uniform drive past on a motorcycle that looks like it is right out of the TV show *Chips*. I feel like I am in a different country.

At least nobody has taken my bike!

I catch a late bus for a four o'clock interview for a teaching position at a school that is located in a southern neighborhood. I have to ask a passenger when it is time to get off the bus because I have never been to this part of the city before. An African-American youth who has overheard my question says that my stop is the next one and that he can take me to the school if I like. The bus is full primarily of elder African-Americans. I decline and stay on the bus. An approving elder woman gives me a nod and a wink and tells me when it actually is time for me to get off the bus and I make it to the interview.

I seem to strike up instant rapport with the elder African-American woman who is interviewing me and she seems to appreciate the experiences that I've had.

"The southern part of Fresno has one of the highest levels of poverty in all of California," she boasts, accurately perceiving that this information will compel me rather than repel me. And when she finds out I like to write poetry, she asks me to recite one of my poems, which I do, choosing one of the few that I have memorized: a villanelle. The woman smiles and says she'll be happy to have me as I am, working as a sub.

❧❧❧

I begin to sequester myself. On several occasions, I sneak out of the house to open a clandestine PO Box that I can use to publish my writing under a pen name. Each time I can tell I am being followed, so I give up.

On a rainy weekend, I stay at home just to spite everyone, even though it pains me. I write memoirs of the ways my father tried to make me into a mobster starting in the third grade. I leap from incident to incident. I fill computer pages with details of my life. I walk outside to a massive rainbow and I feel I am living in the book *Gravity's Rainbow*, which I painstakingly read in college. I feel as though I, like Slothrope, am getting close to figuring out what is really going on in the modern genocidal world, but I can't quite figure it out.

These days, life is a lot like trying to read the complexities of Pynchon. Reality looms on the horizon beyond the rainbow, just out of reach.

The rainbow is not a coincidence, I sense; I am meant to feel this way. I wonder if humans have the technology to impose such an awesome experience. This one feels like it was made to support me.

〵〵〵〵

Not long after this, the African-American female supervisor who interviewed me at the foster care agency calls and offers me the position. She sounds sexual and enticing and excited on the phone. She explains she has to review the pay scale with me and asks me to call and set up an appointment to meet with her.

I feel so aroused that I go to my room to jerk off.

I will be saved from the streets, yet I sense I will really be seduced into being a hornball spy for the government. I hide from the cameras under the covers. When I'm done jerking off, I feel conflicted remorse.

When I share my successful hire with my mom, she sounds concerned and refuses when I ask her for money to help me purchase a car so that I can take the job.

When I talk with my aunt, she also sounds concerned and suggests that I might consider moving up to the Bay Area where she and her husband can keep a better eye on me. She suggests she might be able to arrange a job at an *Italian* Deli she likes to shop at. Her husband is a CEO, an Ivy League school graduate, an Eagle Scout, and some other all-American shit-tistics.

I talk to Joe about my opportunity and dilemma.

Joe seems to know I have recently seen Tom Hanks in *Cast Away*. He suggests the isolation Tom Hanks experiences in the movie might be very much the way I am feeling. "Maybe one day," Joe suggests, "you will get off this island."

Off the phone, I walk across the street to the parking lot of the car dealership that appears to be a surveillance operation. Before I arrive, a man in an off-white business suit steps out of one of the doors of a row of vacant storage units.

I stop and start talking to him.

He tells me in a charming manner that his business was stalled by a hostage situation that was reported on the front page of the newspaper yesterday. This helps confirm that he very well could be FBI.

When we finish our conversation I proceed to the bogus car dealership. I have been eying one of the shitty cars on the lot, a GEO Metro like two of my past cars. I figure this car has been placed there specifically for me.

The only thing holding me back is that the car has a Calvin and Hobbes decal on the back window. I do not want to join in with these CIA images.

Sure enough, the car costs *one thousand five hundred dollars*, the amount I have left in my bank account. When I get in and start to drive it out onto the road, a big truck pulls up on the side of me, stops, and puts its hazard lights on so that I can't pull out onto the street. I back the car up and return it to the fake dealership.

More conspiracy coincidences!

Shoppers at the Food Max appear to laugh at me when they see me vigilantly watching my cart.

I have started getting spurts of the runs along with stomach-aches after eating food in the house. I figure people are entering and poisoning my food when I'm out. I see this as pressure to move to the Bay area.

Every time I walk outside to let Maxine relieve herself, I see U-Haul trucks passing by on the road, giving me the message that I should move.

Moreover, the exact same car that my Seattle girlfriend, Gail, drove has shown up in my carport, signaling to me that Gail's father—a "pharmacist"—may be tracking me down. I calculate all the Italian connections I've had in my life. Most of my girlfriends, like Gail, have been either Italian or Irish.

On TV, which I turn to, as the decision is eminent, there is information about the meth trade. The local news reporter, who barely looks official, reports that 80 percent of the country's methamphetamine is produced in the Central Valley of California. No wonder things are so Mafia-focused in Fresno!

Then, suddenly, the TV screen is interrupted for an emergency update. A voice comes on stating: "Warning—a sexual predator has recently moved into your neighborhood. Please keep all kids indoors."

I cannot decide if this is the work of the Mafia or the CIA.

The message is clear: either I can cooperate or I will be subjected to bogus charges of being a sexual predator.

When it is time for "Saturday Night Live," every channel has this weird industrial show demonstrating how food can get sealed in packaging to keep it fresh. I am not sure what it means. The workers appear to be Italian, perhaps connected to the Italian deli. It seems like some force is trying to guide me to the Bay Area by controlling my TV.

I call my oldest friend, Gary, and he sounds bitterly angry, putting up ridiculous boundaries, saying that he's cooking and that I'll have to wait.

Gary finally says, "Okay, I can talk to you now."

I lay into him about not letting me know all along what was going on in my own family. I tell him about being in the hospital and having to get forensic clothes from the clothes closet. Gary hangs up on me.

Finally, I call my father for the second time and tell him I am scared for my life. I ask him for help. He sounds angry and bitter and says, no, there is nothing he can do to help me out of the position I've gotten myself into.

When I return from walking Maxine, the movie *Dr. Doolittle* is just starting.

Clearly, this is a CIA message. They are telling me with this special broadcast that I can talk to the animals and help them out.

When a dog shouts out "I am Keyser Soze," I instantly pick up the reference to the Mafia movie, *The Usual Suspects*.

This tells me I am destined to work with the Italians. I am valuable only because I can talk to the animals. It is the only skill I have left.

CHAPTER **18**

MY AUNT IS at the door.

I have packed my belongings into boxes. My plan to move near my aunt has strengthened my heart. I am sure there is still Mafia shit up there in the insulated Bay Area suburbs, but I doubt it is as bad as it is in Fresno's meth-infested streets.

After my aunt uses the bathroom, she looks around and says, "You know, Clyde, are you sure you want to do this? I mean, this place is really nice for $505 a month and anything we find you in the Bay Area is going to be almost twice the price."

Now I am sure my aunt can see in my facial gestures that my runt-like heart has melted along with our pleasantries.

Once my bike, my bag, my boxed cat, and Maxine are in her car, my aunt tells me she and her husband have talked and that I can only stay with them for three days. Then I'll have to stay in a motel until I can get moved in.

That ice courage that helped me pack up the apartment is now just a puddle on the car seat next to my aunt.

My aunt makes a mysterious phone call while she is driving and then pulls into a fast food restaurant stating that she's hungry. I wonder if she has called the fast food restaurant to arrange to put poison in my food.

This worry compounds itself in my mind, so that when the food comes I straight up tell her what I think she's doing to me.

Her eyes widen in anger. "Clyde," she says.

This shames me into eating.

At my aunt's house, my cousin has just returned from some high school project in his brand new Honda Civic. He is wearing a Boy Scout uniform. His socks are not evenly pulled up to match on his legs, causing him to look oddly slovenly.

I recall the stress of my junior year in high school, when I responded by becoming obsessed with caloric intake. I recall how before my early hospitalizations, I had been programmed to be horribly judgmental of anything that wasn't upper-crust liberal arts. I sense from the glint in his eyes that that's where he's at right now.

Both of us are slouched in our chairs, not knowing what to say to each other: me, in my studded belt, Montana jeans, punk boots, and Clash T-shirt; me, the miserable failure.

My uncle comes down the stairs and leads me into the garage, which is a wreck, and the only place they will allow Maxine to stay.

After reviewing many of the things I need to know about my three days at the house, my uncle engages me in an old interest of mine, Mt. Everest.

"It's a very risky business," he says.

I agree, even though risky business doesn't interest me very much anymore. Now survival is all I care about. I am sorry for even meddling in the Everest of social injustice at Norton. My uncle seems to get a good read on this.

My aunt comes down the stairs and joins us.

My uncle asks me to please not walk around in my underwear because of my younger female cousin.

My aunt suggests I need to go out and buy appropriate clothing. They can loan me money if need be.

I look at how she is dressed in slovenly black pants and out-of-fashion Adidas shoes and I feel extremely offended. I insist my clothing was not the reason I couldn't get a job. I talk about my interview suit. I talk about the job I got.

My aunt says my current look is not adult.

Plans proceed, as does my powerless slouch in the chair.

Then my aunt accuses me of touching myself in front of her.

The fact that I have done nothing of the sort tells me that she might fabricate anything to put me back in the hospital if she so pleases.

My mind darts from the idea that coming up here was a grave mistake to the realization that I have no other choice. If I don't work with my aunt, attend therapy, and keep my job, my parents won't help me out financially.

My uncle seems to accurately read my level of distress.

My aunt backs off a bit, saying that she has to tell her own son not to scratch his balls.

My uncle invites me down into his den, where he can show me what he has planned. He has found a place for me out in the town of Antioch. It will be a mere ten-mile bike ride to the nearby BART station and then a forty-five minute ride to Walnut Creek, where the Italian deli is located.

This all sounds just fine. These are things I can definitely do.

The next morning my uncle joins me at the table and reads the headline of the breaking story about Robert Hansen, the CIA double agent. He startles in shock.

I have him pegged as CIA.

Outside the house I find two oranges in the street and a white truck when I take a long walk.

After the walk, I am restless all morning. I bounce between my aunt and uncle, trying to move the plans forward as they fight each other over control of the day.

Finally my aunt and I drive an hour on the highway to where the land is flat and barren. When we finally get off the highway, I ask to stop at a gas station to use the bathroom. I approach the attendant and ask for work.

He says, "Well, I can give you an application, but I can also tell you we're not hiring."

I tell him I'll take the application anyway and he hands it to me with a knowing smile. This is a bad sign.

Back outside, I tell my aunt, "I'll be right back." I run into the Denny's down the street and ask for an application. The manager looks at me knowingly and says he doesn't have any positions available.

I've now determined this town isn't for me.

When we arrive at the apartment complex, however, there is a thick-boned, blonde woman, who looks exactly like Michelle, my supervisor from KinderKare, that Pepsi drinker. She sits talking to the complex manager. With imposing presence, she announces she is from the Secret Service. Her job is to protect the president.

My aunt doesn't look the least bit surprised by this information.

My heart sinks into my gut. I ask the woman if she thinks this is a safe complex to move into.

"Oh, yeah, you won't have any problems with crime here," she promises.

Although I cannot stand the pool and the hot tub and the $955 a month rent, the fact that it gets the stamp of approval by the US government means the decision is made.

As we are leaving, I stop my aunt and run in and ask the Secret Service woman to see her badge. "Oh yeah, I'm official," she says flashing me a badge.

The next day, I meet with the Italian shrink my aunt has selected. She will be receiving payment from my parents, who clearly want me hospitalized. With my aunt's support, I tape the session.

The shrink's office is in the back of an antique store in a snooty town called Lafayette. I can get to the office on BART with a bike ride. From the leather couch where I sit, I can see the sign of a local retail store with a: "Big Dogs" emblem. It is visible through the window above the shrink's desk. It makes me think about Snoop Dog. I think that dog is god spelled backward.

It's all Mafia godfather shit!

The shrink sits in a fancy ergonomic chair with her hands atop the hand rests as if she is Abraham Lincoln at the Lincoln Memorial. Her desk is neat and clean. She has a leopard skin handbag. Her taste is very nineteen eighties. It is an era I don't approve of.

At the end of the session she tells me she believes that what is going on with me is extortion. She says perhaps she will see me in the future. I feel slightly flirted with.

The next day before my interview at the deli, my aunt starts in on me again about my attire. Now I am wearing my thick-corded pants with a belt and a turtleneck. I am aware the pants are a bit of an African-American style, but I don't want to hear her encapsulated suburban perspective. She, I have learned, is so uncomfortable mixing with people of the lower classes that she drives all the way out to Walnut Creek to spend top dollar at this Italian deli she wants me to work at.

I meet the manager of the deli, a Chicano man named Mario, who happens to be wearing the same thick cords and a turtleneck—same colors too. I recognize this coincidence as a sign that he is in the know.

He is respectful of me and almost nervous. He asks me to move one of the marble topped tables into the corner so we can talk business, as if it is a test to see if I will follow his direction. He looks impressed that I will work so hard to move a table; his look almost makes me cackle. As he talks to me it seems as if he feels a little bad for me. At one point he suggests maybe they can make room for me to work the cheese counter sometimes.

This does make me laugh.

As if all the extortion that puts me here is only about selling cheese!

Mario looks a little puzzled.

He then gives me a vast amount of reading material about company products.

Now I am puzzled; I mean, I am here to work hard and make a low wage, not to be educated about the region of Italy where these fine fucking olives come from.

But when it is decided I will start on the third of the month, I am serious and thankful.

This time, at all costs, I will not let my personal life interfere with my professional one.

After the interview, my aunt and uncle together take me to a car rental place where I will spend my own money to rent a car. Of course they choose the most expensive company, Avis, and when I complain about it, my aunt tells me that she is trying to teach me something: that Avis is a good American company.

When I see the car they have selected for me, I am dismayed that it is white, like all the trucks that have been following me.

Back at my aunt's house, I prepare to take leave. I console Maxine about her cramped quarters, then go inside. My cat is allowed in the house and will stay as long as it takes for me to get settled. I think about how Maxine and I, the field runts, have a different status. I overhear my aunt tell my younger cousin, who has been hidden away from me as if I am a monster, "He is going to go hiking tomorrow with Maxine because *everybody* deserves to have a vacation."

I want to say, "No, I don't want to spend my last dollars this way. No, I don't consider what I am doing to be a vacation. And no, you are not special because you think that even a lowly person deserves a break."

I feel as though I have become an object rather than a human, a lesson in human decency rather than a relative.

It starts to rain as I follow my aunt's MapQuest directions to a motel just outside of Walnut Creek. At the motel I am alone. I flick on the tube. It is a show on California prisons displaying gang fights and talking about how pedophiles get targeted by the other inmates. It seems like this program is being transmitted purposely to this particular tube, just like the special transmissions I received in Fresno.

I would rather be sentenced to work in a Soviet gulag than an American prison or mental hospital. At least in a gulag, I could find meaning in the work. At least it beats circling on a ward.

These thoughts make me burn. I go out driving until I find a Quick Stop, where I buy a Playboy.

᠉᠉᠉

When I pick up Maxine, I find her cowering in the corner. She has been confined with her own crap all night. When I confront my uncle, he admits they didn't walk her. He just shrugs and tells me where the materials are for cleanup.

I drive through the Caldecott Tunnel and out into the suburbs toward Mt. Diablo. When I reach Walnut Creek, I happen across a sign and start funneling through country roads to look for trails. I end up dead-ending at an adjacent regional park where I can hike with a free map.

I am astounded by the way Maxine instinctually herds the cattle that are grazing in the pastures. I walk up and down graded roads, past the mud pies and the barbed-wire fencing. Toward the end of our trip we end up in more of a wooded area and I note that people in either army apparel or REI apparel are out looking for me. I recall a theory I developed while in Fresno, that a tracking device had been sewn into Maxine when she was spayed. Knowing smiles on the faces of some of the people I see indicate we are in fact being tailed.

Heading back in the rental car through back streets, I see a pack of young children crossing the street with a crossing guard. They are all wearing backpacks. A wave of terror washes over me. I involuntarily duck and hide as I brake the car.

In Fresno, men wearing backpacks were a sign I was being followed; it happened all the time. But here, I can see that these children are just coming home from school with their Spy-Kid backpacks and not following me for real. This makes me want to move back to Fresno and take the job I earned through all my hard work.

The next day my uncle takes me out to eat at a fast food restaurant. He tells me, "You know I'm not like your father; I kill people for a living."

In signing the papers at the apartment complex, the management company attaches a severe financial penalty to prevent me from breaking my lease early. Whether this is the work of my uncle or the government or my father, the message seems clear: this is do or die.

Once I have keys to the apartment, my uncle offers to stay with me and help me get set up, but I refuse. He accepts this, but wants to make sure I know how to catch the bus. His opinion is obvious; I will not be capable of completing my schedule on a bike. It makes me chuckle. I allow him to ride me around in his old BMW.

The two of us end up at a counter in the local mall in order so that I can know where to purchase bus tickets. My uncle announces very loudly to me, the cashier, and anyone else who will listen: "This is my nephew and I am not going to let anything happen to him!"

In my experience, living outside the bubble of the suburbs, this will only make me more of a target.

I leave my BMW uncle behind in the parking lot. I go to a nearby store named MacFrugal's and buy the bare minimum of what I will need to survive in the apartment for a month. Then I go food shopping at the Food 4 Less and buy a week's worth of food.

ﻼﻼﻼ

I arrive to work at a little before eleven o'clock wearing the prescribed black pants. I am granted a nametag, an apron, and one free white-collared shirt; future shirts will cost me twelve dollars. Mario sits down with me and a young girl named Leah, who is also new. Leah smiles as if she knows everything that I've been through.

I figure I will be tempted by many young Mafia chicks looking to marry into a family like mine.

Mario gives Leah and me a test to see if we've read our homework. While Leah demonstrates she's read and respects the material, the inherent stupidity of having reading material for low wage "associates" position at a business like this has caused me to exempt myself.

Performing more poorly than Leah seriously depresses me.

A regional manager, the co-owner of the company, and some kind of Italian celebrity chef (probably a mobster) stop in to meet me. The regional manager appears to be both gay and very disappointed by my mood.

The co-owner takes me into the back of the deli and exclaims, "We are going to make a lot of money!"

He is both sizing me up and trying to change the way I think. I cannot help but sour.

Once I have been accurately assessed, I am told to go home early.

I walk my bike back to the BART, never having felt so utterly oppressed. When I pick myself up at the end of the line in Bay Point I realize my expensive bike bag is missing, along with my Gortex rain pants and a few other items of lesser value. I have been robbed again. Now I am in trouble if it does rain. I cannot replace what I have lost.

CHAPTER **19**

INGREDIENTS FOR EACH sandwich are posted, so it doesn't take me long to figure out what I need to do. Measuring the various dishes is more difficult than I had anticipated because there are different tare weights for a variety of empty containers. Learning the names of the dishes is likewise complicated by the fact they are all written in Italian. And then I have to learn all the different meats as well. For example, there are three styles of prosciutto, a smoked meat that I have never heard of before. Each style bears a long story that explains the level of salt. It is surprising that many fat-cat customers expect to hear each story. I function for the entire day and start to have more respect for the need for the reading materials.

In the middle of my clunky functioning, Len from Danville confides he is absolutely miserable at home and this job is the only thing he has going for him.

At one point he watches me trying to figure out how to put the labels on the meats and says, "Oh, Clyde, I see you are pretty savvy with those meats. I don't think that even I could do much better."

This kind of arrogance stabs me. I have to acknowledge that it was the same kind of arrogance I demonstrated to the people at the Norton when I believed that I could solve their problems.

"You the chicken man?" Len chirps as I am slicing meats. There is a high-pitched distortion in his voice. "Are you the turkey man? I think you are the turkey man, *turkey man!*"

I instantly get the reference. I understand what this Mafia hack means by his bizarre behavior. The chicken man was a famous mobster in Philadelphia who got blown up in his house according to a Bruce Springsteen song.

"I'd be a turkey any day," I tell him. "I'd never want to be a chicken."

He smiles and knowingly chirps *"Chicken man."*

"I guess we have a chicken man," Leah says, as though she too understands what to most people would appear to be nonsense.

This kind of dialogue goes on hour after boring hour.

It pisses me off!

Leah, who was hired right beside me, gets along with everybody in this way. They seem to live to tease and torment my soul. Leah lives in Danville and attends the local community college in her white Volkswagen Golf. She is very smart and always in a good mood. As far as players go, she is particularly hard to take!

Another coworker is Leah's friend, Punk Rock Pablo from Paraguay, a bass player in a number of local bands. He almost always appears to be under the influence of something and criticizes me in a dominant way while remaining pleasant and down to earth with others. He reminds me of my old friend, Gary, for his humor and the way he wears his upper-class shoes in punkish ways. His favorite saying is, "For shizzle my nizzle." Like Leah and Len, he lives in Danville, and he often talks expansively about his father's wealth.

Joy, the assistant manager who is always in charge when Mario is not around, likes to call herself the ship's counselor, which means I am certain not to let her know a goddamn thing about me. Joy takes an instant liking to me and is from Australia and is full of emotion. Her green eyes always sparkle.

Deep down, I will never trust any of them.

On day two, Eduardo, an immigrant from Chile, asks me to take a trip to Chile for him. He will pay. I just need to take care of some business for him.

I figure he is clearly permitted to work here because of drug ties because his English is worse than my Spanish. All day he is permitted to work in the back.

I sort out the Mafia messages in Spanish, and blatantly refuse him. I come to believe that Eduardo, who is reputedly tough, is the unspoken kingpin. I will not be extorted into being his mule!

The only coworker who doesn't join in in this Mafia nonsense is Lauren, an immigrant from New Zealand who works the cheese counter. I am instantly smitten with her looks and am sure I can't hide it.

Pablo has already told me that Lauren is a sex freak and loves to cheat on her husband.

But Lauren speaks to me as if I am a human and tells me that she spent a year living in a squalid rooming house in England before tending bar in Seattle, where she got pregnant by the man who became her husband.

At the end of day two, right before her shift is over, she sneaks some turkey breast into a package and asks me in a flirty way to watch it for her. I instantly read into the meaning of this gesture: she respects that I prefer to be turkey and is ready to show me her breasts.

However, immediately she seems to sense the refusal in me and she never returns to pick me, the turkey, up.

Later, while I reflect on the fantasy of Lauren, Len smiles knowingly and says, "Chicken."

Quite randomly, I later ask Leah if her sun glasses are authentic, are they realy Ralph Lauren.

Leah looks confused when I say this so I stick my finger down my throat as if to say: Lauren make me want to ralph.

Now Leah looks even more confused but I know eventually she will figure it out.

All these Mafia chicks and Mafia dicks need to get themselves to a goddamn punnery in my opinion!

On the third day I meet a young teen named Joel who lives in Lafayette. Joel is a big believer in pot and in upper-crust success. He is fearful yet vies to be dominant.

Joel tries to teach me how to mop, as though I am an ignoramus. Worse, he thinks he'll earn points by teaching me to do a shitty job.

As I leave work, he drives up to me in a brand new white truck he owns and makes fun of the second hand bike I had shipped down from Seattle.

A few days later, while he is in one of his endless conversations about smoking pot, he stops as I am readying to walk out the front door and pick up my bike. He says in a bullying tone, "I am in a play at school; I am getting ready to go to practice. Ya know what the title of the play is? It's 'Bye-Bye-Birdie.' " He laughs as though he is amused by his own toughness.

Anthony, my shift supervisor, is a few years older than Joel. On the third day, he tries to feed me the various dishes so that I know what they taste like. I am petrified he is trying to poison me and I refuse. He laughs and calls over to Adele, the catering manager, to come and observe me.

I reluctantly and cautiously eat in front of upper management.

"See, doesn't that taste good," he says.

Sure enough, fifteen minutes later I am in the bathroom. I am astounded. How could he have possibly poisoned the food in that short a time?

That evening, he calls me out after work and says I'm not respecting him.

I shout, "I respect you!"

I calm myself and explain how I will do anything to make this situation work and don't understand why everyone is so negative toward me. He says he is sorry about my situation but I have to stop taking it out on him and everyone around him.

I wonder what he really knows about my situation, as I act as if I agree. He is a pinch more genuine than Len and Pablo. I figure my facial gestures are out of control.

Mario mostly stays out of it when the Mafia kids are picking on me and works the cash register. Before I leave on the third day, he sits me down and points out I was five minutes late to work and says if it happens again that he is going to fire me.

I cannot believe what I hear and explain to him I am moving up from Fresno to work this job and need it desperately.

He says with fake sympathy, "Oh, I know, Clyde, and if it was anyone else, I would have fired them already."

I feel an enormous lump in my throat this time and sit back in my chair. Then, I lean forward and say, "Being on time is something I can control. I won't let it happen again."

♪♪♪

I am looking out the window at the Big Dogs logo wondering what relationship this Italian shrink my parents are forcing me to see for $125 an hour has with my employers. One hour of her paid time is five hours of my free time (it takes me two hours each way to get to her.) Additionally, one hour of her time is two days of my wages. And there she is, smiling smugly.

"I, too, shop at Lueggio's," she says. So I know for sure I cannot trust her with any important information. In my mind anyone who supports the Italian Deli I work at is supporting the Mafia's repression of me.

I talk about the theoretical orientations I like. Really, I couldn't give a rat's ass about whether she knows my orientation. I am doing to her exactly what she, Len, and the Mafia are doing to me. I am letting her know I know where she is coming from.

I say I am very interested in social constructivism. I say that in my program, I read the paragraphs about narrative therapy very carefully and they were interesting.

"That's my orientation," she says excitedly.

She does not even realize I am trying to be creepy. How could she help me out with the way Len and Pablo and Lauren are being creepy toward me if she is so blissfully and small-mindedly ignorant?

"In fact, I teach advanced trainings in narrative therapy at the Wright Institute," she continues.

I look at her as if to say, "Whoopty fucking do!" and I am relieved when the time is finally up.

When I get home, I eat some food and try to find some freedom. I follow the map of Antioch up to a park. I get on a bike path that meanders around a ball field and then climbs up a steep bank. Maxine and I then pass a woman walking a beagle. I recall one of the government or Mafia plants in the dog park in Fresno telling me he thought Maxine had beagle in her. The beagle here is a message: even here, I am being followed.

We reach a trailhead I discovered with the white Avis car during my "vacation" and there is a sportily clad man sitting there waiting for me with his mountain bike. He talks about how he is hardworking. He talks some bullshit about how he has to force himself to get going on a "mission" like this. I recall the "hardworking" Snickers law enforcement officers back in Montana. He is one of them.

I walk my bike up the path, double lock it to the barbed-wire fence, and cover it up with some brambles. Then I unleash Maxine and throw sticks down into gullies for her and let her chase cows.

﹏﹏

I wake suddenly. I am sitting up and sweating profusely. On the floor in my blanket, I cannot remember why I am so astoundingly terrified; I feel I have just died.

Most nights I am awakening to images and memories of the pressure and pain of confinement. This one is intense and I have no recollection.

﹏﹏

I arrive at work at 6:40 a.m. and Mario invites me to clock in early. Ten minutes after the deli opens at 10 o'clock, a new employee arrives and is introduced to me by Mario as my new supervisor. She has bleached blonde hair with blue eyes and is as skinny and fit as Lauren. At age nineteen, she reportedly just got home from LA where she was trying to make it as an actress. I can see right away she loves to put on a social show as she is able to swiftly join in, dominate, and abuse. I wonder if she was brought in as a supervisor instead of me when I failed company tests.

During my break, I look at the locker she has claimed in the backroom and see she has decorated it with stupid adolescent *frogs* and her name "KaCee Lee Keener." The name itself makes me think of "KKK." The "Lee" in the middle potentially represents an admiration by her family of General Robert E. Lee, the defender of slavery. This is truly an evil empire. I hate it that her last name rhymes with mine.

In this state of mind, I scan the lockers for other clues. I realize the cheese labels Len puts on his locker represent his view of himself as "the big cheese." Pablo has made number associations, tearing up a rap radio station's numbers and creating Mafia fish out of the fours, turning nines into sixes that then represent bigger fishes that eat the smaller fishes. These are sophisticated comments about the *game*. Dominant rich kids like Len, Pablo, and KaCee understand they are big fishes in the Mafia.

Like Anthony, KaCee puts me on lunch last. I wait two extra-long hours, even though I arrived first and biked ten miles.

The deli is mobbed with customers. I think there are many government agents flooding the deli with business so Mario can't justify firing me. Even Joy, who clocks in at eleven o'clock and makes complaints about everyone except me, says she hasn't seen a day like this in a long time.

I am often left alone to make sandwiches. Leah and Len often disappear into the back to be with KaCee. I catch them giggling and talking with each other as only Mafia brats can.

When I finally eat, I choose the cheapest sandwich because I have to pay half price on all food I eat. Even though others don't pay anything for their meals, I fear KaCee will enforce the rule with me and I don't want to give her ammunition to use against me. My job has already been threatened.

After opening the store for three days, I return to my role as a closer. When the store closes at seven, I try to neaten up everybody's station. Joy always complains when there are imperfections with the close. Although Joy never holds me responsible, I believe any problem will ultimately be used by Anthony or KaCee as evidence to get rid of me.

I work constantly against these fears.

One thing in the worker's handbook that every employee in the deli likes to take seriously is the procedure for carrying knives around the deli.

"Behind you with a knife!" one is supposed to shout.

Of course, I instantly get the Mafia message inherent in this and am sure there is no coincidence as Len, Pablo, or Anthony frequently say it to me as they pass behind me whether they carry a knife or not—especially as I am working the slicer. I never hear it said to anyone else in this manner.

While I am in the walk-in filling the drinks, Anthony bursts in, gripping a knife, and startles me. The first time it happens, I do believe I will be stabbed. The second and third time it happens, I exaggerate my natural startle response.

"You okay there, Clyde?" Anthony asks with genuineness he can't help, as he aggressively grips the knife.

Every time a customer orders a Caesar salad, Len says, "Would you like me to toss your salad?" With the word "salad" there's a hint of a higher pitch in his voice.

I immediately recognize the message, as I am aware of the famous Chris Rock *Bring the Pain* comedy routine depicting to the mainstream some of the realities of jail. On the occasional day when Joel works, he delights in the "tossing the salad" routine.

I have no respect for these kinds of antics.

One day, Joy comes to my rescue. Leah is having a bad day and taking out her anger on me. Late in the day, Leah talks to KaCee and Anthony about some hostility they are observing. It's true; I have probably shot them a hostile glance or two. They confront me about it in their punitive, degrading way, and Joy overhears. When they are gone, Joy comes over and asks me why I am mad and I don't know where to begin.

I mention a small example. I didn't get my break on time because Leah came back late from lunch. Joy goes to the back and checks the time clock then returns to let Anthony and KaCee know that Leah in fact was twenty minutes late coming back from lunch.

After Joy is gone and it's just Mario at the helm, Leah, whom Mario always favors, accosts me.

"How dare you tell Joy that I was late? I was late because I was crying, because I broke up with my boyfriend today—I was crying, goddamnit!"

When I fail to show sympathy for Leah's trauma, KaCee gives me extra work and I don't care.

❧❧❧❧

On my way to the Bay Point BART station I look for clues. This is my routine.

One morning on my way to work, right at the spot where I entered the street from out of the apartment complex, I saw a short line of Hershey kisses lined up on the ground. I figured my CIA uncle had them placed there to reorient me toward capitalism. When I think of the chocolates, I think about my favorite movie in College that I saw with Big Brother Joe, *Life is Sweet*, and think about the message of acceptance in it.

Every day I am so aching for recognition for my efforts. The chocolates represent the appreciation I have always yearned for. In a strange way, on that day, I had felt taken care of.

Today, as I involuntarily scan the road, I pass a wrench and realize I have left my bag of tools at home. The wrench is there to remind me I am vulnerable in the event I get a flat.

I am infuriated. I want the people who are watching me to stop breaking into my apartment. Obviously, that wrench came from my bag. They can return my goddamn things themselves; I'm not falling for their game. I leave my valuable wrench in the gutter.

I recall the day I arranged to pick up my cat, Buddy, from my aunt and uncle a week ago. I purposely took the BART two stops past the stop my aunt told me to take. I was sure that, had I gotten off at the intended destination, I would have been followed.

When I suddenly got off at Nineteenth Street I encountered no evidence I was being followed. I biked up to a payphone and called my uncle and told him the corner where I was located. By the time my uncle arrived, sirens started to sound. I remembered Montana. Thus, when my uncle politely asked if I wanted to get a cup of coffee, I swiftly strapped my cat to the back of my bicycle and walked back to freedom. In spite of the chocolates, I hadn't trusted him.

Now, I struggle to bike up the last hill, thinking about this earlier incident. I pedal as rapidly as possible because I don't want to risk being late for my therapy appointment.

"Your parents are paying for the time," the shrink told me. "It shows they care about you and that they can afford it. Why sweat the small stuff?"

I know my parents far better than she does. I know they will hold the fact they spent this money against me.

Then, in one motion, I dismount my bike while it is still moving, pick it up running, and ascend a stairwell. I head straight for the turnstile, past a sign that reads: *"Assaulting a BART employee can really make you late."* I rush down the stairs, afraid.

I remember the one morning I was stopped and my bag was searched. As a result, I risked being late to work and losing my job. I am always afraid I will be stopped by a BART officer and lose my job.

It is true there is a phone in the terminal. I can call Mario who has given me permission to call if I am going to be late. But the cost of the phone call interferes with my budget. Most of my meals come from the dollar store. And I am hungry for every last dollar after my twelve hour day. It all makes me so angry.

My mind is still pondering the shrink's advice.

I recall how my father had sounded gruff on the phone. "I want to give you three hundred and fifty dollars a month, but don't use your credit card and remember I can only do this for a year; after that, there's not much else I can do."

Before I left for the morning, my mom had told me over the phone that I was lucky to be getting any help, that her friends say that she is just enabling me!

I am sure that my mom is just telling her friends her twisted side of the story. Does she bring up the inheritance she is illegally with-holding from me? I suspect she's probably working the shrink over the same way she does her friends.

I am not sure why my mom gives me one hundred dollars less than my father, but she tells me bitterly when I ask: "Your father is not as poor as he tries to make it seem. He won't spend his money on you unless I force him."

On the ground in Lafayette, on this particular day off, on my lengthy cycle to the shrink's office, I pass Adele from work. She is delivering a catering order. Adele just deals with catering and has nothing to do with any of the Mafia harassment or control that goes on in the deli. She just earns a paycheck. I respect her and the look in her dull eyes.

When I say hello she picks her head up and says, "Wow, that's a coincidence that we bumped into each other like this. What are you doing out in these parts?"

Adele is so genuine I don't doubt her in the least. She doesn't have it in her to lie and play spy, but I am sure the whole catering order is probably coordinated this way to send me a message. I have long since given up the idea of coincidence.

As I sit on the stupid leather couch, the shrink interrupts me and asks what I want to work on today. I am presenting her with vital de-tails of my experience, testing her for trust, and she only demonstrates she is not interested in what I have to say. She wants me to start where she's at.

When I tell her about my experience with Joel's "Bye-Bye-Birdie" comment, she smirks. "That is a little weird!" She doesn't even be-lieve it happened to me.

Not knowing what to talk about, I tell her KaCee and Anthony are starting a relationship, as if it sickens me—after all, I am starting to respect Anthony a little.

On a recent morning, when we were both waiting to clock-in, I reached out to Anthony. He had been sitting at the customer tables drawing like a five-year-old child. Having noted that he sometimes had missed an occasional shift, has a low mood, and wears a thought-blocking rubber band on his wrist (a sure sign that he is in therapy,) I approached him in a nurturing way. I saw it as an opportunity to get into the head of one of my tormentors.

I had observed his drawings: a view of San Francisco from his favorite lookout on Mt. Tam and an Aztec coat of arms with a sword stabbing a serpent. I could surmise from these pictures that he felt like an outsider and a dreamer, with an obligation to be a male controller—a mandate that he wasn't always comfortable with.

As if he could sense my empathy and respect, he has been a great deal nicer to me ever since.

The shrink interrupts these reminiscences with a smile and says that Anthony and KaCee are probably having a *sexual* relationship. She says the word *sexual* as if I don't even know what sex is. I figure she has been talking to my mom, who has informed her I am sexually reserved.

I shudder in anger.

The shrink starts asking probing questions I don't want to answer.

She asks, "So when did *paranoia* start to be a problem for you?"

"What do you mean, paranoia? What I am going through has nothing to do with paranoia."

Before she lets me leave, she tells me my problem is I am giving all my power away to adolescent kids who are bullying me.

"Gee, thanks," I say, and remind her that I get a week off of therapy for my move.

She says she is very concerned and wants to see me more often.

I tell her I will only come in once per week.

She asks for permission to call my parents and ask for two hours per week instead of one.

"You're going to do whatever you're going to do," I say facetiously.

I don't get the feeling the shrink is interested in learning anything about me. She knows nothing about what I go through on a daily basis.

ゝゝゝゝ

I have made all the arrangements for the move. I have rented a one-way car and a one-way truck. I feel reassured about this. On a rare occasion I have been given some work to do in the back. I am relieved, because for the past few days the kids have been giving me a hard time about the cheap sneakers I bought at Wal-Mart, among other things. Mario is not too happy about them, either.

I am chopping pepperoncini and Joy helps me out, teaching me how to tuck my fingers in and roll the knife. I chop those suckers up real quick. It's as fine a time as I have had in a long time listening to Lauren and Adele

Adele has just come out of the office and is reading a letter that one of her customers wrote complaining about their catering order. It is a ridiculous piece of hate mail and Adele is understandably upset about it.

I can relate to how Adele feels.

On days that I have had to bike in the rain, customers complain that I look slovenly. Mario comes and talks to me about these complaints even though he knows that I can't help it if it rains.

Then there are the customers who directly address me with their concerns. One just looks at me one day and says, "I think that they should just send them all off in ships and sail them around until they rot and die." The man looks like a working class Italian dude, but his reference is very sophisticated.

He comes into the store repeatedly.

Then there is the short Italian man in soccer shoes who comes in one day and orders sliced turkey from a coworker. When the coworker's back is turned the man looks both ways and when no one else is looking he flashes a police badge at me.

I make these men their expensive sandwiches, but I charge them top dollar for them.

When Adele leaves the room, I speak about not understanding how people have enough time to waste on complaining about their stupid fucking sandwiches.

Lauren snickers. "Oh, I can see doing something like that!" she says. "My friend at the PTA does things like that. She'll even take the time to do something like that for me if I ask her to."

Lauren snickers again.

Now I know why Adele and I bumped into each other in Lafayette. I figure maybe Lauren just wants to ruin Adele's day because she can. Maybe she wants Adele's job.

I go on to flirt with Lauren as I usually do. We occasionally swap movie scenes and recommendations.

Joy looks as if she hasn't picked up on anything that has gone on.

Len comes in the back looking like he heard the whole of the conversation. He puts his fat mobster hand on my shoulder and says, "Chocolate?" with high-pitched distortion. It is something he is always saying to me.

CHAPTER **20**

THE MOVE WITHOUT the help of my uncle and aunt is a true ordeal.

"Why don't you just pay someone," my aunt had suggested when I had asked for help.

When I get to Fresno in an upgraded car I rent from Avis, an Asian man I have never seen before comes up to me and asks, "What happened, man?" He is wearing the same uniform I wear at the Deli.

I know this is a Mafia test so I tell him, "Nothing happened, man. I came here looking for work; I couldn't find any. Now that I found a job elsewhere, I am moving again."

I don't want to expose the Mafia anymore, I just want to pass their tests and move on.

But on my way home, I accidently lock my keys in the back of the U-Haul. Maxine and I have to spend the night in the cab shivering. I know there is no one to talk to about a hardship such as this.

As an adolescent with a six-month insomnia, I used to wake my mom up every night for support. Now there is no use of hope for any sympathy. As a child, I never realized how lucky I was to have such a supportive mother. Now there is no hope for support!

The next day I have to race to get all my belongings up a flight of stairs by myself to return the truck on time.

Then it's back to unsympathetic work, where I wait two extra hours to get on my lunch break. In America, there is no rest or support for the wicked!

A week after my move is complete, I meet my aunt and uncle at a restaurant that bears a complex message in its name: "Left at Albuquerque." I know Albuquerque is an artistic, liberal community because I thought about moving there before I went to Fresno. I can see my Republican uncle, though clearly yanked out of his realm, would appreciate the restaurant, because in a very oxymoronic manner it is exclusive, with reservations and valet parking. It will not matter what I order—I won't care for the taste. Whether it's chicken or chocolate, it is bound to make me sick!

I am in ongoing back pain since the move. I have had to ride my bike, lift boxes, lean and reach over the salad plates, pump the slicer, and stretch my torso to the right in order to cut the breads, all in spite of spasms and ache. There is not even hope for relief. I cannot afford to miss a day of work. Even getting to "Left at Albuquerque" to meet the demands of my family is painful. Nevertheless, I stop at a Kinko's on the way to print up resumes. I continue to resist the cage of the Lueggio Deli in any way that I can.

In the restaurant, my uncle says he is Tony Soprano. I have heard about the show *The Sopranos* enough to know what he's saying. I listen very carefully to many references to *The Godfather* that he, like Joel, enjoys making: he'll just make the waiter "an offer that he can't refuse"; he's the kind of guy who knows what "down to the mattresses" really means.

I watch buffalo wings stain his face as he eats rabidly, like a buffoon bullying around in his preppy, collegiate-collar shirt.

After dinner, I take leave of my aunt and uncle without referencing anything about the move from Fresno. My aunt gives me a back brace. Maybe it will help. This support was unexpected.

Still, biking to work the next day, I get a powerful stomach cramp and an involuntary asshole spit. When I get to work, I have to clean out my underwear in the bathroom sink. Maybe the Mafia uses laxative powder.

ᴊᴊᴊ

Mario is taking leave for a month to go to Chile. He is marrying a Chilean related to Eduardo, the likely drug kingpin.

Everybody in this organization seems to want me to sell out the way Mario does, but it will never happen. I will never treat another human being in the manner he treats me. His ongoing complaints about my service continue to fill my nights with fear.

When a Brazilian named Antonio gets selected to take Mario's place for the month, I plot my ongoing resistance.

Antonio speaks five languages and we have instant rapport. He tells me the good thing about the line of work I have entered is I can travel the world.

To me, this means there is no running away from this Mafia.

But what I really like about Antonio is how he uses racism and the superiority complexes of the Walnut Creek community to his advantage by selling expensive bottles of wine. I feel a strange kind of vindication as Antonio cracks a bottle of wine, "That's beau-ti-ful, eh?" then appears wounded if the fat-cat customer doesn't spend fifty dollars to buy it. It is great entertainment.

I emulate Antonio by playing up a phony class deficiency to sell olive oil. I go on about the rich texture of a fifty-dollar bottle in a fictitious way with an earnest ghetto twang.

Antonio can't help but appreciate me a little when he sees I am learning from him: "Beaut-i-ful, eh?" He smiles at me.

One of Antonio's first days at the helm, he schedules only me on Easter Sunday. It's just Antonio and me and a constant rush. The store is making tons of money.

I work real hard and it is the best day I have had since I left Seattle. As far as I am concerned, the kids can stay home with their chocolate Easter Bunnies and their marijuana parties.

Antonio can't help but be impressed by my good attitude. By loving Antonio and being an angel when I can manage to be, I can resist the kids and the master plan and screw with the organization.

In college, I learned this kind of behavior is the only justice peasants are permitted. I recall the subservient behavior of some of the Norton inmates and make the connection. Why doesn't sociology depict this as a reality in our own culture!

One of the last days I work with him, Antonio explains to me that, "In Brazil, when all you have in the world is grapes, you make wine."

I figure Antonio was pretty lucky to be a Brazilian who owns grapes.

⌇⌇⌇

Another addition to our Mafia family in Mario's absence is a shift manager named Danny. I instantly feel warm toward him.

Danny storms into the back the minute Joy leaves and says he has friends in Pelican Bay Prison. The kids, particularly Joel, look scared. I like this. At least nobody makes jokes about "tossing the salad."

I feel my face light up as I talk to Danny about some of the other prisons in the area. It feels refreshing to interact with someone else who is trying to stay afloat and avoid lockup.

Danny takes to me naturally. On leaving the store the first day he asks me what kind of car I drive.

I pull out my bike, put the flashers on, and bitch about my ten-mile ride.

"That sucks," he says.

It's the only appropriate response I have gotten from anyone in this hellhole.

During his shifts, Danny encourages me to buy some cheap things and make it look good, but to help myself to larger portions of food.

"I've got your back," he says.

I have heard Anthony tell me this same thing, but I have never come close to believing him, given the way he treats me. Danny is a different story. I test him cautiously by having a chocolate milk that I don't pay for.

"Yeah, I like those too," he says.

Still, I am cautious around Danny. When he suggests I take anything I want from the store, I condemn this. "You don't understand, man, I need this job." I am well aware that everything in the store is inventoried.

"I've got your back, man." He sucks his teeth.

I hold strong. I figure his efforts to stay out of jail will fail if he keeps on like this. I understand where he's coming from, though. I realize I am not above anyone who steals; they may not have old money to run back to the way I do.

❧❧❧❧

At home, household items are moved for a purpose to tell me something. I snort when I think of the Secret Service agent's promise that there would be no crime in this complex.

Once, when I am at the library printing up cover letters, I realize my pits stink—I have forgotten to use deodorant. Sure enough, when I come home my deodorant is sitting out on the floor with the cap off.

After that coincidence, there are others: the dime that ends up on the floor suggests someone dropped a dime bag on me; the toothbrush that has been moved is just a subtle sign of control. Every day, I leave it in a different place to mess with my tormentors, and every day I find it has been moved.

One day, I come home from twelve hours of work and my apartment is trashed.

I go over to the management office with rage. One of the assistant managers explains that my uncle came and requested a key, that he is legally entitled to enter my apartment any time because he has co-signed. The head manager one ups me with her attitude. The Secret Service agent who looks like Michelle from Kiddiecare happens to be present. I walk back to my apartment with my tail between my legs.

The bag of kitty litter my uncle has brought over has been slashed open and spread all over my living room. Moreover, other parts of the room have been ransacked, as though my belongings have been searched. The labels in my pants and shirts have been slashed. My closet has been emptied.

This police-style search doesn't appear to be the work of my uncle, but nonetheless I call my aunt and complain. She just doesn't sound genuine in her concern. She tells me that she can tell my uncle not to go into my apartment without asking in the future.

Still, I do what I can to resist. I go out of my way to bike to different mailboxes to drop off cover letters. I mix up other routines.

Slowly and at infrequent intervals, I hear back from potential employers. I accept interviews, remaining very alert for any message that might come to me about the job. Coded comments in the directions that my interviewer provides to the interview site sometimes help.

My first interview is up in Redding with a Catholic agency in a conservative stronghold. I rent a car and drive with Maxine five or six hours north. I interview with a panel of four observers who go through many details of my experiences in Seattle. The sun streams in through the open blinds in the windows onto my face. The well-dressed interviewers are shadows against the light. I answer them with utmost honesty. Though I admit I did not trust my immediate supervisor, I show them written recommendations I've obtained from two reputable coworkers at the Seattle agency. When I lean forward out of the sunlight I can see one of the interviewers looks fairly impressed.

Still, I don't get the feeling that I will be hired.

My second interview is with a local foster care agency in Antioch. My interviewer is aged and competent and the interview is exhaustive. She seems hung up on my comfort level in making house calls. I explain things would be easier if I had the job because I could afford a car. Once I feel I have obliterated that concern to the best of my ability, she explains that I would be the only male on staff and would be taking all my orders from women.

I don't flinch in telling her that that wouldn't be a problem.

I follow up with thank-you letters.

CHAPTER **21**

I TALK WITH my mother frequently. I unkindly spare her no details of my drama. Mostly she ignores it, but she doesn't click over, refuse to answer, or fail to call back like she has in the past. Occasionally it helps when she says she just wishes I lived closer so she could do more to help.

Then one day, when I am starting to get the idea she is really there for me, my mom lets me know she is buying a house for my sister.

"You don't understand, Clyde," she says, "She is managing the house and will be making a profit for me. It's not like it is just giving her the money. You're getting more money than her, anyway!"

This silences me.

In reflective moments, however, I do the math: two hundred fifty a month and the year of bullshit imposed therapy (if it is my mother who is paying for it) still doesn't add up to half the thirty-thousand-dollar down payment.

My mom still refuses me the money my grandfather left me. I cannot buy a car. It seems like my sister always got everything that I was denied: the cross-country skis, the Nike sneakers, the Walkman, birthday celebrations, the private college, attention on prom night.

My father contacts me with his expectation that I attend my cousin's wedding, which will cost me wages. My grandfather has agreed to purchase the airline tickets for me.

When I take my father's request to my shrink, I make up a scenario. I tell her I fantasize about averting the likely poisoning in the wedding food by pulling nuts out of my pocket, and like I am Elwood Blues at the fancy restaurant, offering them to my cousins. *Anyone vant to taste my nuts?* I would say, slapping my grandfather on the back as if I was Jake Blues; cousins would wrinkle their little noses, like the little girl in the movie.

When this doesn't work, I threaten violence to my grandfather, but only if he starts hits me first!

The shrink finally gets it enough to tell me that she can tell my father that it is not appropriate for him to force me to get together with my family.

Though it angers me that my shrink gives me no empathy over the fact that my mother is purchasing my sister a house in the midst of my toil, I accept her help.

My father calls me back and says diplomatically that he understands I am not ready, but encourages me to give my cousin a call.

I talk to my cousin, who wouldn't let me live near him. He appears to get offended by the subtle nuances of my talk about the Mafia. While I am on the phone with my cousin, the call waiting clicks and I take a moment to field the call in the event that it is a potential employer. The woman from the foster care agency says she appreciated my interview and the lovely thank-you letter, but they are just not able to hire me at this time, and best of luck. I answer sweetly and click back to talk to my cousin and try to smooth things over with him.

Once off the phone I realize it is a Saturday and the intrusion of the interviewer's call seems unnatural. It is another piece of evidence of a broad conspiracy.

♪♪♪♪

One day, I tell the shrink that I am upset about the way my parents respond to me; that in many ways, I talk to them like a black person and they react with prejudice.

The shrink doesn't understand my allusion to being blacklisted. Her response is, "Well, if that is the case, don't talk to your parents like a black person."

Though this angers me greatly, it does occur to me that my style of walking like an Egyptian when I am in Rome may not be working.

The shrink continues. "Clyde, I hear you talk a lot about racism—what about racism in you?"

"Sure, I am racist," I say. "Everybody is. Mostly, I have been told that I demonstrate racism by favoring African-Americans. A long time ago a friend in the hospital who introduced me to Public Enemy made me aware of this. But, really, the inner-city minority kids I was locked up with in that hellhole treated me better than any of the kids I went to school with. And I sure noticed how many white people just pitched their noses high when I got out."

I pause, then continue. "But that African-American kid was right. When I was four years old, I stood outside the nursery and looked at all the babies that were lying there and tried to pick out the one I wanted to be my sister. At that time my first choice was a black baby because I thought the baby looked cool. My second choice was my sister because she had a lot of hair on her head. So I guess you're right about my racism."

I think about it more when I get out of the session, and I get angry.

The shrink says that all pimps are evil.

I think about how pimps who favor control over money are necessary to make the world go around; some of them are good. My father could be very good. There she is pimping me for top dollar and I am supposed to learn from her that pimps are evil.

I think about how I am doing better work with her than she is doing with me, and that also angers me.

᷄᷄᷄᷄

When Mario comes back from his drug trafficking expedition, I lose the support I'd gained in Danny and Antonio. The reins are pulled tight on my neck as KaCee regains her utmost confidence in treating me like a slave. I can only make obsequious gestures of discontent.

When I am using the slicer, she walks up out of the blue and talks about how she is better than I am. "People like me; I don't *trip*. I make a commitment to the organization."

I tune her gloating rant out. My shrink's insult rings in my mind: "In reality you are just getting bullied."

I say nothing; I slice chicken. Len walks by and taunts, "Chicken!"

When KaCee has left work for the day, Anthony and I are alone for a moment. We discuss the family pictures that are located in the dining area of the store. We have each pondered them enough to notice Nazi swastikas signs that are present.

I say that I would hate to be a part of the Lueggio family.

Anthony says that it's not possible for either of us to be part of the Lueggio family: "In order to be part of the Lueggio family, you have to have blonde hair and blue eyes."

We both look at each other and I know a major disclosure has happened here.

The only person who has blonde hair and blue eyes at work is KaCee, if that is even her real name. I suppose that KaCee may have taken messing with me a little too far, even for her supposed boyfriend.

Later, I tell Anthony about nearly having my bike stolen outside MacFrugal's.

I saw a man sitting in the shadows as I entered the store and I acted like I was unsuspicious. Remembering advice the bike salesman in Fresno had given me after my bike was stolen, I made a quick U–turn, and sure enough found the man at my lock. I'd strode over to the man and took my bike away.

When I'd done this, the wiry African-American man began crying and calling me Jesus Christ.

"Wow, Clyde, that sounds scary," says Anthony.

"Yeah," I say, relieved to have an ounce of validation. When I had told my mom, her tone had told me that she didn't believe me.

I try to look at Anthony the same way he looked at me earlier.

I believe that the Mafia is paying bike thieves to target me, much as they did in Fresno. Many nights I come out of the deli and find a nail in my tire. There is no way all my bad fortune is a coincidence.

When Joel sees me discover one of these nails one night, I complain people are always doing it to me.

"Oh, that stuff doesn't happen around here," says Joel, turning the key in his plush white truck. "That might happen out in Antioch, but not around here."

Maybe it doesn't happen to people like you around these parts," I say, "but believe me, it happens!"

"Nah," Joel says confidently.

I continue to be unabashedly resentful of poor young Joel.

One afternoon, Joel says, "Clyde, do you know that they say that Freud accused all those neurotic girls of having sexual fantasies and now they are finding out that the sexual abuse was real?"

I think he is showing off. I don't think he is trying to validate or make amends. I think about how in his superiority, he is educating a master's level psychologist about dumbass high school material.

I tell him that it is amazing how youth are so easily brainwashed these days.

❧❧❧❧

Mario does something I appreciate when he comes back from Chile—he hires an African-American kid. The kid lives in Antioch and travels to Oakland daily to attend school. Apparently he is between houses, like I was at his age.

Not only do I sense we are both on the outs around these parts, I know enough about his culture to chum it up.

When Joel and KaCee act out their adolescent encapsulation, I allude to one of my favorite movies, *I'm Going to Get You, Sucker*. I quote a KRS-One lyric.

I know this kid will know exactly that the main character, Jack, is a stick-up artist who goes after drug money that is being funneled out of the community to Mr. Big, the white Mafia.

This kid, Tyrone, responds intelligently and respectfully and we quickly develop a bond.

When KaCee sees this, she immediately offers to drive him home.

The next day, the kid continues to show respect for me. I fantasize that at age sixteen he is a budding undercover agent.

Tyrone starts taking BART with me and talks to me about his military family and future plans.

Meanwhile, Anthony and KaCee become increasingly uneasy. Anthony goes to great lengths to freak Tyrone out when all the adults are gone, putting on weird black-rimmed glasses and raising his voice like a vaudeville nerd. Every day the kid works, Anthony and KaCee double-team him. I watch from a distance, reading dominant body postures and pointing fingers.

The kid shows a diplomatic self-esteem and just mocks them back a bit.

A few weeks into his tenure at the deli, he shows up wearing a gold chain with a Georgia Bulldog on it and has a few friends visit him. His friends look young and studious to me, but they are the only black faces I have seen enter the deli.

Anthony and KaCee are very alarmed. Anthony raises his scared voice and asks the kid why he has friends stopping by the store.

One night, Len, Tyrone, and I are scheduled together on the closing shift, supporting a young culinary school graduate who is a newly hired manager.

Len doesn't do any work, and persuades Tyrone to join him in goofing off. I continue slaving. Out of the corner of my eye, I see Len purposely dropping an expensive bottle of olive oil on the floor.

With the sound of scattering glass, the young manager in training comes out and sees Len and Tyrone goofing off while my best efforts have us still very behind schedule. She yells. She disappears.

The kid gets a feel for what's going on and joins me in my slaving. Len will not lift his fat fingers.

When I get home I cry to my mom about how I am being set up to take the fall. She doesn't seem to believe me. She says I am not pulling my weight. That night it rains. I go to bed thinking about being homeless out in the rain. I wake up in the middle of the night. I am urinating in the bed.

The next day, Joy interrogates the young manager in training, who says she'd done everything she could to get the three of us to work. She says I was the only one who listened to her. She pats me on the back.

Mario and Joy take Len in the back. He comes back very cocky and buddies up to Anthony with a high-five and no worry on his Danville-ass face. When Tyrone comes in to work that day he is fired.

Len turns to me and says, "Chocolate?"

I am devastated. I think about what would happen to me at this joint if I really was African-American.

Weeks later, I talk to Mario about the incident, appealing to the fact that Mario also grew up in Oakland. I tell him Tyrone is a very strong worker.

Mario tells me Tyrone is too immature to work in this store.

Noting my facial expression, Mario tells me: "It is inventory day today. I hate inventory. I would rather fire three people than do one inventory."

From this point on, every month he repeats these lines to me.

꓿꓿꓿

With unsympathetic and moralistic words, my father tells me via phone, "Clyde, many people have to do what you have to do and moreover never have the opportunity to move forward!"

There he is, like the Yale graduate student he once was, judging my impoverished merits as if singing a tender blue-blood tenor version of *Going Back to Nassau Hall*.

Meanwhile, as I bike through the community, the master plan plods forward.

An old Mexican-American man who looks like the healer at Campo Verde comes up to me in Food 4 Less and says bitterly, "Now you know what it is like to be a Mexican immigrant."

A couple of African-American youngsters cross the street. I suddenly swerve to avoid hitting them. They lift their heads and say, "Yes we *are* trying to get in your way."

On the BART platform, the Santa Claus man from the Norton who once clucked at me like a chicken stumbles up to me with handcuffs in his back pocket and a sign on the pocket of his jean jacket that reads "CIA Officer." He sits in the disabled seat across from me and my bike and stares at me. I don't care if he killed somebody once, I pay him no mind!

My father hangs up after I finish telling him that I won't make it to another cousin's wedding, and I hear Len's voice in the receiver calling my name with a great deal of laughter in the background.

A large African-American man on BART who stands opposite me looks normal one minute. The next glance I see his zipper down very blatantly. A glance later, his zipper is closed again.

The day after I finally squander money on a pair of shoes, a clean white boy who is dressed with the homeless Haight-Ashbury look gets onto BART with me with a new pair of shoes tied around his neck. He gets off at my stop and encircles me as if he is Green Day's Mister Whirly. I pay him no mind.

At the Food 4 Less, after my stepfather has just told me on the phone that he was listening to Elvis, the music is interrupted and an old Elvis tune starts playing over the loudspeakers.

Exercising Maxine with her favorite rubber toy in the back of the apartment complex, I see three cop cars roll in. I run back to my apartment. I reach for my bike and find that it has a flat tire. I waste no time pumping the tire up with air and take off pedaling as fast as I can. When I make it all the way into work without a flat tire, Len and Pablo both show up twenty minutes late; Joy unleashes on them for being late. I am left to conclude they are getting yelled at for not slashing my tires.

These are all part of my daily realities that I cannot explain to anyone.

All roads for such grotesque harassment lead back to my poor father.

Finally, I call my father and rage at him. I am not even sure what I am saying but am aware of my abrupt, accusatory tone. There I am throwing him down the stairwell!

Suddenly, my father is yelling at me with uncontrolled rage. "Goddamn it, Clyde, how could you do this to me?" He rants a little while.

I resort to a calm, detached, and judgmental listen. When I speak I sound like a factory worker who despises the CEO. I keep myself calm but leave tons of judgment in my tone.

His sudden silence speaks to me.

CHAPTER **22**

THE SUMMER SEASON progresses at the deli. I grow tired of the commute and the whole of the Mafia mess that continues to whittle away at my soul.

I mess up giving myself a haircut. A new coworker at the deli, a hippie girl, makes some harsh facial gestures at me the morning after I had to resort to the buzz cut, I have a meltdown, crying with uncontainable sobs that I cannot explain, forcing Joy to send me home early at my own expense. The hippie girl smiles at me kindly the next time she sees me, even though she had to cover my shift.

Days later, Anthony departs his supervisory position. KaCee sings praises about Anthony's mission to go train athletes back in Texas, where he's from. Even though I can just about smell the horseshit in the pastures, I will miss Anthony.

Joel then takes KaCee to his prom as a date. It makes me laugh because I sense it is a ridiculous Mafia effort to make me jealous.

I respond to this by telling Joel about my prom night encounter that involved fear of a first kiss, a pacing, pissed hyena at the zoo, a lifted leg, and sprays of urine.

I am actually trying to be brotherly toward Joel for once, so I ham up the story in all its real but ridiculous glory.

Joel responds in his typical fashion, carping, "Uh, no, that didn't happen to *me* on *my* prom night."

Sure enough, not long after this, KaCee passes me a note that reads: "I think you are cute."

I can only smile, because this only confirms the caged Mafia dynamics I have been imagining. Sure enough, her recent humming of the theme of the movie *Sweet November* is done with the intent of seducing me.

"Don't you ever get horny?" my shrink says in therapy, as if she herself is trying to sound seductive.

I suppose it is another one of those "coincidences." It's true; I fantasize about Lauren in my spare time, a married woman.

One afternoon when I am visibly down, I get double-teamed by Lauren and KaCee, who flirt with me, shaking their seductive bodies on either side of me like I am a long shaft. I feel like I am nothing but a long shaft these days and resent that this treatment does function to pep me up. I just want to keep my job so I make no complaints. I only feel cheap and resent my testosterone.

Around this time a rich girl from Idaho gets hired. The first day she is working, Joy picks her brain about whom she is dating, as though she is fixing a report. The girl spews out details of her life, as though they are a public joke. Mario comments to me that he is afraid of her because the epicenter of the modern Klan is in Idaho.

I would be confused about how a girl, who scares her boss, gets hired; but I know it is a Mafia joint.

The rich girl is dating some lower income dudes, who are clearly using her for money. "Oh, we'll just take daddy's credit card and go to a bed and breakfast," she says, "I don't care. Oh anarchy, yeah I like anarchy. My boyfriend is into that."

Unlike the others, she even tries to be my friend.

Really, I am relieved to have another political hostage amongst us, even if she is totally annoying.

One day, while I dust the bottles of expensive wine I would never be able to afford, the rich girl neatens the bags of potato chips she would never lower herself to sample. We talk as we are working and she says something. I think it's so pathetic that I turn to pat her on the shoulder. She has just gone from standing to stooping in front of the chips so my pat doesn't land. Then, I spin around very embarrassed. Somehow my hand swung down as she was standing and brushed against her ass. I pick my head up to see Mario glaring at me like a bull, as if I have just licked the glass display case at a chocolate bakery. He charges, grabbing my hand and leading me to the back, where I am ordered to wash dishes out of sight of customers.

The rest of the shift, I have the clear sense I am being talked about. I cannot even endeavor to explain myself to anyone. I cry to my mom when I go home that night.

The next day, when I am in my Sunday morning ritual, pulling chairs and tables from out of the shed, the rich girl's boyfriend and his male friend come at me, cornering me in the shed. I am terrified as the anarchist asks me, "Hey, Clyde, what's this I hear about you touching my girlfriend's ass?"

I blurt in full Mafia drawl, "Hey, she just keeps on trying to hitch a ride back home with me, and I am not going." The boyfriend just looks at his friend and leaves as I try to make sense of what I blurted.

In love with being the epicenter of attention, the rich girl tells me she asked her boyfriend what happened when he came to talk to me. She says her boyfriend got quiet and said, "Clyde is cool." She says her boyfriend's friend immediately concurred, saying, "Clyde is cool." The girl mimics their masculine nods as though she could care less.

Mystified, I offer her quite a sincere apology.

She looks disappointed.

ↄↄↄↄ

A letter comes out one morning from Jack Lueggio about one of his workers who was recently killed. I skim through the loving portrayal of an all-American boy to the admission that the death may have been due to drugs.

I fear my father is responsible.

I still recall how my father told me in the hospital, "I love you more than life itself." Still, I just can't believe he and my stepmom would stoop so low. I wish the death could have been mine.

I imagine everyone directing energy against me that day, throbbing, sobbing, and pleading: why couldn't it have been the crazy person who died, not someone who was loved by others?

After work, I talk with Len, who looks pained and says he knew the deceased.

The next day, an older lady with two young adult children is particularly nasty to me. She complains that she found plastic in her turkey. She has never experienced someone so incompetent in her life.

I fear she is the mother of the deceased. Len, seeing my distress, pulls me aside and admits to me he is a good friends with the woman. Then I understand.

"Buy her a little chocolate for your mistake," he suggests. I honestly don't believe that I made any mistake at all but I do as he says.

I would never consider wasting my money on chocolate for myself, but I pay for it anyway to make up for the death. Maybe this move will help Len forgive me.

Shortly after this, a real plot to get me fired is revealed. It happens on a day when KaCee leaves her car with a local mechanic.

I hear her ask Joel for help.

"What's in it for me?" Joel asks.

Then, Joel and KaCee disappear for an hour in the afternoon, leaving all responsibilities to me. KaCee comes back and rides me particularly hard to get things done so Joel can lounge at the cheese station. Exhausted from the bike ride and all the extra work, I am livid. When Adele comes by briefly, I say nothing to her.

The next day, Mario calls me over and tells me KaCee is my boss and he will fire me if I ever give her any more trouble. Mario explains poor KaCee called him in tears after the shift and told him she was afraid of me and I often give her problems.

I deny I was *that* angry or scary. This doesn't make any sense to me. He doesn't ask me for my account of what happened.

"Clyde, I have a member of the senior management staff who

came in and said you looked very scary and defiant; if it happens again you are gone. No questions asked."

I remember back to how Mario used to criticize my hygiene during the rainy season. I made it through that; I can make it through this.

Later, once I am collected, I communicate with KaCee. I let her know I need this job and will probably end up homeless without it. I tell her she left me stranded for an hour when she went to pick up her car with Joel and then expected me to do Joel's job without any questions. Of course I was angry. But when else have I ever given her any problems?

She speaks in a detached and unfeeling voice. She mentions the time I responded to one of her demands by motioning like I was peeing on the floor.

She has a point. I did that one day after Mario returned from Chile.

I tell her I hadn't been aware I had offended her and I had only been trying to be funny.

She mentions the time I made fun of her when she sniffed from a cold. This shocks me. I thought she had known that my gesture meant that I knew she was using cocaine. I apologize and I ask her to tell me when she is offended so we do not have this kind of miscommunication in the future. She does not dignify this with a response.

ﾉﾉﾉﾚ

My grandfather follows up a conversation I had with him in which he accused me of lying about the hundred-and-five degree temperature out in Antioch with a care package of dried fruits and nuts. Figuring the package to be spiked with laxative powder, I open the attached card to find a pencil sketch print of a rabid wolf, poised and ready to attack. Inside, my depression-era grandfather has scribbled in his violent hand writing: "If you are in fact not going to eat these, please give them to someone else you know!"

When I show the shrink the card, she only makes a small face and suggests I not throw the food away. I listen to her. I honor the don. I store the shit in my cupboard.

I tell myself I will never ever give these fruits and nuts to anyone, knowing that they could make others sick.

The summer lags forward until I reach a new low. When I feel I will never escape and am just sick of looking at the nuts and fruits in my cupboard, I surrender to the rabid evil of my grandfather and the shrink. I clear my shelves and bring the nuts and fruits in as a gift to my peers.

I, who some might say once hunted the wolf at the Norton, now have succumbed to becoming part of the pack. As I watch the Mafia players chowing down, I know I will never forgive myself for this action.

Surprisingly, there are no signs of laxative poisoning and I find myself feeling more accepted. Leah is particularly thankful, saying she loves this stuff.

ᴊᴊᴊᴧ

At the library these days, as I continue sending out resumes, I keep running into the same toothless African-American man. Repeatedly, he comes in while I am working and gets onto the computer next to me.

The first time he meets me he cackles and takes out his partials and wags his tongue insidiously. "I can read all of this, because I am wise," he blurts.

I look over at his monitor, which is covered with nonsensical markings.

When I look back at my monitor there is a mark at the bottom of my resume that I cannot get rid of. I look over at his monitor and he cackles again at me, then he leaves.

The third or fourth time I run into the black man at the library, he approaches me, appearing very solemn. He tells me he is a CIA agent and works for the multinational corporations. I look deeply into his eyes and can see he is fully brainwashed.

I explain I have learned a lot from my mistakes but I don't have a lot of computer skills.

The man's tone has shifted from homeless hobo to college guidance counselor, and he advises me to get those computer skills because all the employers are looking for them.

〜〜〜〜

I take my driver's license exam twice before I pass it.

As is the case everywhere, there are many signs that I am being followed at the DMV. The first day there is a wild-looking young man wearing a shirt with wolves on it. He paces the aisles of the old, dingy building while I take the test in a standing booth and then he follows me around back after I fail, to where I unlock my bike.

The day I am successful and obtain my license, KaCee stops by the DMV and acts like she is surprised to see me. I know there is more to her presence and the wild man's wolf T-shirt than just coincidence.

When the government employee hands me my license, she says, "Keep biking everywhere, and you will be the *strongest man in the universe.*" I recall my words to the runner back in Fresno.

I often think about joining the army these days. I pass by the recruiter's office when I am biking home from the DMV. I would be grateful for the security of three-hots-and-a-cot, as food is always scarce. Of course, I could never allow myself to be trained to kill other people, but what better of a way to send the government a message that I am not going to ever go against them?

Then, I use my license to do something else that is almost unheard of: I register to vote as a Republican! What more could they ask for?

〜〜〜〜

In therapy, the shrink asks me my opinion about the OJ Simpson verdict and then listens to me in a very judgmental fashion as I say that even if OJ was guilty, which I never cared enough to even explore, so many white people get exonerated for so much worse; it's about time a powerful black man gets exonerated too.

She bites on this needling. She says that a young white kid she knows got a broken arm on the BART for just trying to deal some pot; white kids don't always get away with it for free!

"Yeah, some would argue that a white kid who lives out here and doesn't really need extra money deserves to feel a little of the pain of the ghetto for trying to profit off a dime," I say. "Maybe he was disrespectful. He'll probably never go to jail for what he is doing."

I can see that these comments only offend her. Anyone could sense the judgment gaping out of her.

It angers me that she is using my compromised position to impose racism on me. Her whole enterprise seems pointless.

﴿﴿﴿

When my mom comes out for a weekend for a therapy appointment, the session is pointless. I tell my story, but neither she nor the shrink listen. The shrink cuts me off crudely and asks for my mom's version of events. In spite of all the suffering I went through, I bite my tongue.

My mom tells the brief story of how the whole family rallied together to come out and see me in the hospital, paying for expensive plane tickets, only to get rejected. My mom emphasizes the unity they had.

My mom continues: she was very mad at the doctor in Helena who didn't commit me at their command. I am silent and contained and let her repeat herself several times. She says the policeman who briefly picked me up was good because he'd called them and assured them I'd end up hospitalized.

When it is finally my turn, I start to talk about the damage the family unity has done to me.

The shrink cuts me off and says she thinks I should listen to mom again. The same ignorant and hateful take on my reality gets imposed on me again.

I soothe myself during my mom's second speech. I think about how, in reality, I am doing notable charity work, making expensive sandwiches for rich people like them, while going to bed with an empty stomach myself.

The next time I meet with the shrink, I again find myself talking about how hard I am working just to go to bed hungry.

"Well, I believe your head is working hard," she says, "but believe me, working at a deli is not so bad."

I get a strong sense she has never worked a minimum-wage job in her life.

Indeed, she tells me that her first job out of school was working at a prison. I don't think she realizes how lucky she was to go home to a middle-class lifestyle with the pay she received at the prison.

When she tells me about the prison, she tries to impose her version of true evil on me. She says a *black* man from prison told her, "Look, lady you have no idea what it's like; when I go back in that hell zone I would kill a man over a cigarette."

"That's true evil," she says, "These claims you make against these poor teenagers and your boss at the deli are not."

I refuse to comment. I have a strong sense that that evil prisoner was just testing her out to see if he could talk to her. It's likely just wuff talk depicting realities of incarceration. She is not safe to talk to. She knows nothing about the America you've experienced.

She says, "Well, if it's not safe to talk about it here, where is it safe to talk about?"

I explain Pac Bell has a truck outside right now and is playing with the phone lines and God knows what else.

She replies, "Well, if that's your reality—that it's not safe to talk about things here—then I feel bad for you. I really do."

❧❧❧

The next time I meet with the shrink I can't take it anymore. I let her know how utterly unhelpful she is. I go on and on. Now that I have health insurance I have been calculating the cost of these sessions. She has already taken from me over seven thousand dollars that could easily be spent on a car and vastly improve my functioning.

I keep my eyes down as I am attacking her and when I pick my head up I see her posture has sagged in her chair and her legs spread apart. I see through her panty hose to her gaping vagina. Immediately, I look away and feel violated. I halt my criticisms.

When I stop, she apologizes—for what I am not sure. Was her behavior purposeful?

She agrees with me that she feels lost and doesn't know how to go about establishing a rapport with me.

It seems like the first helpful thing she has said to me in a long while.

❧❧❧

My mom informs me my sister is pregnant and going to get married.

I complain about therapy and ask if I can please stop going. My mother insists the shrink is helping me.

I cannot contain myself any longer. I complain about the series of raw deals I've been given throughout my life. I don't stop. I repeat complaint after complaint.

My mom calmly explains that my sister gets more family resources because she asks for things and I don't.

I say I need money to buy a car.

My mom pauses and says coldly that I haven't asked for a car.

"Mom," I say once again, "can I have money for a car?"

Mom says she is afraid to defy my father, who clearly does not want me to have a car. She pauses. It is a long, cold silence. Then she agrees to send me three thousand dollars.

I scour a car magazine called the Diablo Dealer for deals on simple, low-mileage vehicles. I note an increase in parked cars for sale on my route to and from work and this makes me convinced that a crook will set me up with a Mafia lemon.

I go to a dealership and find a Ford Escort for five thousand dollars but give up on that when I can't talk them down a penny. I figure there likely are corrupt Montana marks on my credit report.

My aunt, upon hearing of my three-thousand-dollar capability, offers to help drive me to the cars I want to see. I fight with my aunt about her values at a few different dealerships. She thinks air-conditioning and electric doors are something I should consider, even if I've never needed them in the past. She doesn't think it matters if I can only afford a vehicle with 200,000 miles on it; I deserve to drive in luxury.

Finally, I find a 45,000-mileage vehicle with a stick shift, crank windows, and no air conditioning at a dealership close to my job.

I even get the car checked out at the local car repair and it checks out very well.

Deciding whether or not to buy the car torments me. I visit the dealership on my break from work the next day, wondering how the owner can afford to live in such a wealthy area selling such cheap cars. I tell him about my situation.

He lowers the price of the car by three hundred dollars and says, "You know, I do have things like profits to worry about!"

When my plates finally come in, I ride over to the dealership.

Getting insured has been quite the ordeal. A sudden lawsuit caught up with me from a firm named Norton and Tremble. The coincidence of it delayed me several weeks. Plus, several insurance agents tried to rip me off for no reason I could fully uncover.

At the dealership, my car's new key, which is supposed to be in the mailbox, is not there. In a panic, I turn up the welcome mat and find the key. Then, when I finally go out to the street to start up the engine, it won't start.

Down at the gas station, the mechanic I previously paid is just getting off work. When I tell him what has happened he offers to come look at the car with his wife. He takes one look at the car and says that the battery needs a jump. And that works.

It is like the Emancipation Proclamation.

CHAPTER **23**

I ENVISION BECOMING a Veterinarian Tech, an EMT, a postal employee, or a supermarket checker: anything that will give me independence from my family. With every siren I hear I imagine myself out chasing traumatic accidents. I inquire into taking the civil service exam. I apply for work at the Safeway across the street from the deli. Now that I am in possession of a car, I might add a paper route to my current schedule. With the year of financial support from my parents coming to a close in six months, I need to find a way to increase my income by any means necessary.

In the mail, I receive a Social Security notice that tells me that the SSDI monthly payments would be three hundred dollars higher than what I make at the Deli.

While I was still on my bike, I risked hospitalization by going down to the police station to get my quivering fingers printed so I could be registered as an intern with the Board of Behavioral Sciences. Now, I receive a letter in the mail that simply reads: "THE FBI HAS REJECTED YOUR APPLICATION FOR REGISTRATION!"

Containing my fear, I call the Board of Behavioral Sciences for an explanation. I send in my corrected application and wait. I hate the way the gocernment taunts me so! They want me to give up.

I call mom in desperation one night and beg her to let me move home. She says I would have to get my own apartment if I move back east. She suggests that what I am now earning is substantial enough to warrant continued investment in my future. "Just try not to lose that job at the deli!"

Then I'm shocked to receive a letter from my father that compliments me on my hard work and expresses faith that, if I continue working hard, things will work out. I review it carefully and have a hard time finding anything negative in the wording.

I also receive letters from my grandmother that appear to be supportive. She has been writing me from the Laundromat near her vacation cabin in the Adirondacks, talking about the poverty that surrounds her. I respond with a thank you letter.

The week before my father's visit, grandma sends me a T-shirt that reads, "Hiking the Appalachian Trail in the Adirondack Mountains." But everyone knows that the Appalachian Trail doesn't go through the Adirondack Mountains!

My cousin in Colorado assures me that our Grandma made no special effort to create this malapropism. But why should I believe him!

"Coincidentally," a T-shirt gift arrives that same week. It's from my mother, who's vacationing in Spain. It's the yearly vacation T-shirt I always get and resentfully would never wear. This year, the T-shirt has marijuana emblem palm trees with matches as trunks. Just as I am aware that mom and my stepfather are potheads, they are aware that I think the illegal pot business is involved with the enslavement of whistleblowers like me.

The two T-shirts set my mind ruefully spinning . . . Who is really sending me these obnoxious items?

At the shrink's office, I wish I could trust her enough to speak of the shirts. I will be meeting with my father and the shrink during his upcoming visit and I am still angry about the meeting I had with my mother. I verbally dance around, trying to decide whether it is safe to talk.

The shrink cuts in and directs the session, as she often does: "I want to talk about accusations and allusions to sexual abuse that you have made."

I cannot recall ever having made such allegations to her. I figure she is reacting to records in Montana. I was shooting out my suspicions there on the phone to Big Brother Joe. Or maybe she's talked to my mom without telling me.

I respond by telling her three or four memories I feel may have hurt my sexual development.

"That's it, Clyde!" the shrink says. "It seems that you have been throwing around a lot of hurtful accusations here."

I wonder if my mother put her up to this.

"Well there's a lot I don't remember," I say. "I am suspicious that what is happening to me is more trauma-related than psychosis. I've been diagnosed with four or five mental illnesses and I have come to a realization that I am a valid person."

"Well, Clyde," the shrink says. "I've heard many real stories from *women* who have graphic stories of exploitation, and I don't think your stories compare."

When I get home, I call my sister.

My sister has been caring enough to send me a letter while I was in Fresno apologizing for being so selfish. Still, I have rejected her effort because of precocious puns, a clear reference to and endorsement of the realities of Mafia abuse.

She's in the house my mother bought for her. Her marriage is in a few months. It's about noon on my day off, which means it is three o'clock on a workday for her, but she is home. She explains that she is not yet dressed and has a knock on the door that is the mailman dropping off something. I wait on the line. When she is finally ready to talk she is in a jovial mood and asks how I'm doing.

I mutter. I don't know what I'm doing. I'm talking about my latest Mafia experiences. I suppose I'm testing her out.

Suddenly, my sister is *laughing*. She laughs and laughs. She seems to be gloating!

I recall taking my sister out walking with the family dog after our mother had passed out for the night. I had been so careful to be good to her. I explained what drunk people were like so she wouldn't judge our mother for admiring me in comparison to the creepy men who come after her wanting dates. I can still remember mom's words, "Oh come on, Clyde!" she'd pleaded, coaxing me to go out with her, driving illegally.

I think of how her total dropping of her parental duties since then has conspired to make those words sound seductive in my memory.

Still, with either hope for the redemptive power of karma, or just to disrupt heinous laughter, I, with greatest of need, ask her if she remembers anything about that night.

She turns serious. She says she doesn't remember anything out of the ordinary at all, ever.

"No, Clyde, I just think you are really sick."

ﺩﺩﺩﺩ

I have never driven my new car so far as when I pick up my father at the San Francisco airport. I worry about it breaking down. Then there is the parking issue; I have not wasted so much money since Fresno.

When my father walks past the security checkpoint, he is wearing a blood-red baseball hat and sunglasses. He is thinner than I remember.

Once I've paid the attendant ten dollars, without comment or acknowledgement, I end up agreeing to visit the Haight-Ashbury district.

My father, for some reason, wants to see the Haight. I think of my fear of becoming Mister Whirly. It seems like my father knows all about it.

On the way, my father is hungry and requests a stop. I find a little spot off the hilly road we're driving up so we can walk to a bakery we just passed.

I've been looking every which way to see if anyone has a tail on my car. The street is throbbing with people and the Mart that holds the bakery is likewise. My father walks right into the crowd of people and opens his wallet so that the whole room can see it is full of twenty-dollar bills

Concerned that the people following us will punish me for this disrespectful behavior, as they often do, I leave my father and rush back to the car to protect it at all costs. In the event that I am wrong about him, he needs to be responsible for his own damned arrogance. I lock the doors until my father stumbles mindlessly back to the car while wolfing down some baked goods.

At the Haight we walk through Golden Gate Park, looking at the homeless, and I assess my father's street smarts. He seems not to understand, but I think it's a brilliant con. I sense that he wants me to know what would have happened to me if not for his help.

After the long ride home from the Haight, my father takes me out to the Burger King near my apartment.

I think of how my aunt tried to teach me how to order from Burger King like an upper-class Californian—using first names and asking intellectual questions. My father rudely keeps the workers waiting for his order.

I impulsively blurt: "Don't worry, dad; if you don't know how to order, I'll take care of you. I know how to order food from Burger King."

My father looks absolutely pissed. When he orders two cheeseburgers and looks knowingly at the African-American workers, I catch on to what is really going on.

This isn't about bad manners! This meal could be destined to be more than just a burst of diarrhea spitting out of an asshole. This would be the perfect time for my father to prove his ruthlessness.

When I get back to the apartment I get very angry with his godfather shit. He, in turn, gets very angry back. It is like it was back in Philadelphia Child Guidance Clinic, when he bullied me into eating in front of the therapist. He may have got that bagel down my throat but I sure as shit wasn't going to keep it there! Now, I at least want him to know that I didn't die stupidly.

Weak and angry, I bite into the Whopper—but I live.

دددد

In session with the shrink I talk and talk about the recent ills I've experienced in the relationship. My father sits stiffly.

After some time, the shrink interrupts, "Clyde, I think you are working too hard here. I want you to give your father a turn."

She questions my father, who is resistant.

Finally, he says that when I was in eighth grade, I tried to build a Windsor chair—a project that was way above my capabilities, a reach.

I remember the project I never finished. I'd wanted to use the lathe and make my father proud. I was just seeking recognition.

My father then says it occurred to him back then that I was trying to outdo him—competitively working at being better than him. He feels that much of my life I have been competitive against him.

I look at the shrink for some support. She just looks at me with anger, as though my father has just hit on something that she feels, too.

I think of all the putdowns my father has given me over the years; now I understand why. As the don, like Napoleon, he has to be the best at everything.

I recall sinking nails for him when I was five years old. No matter how well I accomplished the task, he'd always finish the job, whether it was necessary or not.

Whether the shrink gets it or not, I know he is projecting.

After the session, we visit my aunt and uncle, who busy themselves making suggestions about what my father and I can do in my free time. I am appreciative. My father looks offended and suddenly exclaims, "Clyde and I have never had a hard time finding things to do together!"

I am surprised about his inability to conceal his emotions. It does not match the contained mastermind of the criminal network I have been up against.

The next thing I know, my father is telling me where to go. I am driving into the Berkeley Hills as I start to worry about the long-term health of my car. When I mention it, my father tells me not to worry.

We get to a fire road; I pull over and park the car. "This is as far as we go," I tell him.

The two of us follow the fire road as far as it will take us. We cross the road and bushwhack. I tell my father about some of my ideas about the personality: how it is divided into the pimp, the whore, the John (or trick), the police, and the vigilante. Life is more complicated than just the id, ego, and superego, I explain. Having spent a good deal of time working these concepts through my mind during the long bike rides to BART, I pontificate.

My father listens, less judgmental than the shrink. I haven't been able to share mental wanderings with anyone in this way for a long time.

Then I listen to him talk about the limits of science, a central theme throughout much of my unread poetry. When I return home that evening, I have a much better feeling about my father.

The next day, my dad and I take a seat on the BART: I to get off at Walnut Creek, he, at SFO airport. On the train I maintain a low profile, worried about the public statement being made to the people who follow me on BART. I feel some degree of conflict about my embarrassment as my father speaks in an elevated voice about environmental issues. He rants on about the idiocy of the American Empire. I notice a man in a business suit listening very carefully, trying to stare him down. My father just continues.

❧❧❧

Seven days later, when I have again been scheduled off two days in a row, my mom arrives with my stepfather for their annual post-vacation trip to California to visit my stepfather's relatives. They bring themselves to my apartment by lunchtime. I have been cleaning and working on cover letters on an old computer I have up and running.

Once in the house, Dick Wigglesworth kisses my mother, then looks up at me and says, "Don't get jealous of the ox!"

As I try to make sense of this, Dick Wigglesworth offers to buy pizza for lunch.

My mother and I prepare to leave to pick up the pizza, and my stepfather asks to stay behind.

My stepfather, Dick Wigglesworth, member of a Masonic Lodge and a World Federalist, is totally devoted to the corrupt upper echelon. Now I am hip to the fact that he is probably going to run drug deals off my computer.

I tell Dick Wigglesworth that if he is going to stay back, he is not to go onto my computer.

My mom criticizes me for rudeness but Dick Wigglesworth agrees.

At the pizza shop, however, I get a strong sense.

When the cashier tells me that the pie will be an extra fifteen minutes, the obsessive intuition escalates. I walk out the door of the pizzeria and mom follows. We drive wildly back to the apartment and I start running. I burst into the apartment, and sure enough, my stepfather is typing away.

He can be sneaky—well, so can I.

I tell Dick Wigglesworth I want him to leave my home.

He interrupts and says that I'm right; he is sorry. "I only wanted to play foosball," he says, "but you are right, I shouldn't have disrespected you like that."

"That looked like a lot of typing for playing foosball," I reply.

After lunch, it somehow feels like I've made my point. Once we've eaten, it occurs to me that I've stirred up enough evidence for the hidden cameras so that the Feds will know that it wasn't *my* illegal computer doings all these years.

Maybe somewhere along the line a corrupt person who likes drugs will hire me.

After lunch, I take Maxine and my mom for a long hike in the Black Diamond Mines, the Regional Park that I have begun exploring more extensively now that I have the car that mom, after all, did buy for me.

Hiking with her takes me back to Montana and the two of us do a bit of talking.

By discussing my cousin who plays polo and wants to be an investment banker, she is able to demonstrate how far she's come from my father's moralistic simplicity and her own hatred of the nouveau riche. My cousin, who grew up admiring Michael J. Fox on *Family Ties,* is okay.

"Well, that's good for him," I say diplomatically.

"Yeah," says mom. "I really like *him* because *he* likes *family.*"

This stabs me.

I make an effort to contain my feelings, given her a compliment. I recall how when I was five, she broke down and bought me toy guns. I recall how unsatisfying those guns had been and how great it had been that I had been given the freedom to explore that ridiculous desire.

"Oh, that was your father's idea," she says. "He said that he hadn't been allowed to play with guns when he was little, and how he didn't want to see you regulated in that manner."

I am shocked, because that sounds like something I would do. I recall all the restrictions I had grown up with: not allowed to watch *Speed Racer, Star Wars,* or *The Bionic Man.* I was left out when my friends would talk about these shows.

I can see that perhaps much of what I have become stabs my mom in the heart.

As if she can read my mind, she looks at me and says, "I am really glad you stopped wearing that cross around your neck. I really hated to see you wearing that," she adds. "I think you are getting better."

I think about how the chain has broken and how frustrated I am that I cannot afford to replace it.

❧❧❧

Back at work two days later, I have grown taller for enduring the visits from my family. I sense that new understandings I have gained can translate to better work relationships.

I start to explore a relationship with the boss man, Mario, someone I have spent hours privately shunning.

In the past, when he saw that I owned a Mexican wallet, Mario asked if I knew what the logo meant. Knowing it was a logo for a Mexican football team, "Why, gee, I know what it stands for! Let's see . . . CA . . . stands for . . ." with a dramatic pause I chicken-balked, "*California Avocado.*"

Now, when Mario seems to reciprocate testing behavior with me and asks how I could be a Republican, I roll smoothly with the new information and play stupid.

Seeing that my desperate message to the CIA of fake personal reform actually didn't go to the CIA but went to Mario, I contain my shock. I tell Mario that I actually I am in favor of the Green Party.

Mario looks like he realizes he has been played.

I mentor him, quoting a Cool Moe Dee rap lyric.

He challenges me again. "Clyde, do you even know what that means?"

When I demonstrate my understanding—it is Cool Moe Dee dissing LL Cool J in a way that fits the way I just dissed him, Mario retorts, "Well, I went to school with Too $hort and we all used to pick on him and call *him* a goody goody!"

"I hear you. Too $hort, like most of the rappers, poets, and English Majors, probably is a goody-goody."

Len appears not to understand Mario's faltering.

Bullying, he cuts in knowingly by telling me his favorite movie is *White Men Can't Jump.*

I note the coincidence (I had just recently rented the movie from my video store.) Len might want to silence my power in this conversation, I think, but I just can't picture his chubby legs being able to do so much as an inch high spread eagle without damaging his groin.

Shortly thereafter, Len is alone in the open office, tapping phony numbers into the calculator. He calls me in. He says in a mimicking tone, "I am just figuring out all the money I am earning from selling drugs—let me tell you, it is a lot.

"I am trying to earn enough money," he adds with a little more sincerity, "so that I can put myself through medical school, so that I don't have to rely at all on my asshole father to be a doctor."

I instantly feel ashamed. I, too, insisted on earning my own money and on putting myself through graduate school, resenting those who did not have to work their way through. Now I can see this as being prideful, my own artificial ghetto mentality.

Not long after this, Mario fires Len for coming in late. It was his last chance, according to KaCee, although I had rarely noticed him being late at all. She says with a tragic air, "Yeah, Len had finally said he was clear about wanting to commit to working here and then he said his alarm just didn't go off."

I call my mom in tears that night, afraid I will get stopped at BART so that Mario will fire me like he fired Len.

When I talk about this in Spanish to Eduardo's Chilean cousin, she explains to me in broken English that Mario and Len are like brothers and that this move is not personal in any way.

Everyone in the deli will always love Len, as though he is family. Indeed, a week after he is fired, Len shows up dressed in expensive clothing and invites Mario to go golfing with him, a proposition Mario proudly accepts.

"We're all like family to each other," Joy explains to a customer.

If you can't keep it in your pants, keep it in the family! That is the mentality of this whole damn clan, I am starting to sense.

❧❧❧

When the hippie girl and the openly rich girl leave quietly to go back to school, a new woman gets hired who is a recent college graduate with a teaching certificate. She has moved to the Bay Area with her boyfriend, who grew up in Lafayette. I figure the boyfriend used family connections to get her this job while she interviews for a position as a music teacher for the upcoming school year.

When she reports success with all her interviews, I am certain not to be jealous. She is open with me that she does not like California elitism. She washes her hands all the time and kisses the customers' asses, but behind their back she rolls her eyes.

Not long after she starts working, she shocks me by defying all the other kids and inviting me to go hiking with her boyfriend. On my day off, I drive in and meet her and her boyfriend after she gets off work. Her boyfriend leads us back through Moraga to this trail that heads up into this park named Sibley.

I ignore the vibes from her boyfriend. During the conversation, my new female friend reveals to me that she is impressed by how much drug talk goes on in that deli. "Yeah, I've heard Pablo talk about visiting meth labs all the time," she says casually.

I note that Pablo hides that stuff from me but tell her that it cracks me up the way acts as if he would never use pot, when he is clearly high on meth half of the time.

At one point the boyfriend looks at me smugly. He ends his silence and starts talking about how cults come out to this Sibley Park and worship the devil.

I look at him as though he has just pulled a knife out on me.

He looks back, seeming to have personally confirmed something. I continue to pretend that I have nothing against this pompous asshole.

The next time I work with my friend she apologetically lets me know that the three of us won't be getting together again. By this time I have learned not to let this fact sour the working relationship I have with her. When she lands her first professional job in time for the school year, I am happy for her.

CHAPTER **24**

IMMEDIATELY, AS I walk in the office, the shrink has a curious affect: she appears to be welcoming. As soon as I am seated, she tells me that terrorists have demolished the World Trade Center towers and that the Pentagon has likewise been attacked. I have an odd sense that today she appreciates, rather than dreads, my company—as if she's somehow been wounded. She tells me this is a game-changer; the world is going to be different after today.

"These are problems that the CIA is going to have to deal with," she says.

Great, I think, maybe they'll get off my back.

At work, things are unusually busy. I think it's like the way it was on the Titanic: I am one of the men locked in the bottom of the boat while everyone else is out on the deck listening to violins play.

KaCee picks her head up at one point in the day and talks to herself, saying, "Wow, I am very angry!"

When I hear this, I realize that her take on the issue is just about as ridiculous as my own.

I also hear an uncharacteristically sober Pablo talk out loud to himself, sadly saying that he is prepared to defend this country.

A day or two later, as the world is somehow becoming consumed with American flags, I hear Pablo renege his statement of loyalty. He states the same thing I heard a rich Walnut Creek resident at the bank say: "You know, if our money isn't safe in this country, we will just have to go somewhere else."

As flags appear on the doors of my neighbors' apartments and on the antennae of cars, I observe how they contrast with the flags that appear on the kids' lockers at work. Some flags point up, as in "America will rise"; some point down, half-mast. Mourning? I wonder what flags hung up backward mean. There is a backward flag now pointing directly at the deli. Is it a symbol put out that targets the Mafia store as being anti-American?

In the car on the morning commute, I hear on NPR that even drug-running Mexican culture has been disturbed by the attacks on American power.

I purchase a flag and put it on the antenna of my car so my true feelings won't put me at odds with the social mainstream. The flag means nothing but internment camp existence to me.

◆◆◆◆

On the first Saturday after the New York City attacks, there is a wine and cheese festival going on in Walnut Creek, taking over the main street area. I am awed people can still afford to spend money on wine and cheese in this time of crisis. But as I walk from BART to work through this stupidity I spot a Muslim man who, due to menacing looks shot my way, has already identified himself to me on the BART train as the man who is following me today. Suddenly, he appears from behind a booth, as though trying to scare me. I watch him disappear like a soldier through other booths and I hasten to work.

In one sense, I could care less if there was a bombing at an idiotic festival of privilege, even if it hit me. On the other hand, even though these over privileged folks have been complaining about my hard work for the past ten months, it doesn't mean I am in favor of them being blown up.

In my gut, I don't think this Muslim-looking man following me is there to blow up the festival. I imagine that this following stuff is more like counterintelligence run by the CIA. If it is CIA, I feel, this could be a test to see if I am so anti-American that I would turn a blind eye to the danger.

KaCee is sitting in the office alone when I come in. Maybe she believes the fake fear and determination in my eyes. She acquiesces when I ask to make a private call. I get out the Yellow Pages and call the FBI.

The telephone operator asks me, "You are not just afraid of seeing Muslims in a mosque or anything?"

I tell the man a little bit about having experienced some stuff in Seattle and that I recognize that what I saw appeared to be intentional and weird.

"Okay," says the man knowingly. "Thank you for calling."

And then I am done and I feel relief.

I work the day in peace, feeling balanced, as if the call were an act of faith, a gesture toward growth.

When I am ready to clock out, Mario pulls me aside and asks if I am all right. "I heard that you saw Osama Bin Laden on your way to work, or something."

I tell him it is not true and I am just fine. I figure that KaCee had probably made the rumor up.

On my way through Main Street, I see tons of security. America has heard my message of reform and has validated me!

At BART, I see two clearly Muslim men rushing through the crowd. When they see me, they glare and then leave the platform as though they were only there to send me a message.

I cannot deny I fear having done harm to Muslim people. I struggle with my mixed feelings all the way home.

❧❧❧

"What on Earth did you see that made you feel like the man you saw was going to blow up the festival?" says the shrink in about the most judgmental voice I can imagine.

The part of me that feels guilty swells.

I have this sense that what I have done, so too would a real live mobster like Tony Soprano. But I have not yet seen the Sopranos so I sulk.

At the end of the session, in a threatening tone, she says, "Clyde, if you keep on doing what you are doing, you are going to end up getting in really bad trouble!"

I feel very threatened. I am afraid the shrink is going to hospitalize me.

Days later, I see the Muslim man on my way to work. I ignore my incredibly complicated feelings, walk up to him, and chum it up.

He says he is a dishwasher around the corner from the deli. I know there is no restaurant around the corner.

It is the only other time I will ever see him again. In parting, I tell him to have a good day and that I am sorry.

Furthermore, I take my car to a Muslim mechanic to get the oil changed and take Maxine out onto a patch of grass and play fetch with her in front of what I imagine to be the Muslim community. It is my way of making peace with those who are following me.

꜀꜀꜀꜀

Back in Jersey, my father is marching right into mosques with his Quaker volunteer work. He seems very confident about the fact that he is free to do such things.

I caution him on the phone one day. "Be careful, dad."

He does not respond.

Then he tells me he is in the process of getting money from my grandparents so he can continue to support me as long as I am working hard. This is a huge relief.

When I report my thankfulness about this support to my mom, she reminds me: "Don't believe your father! He has more money than he likes to let on."

I think of myself and my father as being old money Al-Qaida wolves preying on the weaker members of the lower social strata primarily because we are hungry ourselves. It makes me ashamed for my previous choices in life. Never again will I willingly choose to live with roach infestation simply to justify my feelings of deprivation like I did in college.

Around this time, I am hiking in Black Diamond Mines with Maxine, on a ridge looking down on a field. Suddenly, a coyote howls from down in the valley. My innocent Maxine starts to run down to greet the coyote.

"No!" I scream, so that I can hear my voice echo throughout the region, and Maxine listens to me.

I endeavor to hike around the valley to get back to the car safely. I find a big stick to beat off any attacking predators and think about the viciousness of nature and the complications of peace in a time like this. I will beat a coyote with a stick to protect Maxine without hating the poor coyote that is starving, uncared for, rabid, and jealous.

Still, I don't believe that Al-Qaida wolves are pure evil. The coyote's con seems natural and necessary. I am starting to appreciate that starting a war comes with powerful sentiments of need and justice, just like my dumbass actions at the Norton.

Getting back to the car is a lot like walking around the lake in Seattle. I imagine coyotes streaming over the rocks or around the corners, and I am ready to fight. I wonder how Quakers can be so protected that they simply wash their hands clean of nature's calls to violence. I feel my dog is worth it.

When it's over, I can see there was no real danger. Maxine listened to me. In reality, it is up to God what happens, not me!

꒱꒱꒱

A foster care agency calls me for an interview. A woman by the name of Brenda Wolfman sets up an interview.

Brenda Wolfman, the spy inserted into the nonprofit world, seems like a sweet and peaceful woman. In spite of monumental efforts to stay professional, however, I get the strong feeling after an hour that she will not be hiring me.

I remember some advice I once got in graduate school about interviewing. I say, "I've been interviewing in the Bay Area now for ten months now and am a little perplexed about why I am not finding any work. Do you have any suggestions or feedback about my interview?"

Ms. Wolfman looks at me. "Well, most social work positions want to hear that their workers are nice and organized."

I have been honest about how clinical considerations are my strength and organization is not. But I did not go into depth about my organizational impairments.

At a second interview at a San Francisco homeless shelter, I get another sense that I may be point blank wrong about the way I am seeing things. The interview is packed with a large team of potential coworkers. I answer a question about why, with a master's degree, I would even consider being underemployed at a front-lines type of position. I talk about how, though $30,000 a year would barely cover my expenses, in the past I hadn't been able to master the environment because I had been all alone without a team. I say that I want to be successful and do justice for street people.

As I am fielding other questions about my interests and my social life, I hear the slightly bizarre shrill voice of a Latina woman.

"Oh my God, suddenly I was getting a flash from a movie called *Stigmata*!" she gasps. The woman's friends who are sitting next to her acknowledge her comments as if they are normal.

When I get home from the interview in the evening, I rent the *Stigmata* movie. It makes me think when I see the way a woman is shown on a subway, screaming as her palms bleed for no apparent reason. It occurs to me that many people who are Christ-like figures in literature are symbolic stigmata! The woman is right—some of these coincidences going on with me may not always be a Mafia following. Maybe I am a spiritual man!

When I am called back for a third interview a few days later, I explain that I cannot take another day off work, as Mario has threatened to fire me. The young Indian administrator presses me to attend. I have been feeling overwhelmed with memories of the tragedies at the Norton Hotel and refuse the interview.

During weekly hikes in the Black Diamond Mines there are always circling, ghetto-bird helicopters and people on bikes stopping to check in with me. I am starting to see everything as an apocalyptic battleground.

On my way to therapy one day a local cop tails me all the way to Walnut Creek. Am I Jesus, or something?

I visit a Lutheran Church because it sits around the corner from my house. Sure enough, the preacher catches my eye every time he talks about Jesus, smiling as though he knows something about me that I don't.

In therapy, I bring in the key evidence that the government could use against me to suggest that I am a child molester, a story that I wrote in college about a white man I delivered a sandwich to at a halfway house. I am concerned that the story of this man who I envisioned as an institutionalized schizophrenic man is suggestive that he may be a child molester, therefore incriminating me. My writing teacher in college had brought her child to a school Christmas function after reading my story and had gotten very uncomfortable with the baby being close to me.

I hand the shrink the story without explaining my motives, just to see what her reaction will be.

I recall other stories I wrote about rape. I worry about myself that I have always had such an unconscious focus on such things.

I tell the shrink about my ability to see things like trauma in peoples' eyes. Finally, I tell her about the eyes of Elvis Smeidecamp on the BART, a Cal Fed advertisement that has changed daily (Elvis Smeidecamp is listening: it once read to my shock.) I tell her about the eyes of this boy I have recently seen in the newspaper that shot up his school.

"I see something similar when I look into the eyes of all these individuals," I say. "I can even sometimes see it in myself," I add.

The shrink asks if I have ever thought of shooting up a school.

"No. I have always responded to rage and anger by hurting myself instead of others."

The shrink says she is glad for that and she thinks that is better than hurting others. Then she asks if I trust myself.

"Yes, I trust myself," I say, a little miffed that she still has no understanding of me. "I trust myself but it is other people that I definitely don't trust. I would never intentionally hurt another person or myself."

The next week, when the shrink hands me back my story, she says she is really impressed by my writing abilities. I tell her I want to know if the story makes her at all concerned about me.

"No," she says. "I just thought it was good to read."

I breathe a sigh of relief, but the shrink doesn't let me get away with such comfort. Later in the session, she says, "Clyde, you are a person without a friend or support in the world. I hear you talk about the evil in other people all the time. What about the evil in you?"

Later that day, I pass a bookstore in the small mall in Antioch that is displaying a new book about Hitler. I read the first page. It describes a man who came to Germany without a friend or support in the world. I can see how the shrink believes that I am the bad one, like I am in danger of being a controller like Hitler, or a Columbine shooter.

Finally, I can own that I am sometimes wrong as society's blood drips down my face. I know I am not a schizophrenic. I know I am not really a spiritual man. I know I am someone apart from all this Armageddon hell.

CHAPTER **25**

I DECIDE TO take the shrink's advice and take a break from looking for work. I focus more on social activities. I go to poetry readings. I go climbing at a famous bouldering rock in Berkeley. I get a book of outings from the Sierra Club and start going on canine hikes with other lonely dog owners. Each outing is its own taste of Americana during which I stay alert, waiting to be struck down.

After work one Wednesday night, I drive south on 680 to the town of Freemont, which is south of Antioch toward San Jose. At the trail- head of a small regional park, I meet the leader of the hike, a woman who works for the fire department in San Jose. Though I like her dog, I think that she is capable of cooperating with a sacred conspiracy to keep the oil and money flowing in spite of the apocalypse.

Another man shows up with two dogs: an Australian shepherd and a Brittany spaniel. This identifies him to me as an elite spy. People who are breed focused have always made counterintelligence efforts. I recall the chip that may be sewn into my dog.

Though I expect to be neutralized (on "Mission" Peak, none the least) I allow myself to be reeled in. I stay. We begin the mini two-thousand foot ascent and they stop repeatedly to gasp and swallow water. In the dark, at eight thirty or so, as I am approaching the sum- mit slightly ahead of them, I notice that the man sniffles as if he was snorting cocaine or trying to sound like a pig! The woman counters his sniffle with a snort of her own. They go back and forth like this a number of times.

Pigs!

Now, as gale winds whip across the ridge, I see the lights of the entire Bay Area, and I am expecting to get shot. The government could do it any time!

Instead, the woman talks about her lonely life and the man comments on the beauty. I, reaching for my first sip of water, accidently pick up a dried mud pie sitting on the dark, dry, grassy earth. Otherwise, the ridge top is uneventful.

On the way down, my two companions start snorting again, and the three of us get lost for a time. I wonder about the directional capabilities of pigs. They start a debate, and somehow the three of us get back on track.

The man is talking about Barry Bonds. I can hear straight through what he is saying about home runs and steroids and see that he is talking about himself, the financial bondman spy. His comments are actually about legitimized crime that props up the monetary system.

The world is ruled by the cheaters!

ꜱꜱꜱꜱ

My thirtieth birthday comes without much fanfare. Mario lets me eat lunch for free and Joy gives me a hug and an extra special thank you for the thank-you card I have given her.

Joy had recently revealed to me that her family had been so abusive that one of her brothers had been driven crazy. "One time, my father took a knife to my brother's warts and threatened to cut them off," Joy said, pointing to my warts. "It scared him so much that the warts went away." She'd held up some salami. "You see this hunk of meat; now I want to rub this meat over your warts and make them go away."

I can see now why Joy sticks up for me, though I am certainly not crazy like her brother, as she appears to be suggesting.

Still, I find Joy's gesture to be abusive anyway. Having hunks of penis meat aggressively smeared over my hands reminds me of the clip of the Asian porn star on Kathy's wall.

Lauren tells me I look good for thirty—it is the nicest compliment I have had in a long time. It is nice that Lauren continues to flirt with me, because I sense that KaCee is still waging her rumor campaign against me.

Lauren comes into the deli on her day off with her husband and her kids, all dressed up with her eyes on me. Her husband gets jealous and stuffs a hundred dollar bill in her pocket. She then tells me all about it. While part of me finds this drama disturbing, Lauren is definitely a boost to my thirty-year-old ego.

One day a manager that I recognize from Safeway, where I have applied for work, comes over to the deli to get a sandwich for lunch. She spends time conversing with Mario over at the cash register. Later in the day, Mario calls me over. "Clyde," he says. "We'll always have a job for you here, but you are not allowed to work anywhere else."

One day, Pablo tells me that I should listen to the Michael Jackson song "Cool Criminal," and then sings it for me in a meth falsetto. While I still resent Pablo, the song validates my perceptions about the corruption at the deli.

When I notice that Pablo is drawing penises throughout the kitchen and counter areas, I get mad at him. I know KaCee will think I did it and complain to Mario, and I will get canned. When I confront him with this he does not deny doing it but says, "Wait a minute, why do you think you will get blamed for this?" His tone sounds like he is truly trying to correct a delusion of mine.

That night he offers to drive me to BART. It is the nicest thing any of these Mafia creeps has ever done for me.

In his truck, I lose it a little bit and I just start spewing out abuses I have suffered at the hands of my parents who are leading this conspiracy against me.

He just says—heartlessly—"I got to go."

I realize I am ranting, and embarrassedly get out of the car.

The next time we work together he says, "Okay, now I am going to come clean with you. KaCee has been telling everybody that you are a pervert and I can't take it any more so I am telling you, and I am not standing for it." He tells me some of the details of the plot.

I, of course, don't trust what he says to me. I even consider the possibility that I have only been paranoid about my sense that KaCee is calling me a sexual predator and reason it is possible that Pablo knows my inner thoughts.

A few days later, however, KaCee grabs a rag and walks up to me and aggressively starts scrubbing at my groin, not actually touching but coming pretty damned close. She scrubs the counter a minute and then she is back at my privates.

I helplessly drop my hands and look around for help. I know as well as KaCee does that I can do nothing about this. I just put on a sad helpless face and wait for her to stop.

When it's over, Adele comes back out of the kitchen. I lose my powerless face and pretend that nothing at all has happened. Politically, I know better than to accuse KaCee.

The next time I close the store with Pablo I confess that I hadn't trusted him when he had come clean with me.

A few days later I am working with my friend, the teacher. I have just recently watched *So I Married an Axe Murderer*. A group of young women come in and one quotes the movie and asks if I have ever seen it. I am standing behind the meat counter.

I tell her, "No, I haven't."

When she leaves my friend says, "Wow, that girl was flirting with you."

I feel validated, as it seemed to me she was, but I do not tell my friend my suspicions that she is another Mafia plant who happens to know that I had just rented the movie.

Lauren, who's been listening, shouts from the back, "Shut your damn cakehole," like the Scottish father shouts in the movie. I recognize that I am the axe murderer to the Mafia chick and the spoiled rich boy to Lauren, who is funny as hell even though she is married to money.

The next time the shrink hassles me about sexuality, I tell her: "If I were to get with one of these young rich girls, I would just end up being accused of being a pervert. They are nothing but jailbait to a guy like me." This is all I will trust her with regarding the incident with KaCee.

Meanwhile, I buy new work clothes—clean white-collar shirts from the company and black pants from Wal-Mart. I have an old pair of dress shoes that I start to utilize as well, knowing that I cannot afford to replace them when they run out. I start focusing on outdoing Mario in his pursuit of virtuous hygiene.

One day, the regional manager, whom I believe to be gay like Jack Lueggio, says I am exemplary in terms of my uniform. As a reward, he offers to teach me about the cheese case, as Lauren is off on this particular day. I am grateful for the attention and try to flirt a little through my fear, like a latent homosexual. It is my way of communicating that I am willing to go into management.

When Lauren gets back the next day she comes after me in the back and calls me an Uncle Tom.

She is right; I have encroached on her space, trying to make it into the big house. It makes me reflect on my own process and change. I could never have behaved this way in the past.

This makes me think about the wisdom of the Uncle Toms of the world, if they would only just use the power and trust they earn to free the serfs. I suspect that not all who worked in the big house took advantage of those who slaved in the field. There is something to accepting reality and striving to be the best kiss-ass you can be; I think that I can trust myself not to betray my brethren. It is like selling overpriced olive oil to the customers who anger you. It's like turning the other cheek. It empowers you to make the world a better place. I start to feel a sense of dignity in learning phony-ass house skills.

Since I have stopped reaching out to my mother, I have slowly turned to leaving long, complex messages on the shrink's answering machine. The messages are partly meant to torment the people who are listening in, partly meant to reach out for help, and partly meant to annoy the shrink, whom I can't stand. The shrink, to her credit, never mentions them or complains about them.

One day I try a new tack with the shrink. "Yeah, I don't blame my parents for refusing to support me."

The shrink's body language responds very positively to this.

I continue. "I mean, what's in it for them? They don't get anything but complaints and anger from me. Why should they bother?"

A moment later I shift to talking about how hard things are for me and sense, once again, her attention fading.

Suddenly the Uncle Tom skills are out the window. I amplify my voice and tell her that I have been resorting to eating out of the trashcan to save enough money to get by. It's not true, but it is just about how desperate I feel every day.

The shrink's attention comes back and she says she is sorry to hear that I am suffering, in a phony voice.

The next time I meet with her she acts as if she has had an epiphany of some sort since our last meeting.

I am explaining to her that I don't like being under my parent's control because it reminds me of what it was like to be under their control when I was little. It seems like the fortieth time I've made this point to her.

She says, "Well, then I hope you can get a job so that you don't have to be under their control."

I use my best Uncle Tom skills. "Thanks," I say, through utter hatred!

Now, for the first time, I have an agreement with this Mafia chick. I will put up with bullshit without complaints as long as she supports my independence. Finally, she's ready.

Seeming to sense this unspoken agreement, she finally refers me to a psychiatrist.

I park in Berkeley and walk to the psychiatrist's office on Hearst Street. Yes, I think, this may be the death of me. On the way, I panic. I have parked in front of a school, potential evidence against me that I am a child molester.

When I finally figure out the code and get in through the building, after the standard long wait in the office, he listens to me talk for a half an hour about the Norton and how I want to land a better job; then he talks with me about what my diagnosis should be based on what I am willing to tell him at this point. He suggests I have social phobia. He prescribes no medication. I wish I could talk to the psychiatrist instead of the shrink.

The next day off, I follow directions toward a park called "Tilden" or " Till Then."

On the drive, however, I am being followed, so I turn off at a side street that puts me dangerously close to the San Pablo Reservoir. I am afraid that the government will think I turned down the street in order to poison the water supply. I make a violent U-turn and find the right turnoff to " 'Till Then" park.

I have become acutely convinced that the government uses the numbers on my license plates to identify me. Lately, I have uncovered secret Mafia meanings behind each number up to nine, based on the sandwich specials at the deli and my qualitative experiences with them. For example, one is a chicken sandwich with Parmesan—clearly indicative of the Italian drug kingpin. Three is a vegetarian cheese sandwich, which is good because De La Soul raps about how three is the magic number and Jesus died at age thirty-three. Four is an eggplant vegetarian sandwich that is related to Jesus, because when you turn four on its side it looks like a fish. Numbers like six and eight are bad numbers because they represent Satan and drugs. Nine is the innocent truth—it lets the devil suck its dick and also functions as a gun in the ghetto.

What is really remarkable is that I lived my whole life without this knowledge.

Now at least I know that Mafia numbers on my license plate are sequenced to forever label me as a Mafia slave who listens to Satan and drugs and this depresses me.

Nevertheless, I enjoy chatting with the strange hikers while I walk Maxine. Maxine looks back at me to check-in during the hike, which embarrasses me because I see it as a sign of an insecure attachment, a sign I am not a good parent. When I comment about this to an Asian house mom I am hiking with, she says, "Your dog just loves you; there's nothing wrong with that!"

On a later hike in this same park I tell a female hiker about the TB scare back at the Norton. The worker, a real government spy, says that she works in public health for the government and that PHA handled the scare appropriately. She said that going public with a scare as such is not appropriate.

I tell her, "That's interesting." I hope this exchange will lead to future employment.

ＪＪＪ

The next day off, I have an interview. Apparently, Ms. Wolfman recommended me for an intern position after my failed interview with her.

I meet with a large Irish man named Jack. He asks me about what went wrong between me and my supervisor in Seattle. When I don't want to tell him, he invokes some Gestalt techniques designed to get me to emote feelings. I fake my way through this because I discern it's better not to tell him that my supervisor was a cocaine user.

He asks if I am okay working with him and of course I say yes and so he hires me. He says I can earn about five hundred dollars a month on top of what I earn now if I am good at this internship.

"Hey," he says, "I get something from you. I'll bet you've been in real poor areas when you worked back east."

I am a bit shocked by his intuition and think about all the lumberjacks in the northern Adirondacks who toiled for my great-grandfather and the money that is coming my way from my father that is keeping me out of the social service system. I realize that my inadvertent Mafia drawl is deceptive.

I am honest and deny his intuition.

He looks at the Band-Aids I have over the warts on my hand and adds, "Man, we have got to get you out of that deli soon, before they cut off your fingers."

Before he dismisses me, he looks me in the eye and intones, "Son, you have got to make friends with the *things* that are following you around. I think that's what's keeping you from working!"

❧❧❧

On the BART ride home, an African-American man approaches me when I arrive back at Pittsburgh/Bay Point. He says, "Man, I have been following you ever since you got on at San Leandro. I have come all the way out here just to talk with you. And now I just want to know your name?"

I'm a bit shocked but decide to ham it up a bit with a stately white man's drawl: "Why, my name is Clyde Dee." The man smiles with appreciation and I take leave of him. I wonder if I'm really ready to make friends with the people who are following me around.

❧❧❧

On my first day of work at the new job, Jack explains he was raised in South Boston, home of Whitey Bulger and the Irish mob. My new coworkers are doctoral students. Some have driven into this drug zone in their SUVs with their clean, fluffy hair.

There is also a PhD who can't even speak in clear sentences. She talks and talks.

I don't judge her.

After about a half hour, she says clearly, "The core of any psychological issue, it all comes down to instincts."

This identifies her as sadly stuck on Freud, the cokehead pimp of psychology.

When it is my turn to make a comment, I say I am aware that many of the kids we will work with will be impacted by the drug war as it is played out in the community.

Jack's face gets instantly red and he states, "I'll tell you what we need to do to get all these guys to stop using drugs—just turn on cool showers when things heat up!"

Suddenly I am in a panic. I am afraid that this is similar to something I had once told my father over the phone. I hadn't meant it; I was only being sarcastic.

Now, hearing my words applied out of context, I feel particularly guilty.

In this context, talks of showers remind me of Hitler's showers in the concentration camps. People dealing drugs on the street are in concentration camps and need a break, not a shower.

I get off at the Concord BART Station, where my car is waiting. I change into my suit and drive to the downtown square where I find the Regional Center. I am trying to become a case manager for developmentally disabled individuals. I realize I have forgotten a pen. This might make me look incompetent! I borrow one from the secretary and there are a host of forms to fill out.

When a young Irish lady comes in to interview me, I'm a little flustered. She immediately notices my anxiety, stating, "Wow, it seems very hot in here." She cracks a window. When asked what I would like to see in a supervisor, I talk about a trusting relationship that is supportive and work-focused.

She says, "Wow! That seems like a lot to ask from a supervisor!"

I try hard not to look distressed.

"It sure seems hot in here!" she says, cracking the window a bit more.

I excuse myself and explain I had just had a first day of work at an internship.

"Yes, the first day of a job can be very stressful, I suppose," she says, "but at this job you will be incredibly busy. You will barely have time for lunch. I am not sure you can handle that."

Defensively, I tell her that I had a 3.9 GPA in college and prefer to be very busy.

But it is no use; this woman's mind is made up. I can tell.

At night, I can't sleep a wink. I am amped up by shame over Jack's comment and the failed interview with the Irish woman. When morning finally comes, I have already left my fill of distressed messages on my shrink's voicemail. I don't know if I can make it through the day.

I call my father in crisis and tell him that even my apartment is a mess. He responds empathetically and asks if I would like him to come out and help me get my apartment together.

I stop. I look into the mirror by the washbasin. This is a rare opportunity to make a change. I accept the invitation. I make plans.

I get off the phone and call off from work for the day.

ﬤﬤﬤ

The psychiatrist has me in his office and is hunched over, ready to listen, and I just don't know where to begin. I know he won't believe all the things that have happened to me. Without making any real decision, I blurt out, "I think the people I work with are in the CIA." It is my most honest feeling in the moment.

I watch the psychiatrist's eyebrows shift from calm to severe and pointed.

I can see that he has made all the necessary conclusions about me. He looks mean and harsh.

I tell him that I had been fine when I was on six milligrams of Trilafon.

He prescribes sixteen milligrams.

I clean and organize my place for my dad's visit. I call him and he says not to worry about cleaning up, he'll help.

I tell him that I want to use his help to get myself together in other ways. Knowing that he is coming helps.

Before I go to bed that night, I do the psychiatrist the favor of trying his dose for one day.

The next day at work, I have a calm and easy day. I don't feel any differently about what I've been through, but it is much easier to focus and stay calm. When I get home, I think about how easy the day was and how tired I am and how I doubt that I can keep up with my job, feeling so sedated for days on end.

I purchase a pill slicer and take a half a pill a day.

My father stays with me as I am adjusting to life back on medication. When I am at work, he works in my apartment. I listen to him on our walks and at our dinners.

One night, he takes me out to eat at the Chinese buffet restaurant right around the corner from my apartment. I have become accustomed to looking at the buffet's leftover food in the dumpster. It is nice to sample it fresh at long last. I recognize that it is my father that saved me from real dumpster diving.

CHAPTER **26**

CHRISTMAS TIME COMES to the deli and I become increasingly impressed by and collaborative with Mario. Some overpaid interior decorator goof who profits off the sweat of my labor comes in and stacks up Italian sweet bread in triangular designs throughout the store. Customers come in and build themselves gift baskets that Mario or Joy prepares with clear plastic wrap using a machine that looks like a hair dryer. Adele gets particularly busy with catering orders and often requests help. Through it all, Mario is so busy he never bothers to eat.

Mario's attitude toward me has changed with the medication. Whereas he used to send me out to do cold, dirty work in the rain with a cold shoulder, he suddenly starts to make pains to acknowledge the thorough job that I always do. Under the direction of a chemical agent that takes the edge off the anger in my eyes, he respectfully says, "Good job," when I get back inside.

The medication doesn't change my feelings about what has transpired. However, Mario's acknowledgement is extremely important to me.

One week I lose one of my miniscule checks without noticing it. Joy and Mario make a big deal about my carelessness. They suggest I go thank the person who returned it to them. I don't truly believe that I dropped it on my way out to the car as they suggest. Nevertheless, I oblige.

Sure enough, the woman who found my check works in a nearby service joint for developmentally disabled individuals. They happen to have an opening for a "teacher" position that pays twelve dollars an hour. I apply.

As I prepare to interview, it occurs to me that perhaps what has gone on with me my whole life is that I have been in some way developmentally disabled. Maybe the management of the deli is trying to tell me that is my problem. I can admit that I have asperger's syndrome. I am willing to accept any label other than "schizophrenic." That word just does no justice to what I have gone through.

The interviewer is the woman who found my check. She says, "All the adults who come here are 'well taken care of.' Are you 'well taken care of?' "

I find this to be extremely classist. I bite my tongue and tell her yes.

Later that week, Mario talks to me about the reference he's given me. "That's right, Clyde, I told them that you're a team player, that you get along with all the kids here, and that you're well liked." The tone in his voice tells me that we both know none of this is true. I feel ashamed, in part. I also feel motivated to improve.

Before I start the new job, I go to the doctor of the new company for a physical in a fancy building in Concord. I carefully look over at the physician, who has the power to keep me from getting a professional job away from the deli. He is very unprofessional, wearing an obscure piece of medical equipment on an elastic band that sits crookedly on his head. His hair is not combed and he looks at me cross-eyed. I wonder if the man is even a real doctor as he swings his stethoscope around from where it is backwardly hanging on his back. I don't tell him about any medication I am taking. I am still so afraid my drug test will come back dirty. Every doctor that I have seen has caused me to quiver like a dog.

On the morning of second day of work at the developmentally disabled outfit, I can't get myself out of bed. I drive in to the deli and beg for my job back.

"Clyde, what were you thinking?" says Mario, "Of course you can come back."

Back at the deli the next day, KaCee circulates a joke all day long: "Hey, what's better that winning the Special Olympics? Not being retarded."

I know the joke is in my honor and everybody seems to feel obliged to laugh at it. The stigma of it eats at me.

At the deli Christmas party, Anthony shows up and hangs out with me. KaCee looks at him from the top of the swivel stairs in Joy's immaculate household and clears her throat, indicating she doesn't want her boyfriend betraying her by associating with the pervert. Anthony simply ignores her.

He tells me that I should counsel young adolescents. "You'd be really good at that," he says.

I am overwhelmed by this compliment. I have given up on the idea that I could ever do counseling again with all I've been through. Just seeing this kid, who had to put up with all my shit, expressing hope for my future is enough to nearly reduce me to tears.

I tell myself that if he has amends to make to me, he has just made them. He still owes Tyrone an apology, though!

♪♪♪

I take a trip to Napa with Timothy, a high-end dog food salesman, who takes a rare day off with his girlfriend. I befriended Timothy one evening seven months before, when he was moving in to our apartment complex, immediately suspicious of the spy-like twinkle in his eye. I had helped him for hours in spite of my exhaustion, and ever since, Timothy has been supplying me with bags of his competitors' dog and cat food. He claims to steal them off the shelves.

Timothy makes over a hundred thousand dollars a year. He is in love with being the boss of sales. His girlfriend is accustomed to criticizing him when he shows sensitivity. "Don't worry, baby, just keep on bringing in the six digit salaries," she says. "You are just fine."

On the ride to Napa, Timothy's girlfriend respects the fact that I was once a shrink. She asks for an interpretation of her dream.

I am not honest about what I really think about the dream because the dream does not say much about the strength of Timothy's bond with his girlfriend.

Timothy tells me I am smart and should get a PhD.

I say that all I care about any more is making money to survive.

When we finally get to Napa, Timothy and his girlfriend are such great hosts that, when I refuse to drink more than a few sips of wine, they too refuse. The three of us end up back in Antioch watching the latest Kevin Smith movie.

I can see Timothy trusts me, because he makes a point of letting me sit next to his girlfriend. She has explained to me she thinks he is paranoid. I just feel he is intuitive.

Coming out of the theater, I try to conceal the fact that I have just seen a thousand allusions to my illegitimate hospitalization, as if Kevin Smith has followed my personal story. I believe the movie Clerks was actually written about me at the Korean Deli in which I worked in Camden, New Jersey. I have re-rented the movie and seen all the marvelous connections.

In front of Timothy, I don't care. It helps me understand and accept what has happened to me.

When we part, I am sure to look Timothy in the eye, and with the hard-earned wisdom of my friend, Mr. Wilson, from Seattle, I thank him for the mini vacation in Americana.

‿‿‿

Before I know it. I am taking the BART home on Christmas Eve. I look at all the other people, yearning like me to get out of the cold. Walking to my car, I see people waiting to take the bus and I feel a part of a larger world.

Even though there is no Christmas waiting at home, it is a triumph to feel grateful for what I do have.

Of course, it helps that my father is coming to town again. He is staying with my stepmother's niece, Amy, and her husband Calvin—they happen to be spending the year in San Francisco where Amy is clerking for a federal judge. I will meet him and my stepmother at the Civic Center Mall at 9 a.m.—a clear improvement over my experience last Christmas.

It takes a long time to find my father at the mall, as he is very late. I walk around the large mall and observe the homeless Mister Whirlies and reflect on my sellout.

As the leader of the Service Committee at the private school I attended, I had led my peers through many different activities. One activity had been going onto the streets of Philadelphia and feeding the homeless.

I still recall a man to whom I was giving a sandwich. He had told me: "Life is hard for the homeless; you better hope it doesn't happen to you."

I recall thinking the man didn't understand. I worked twenty-hour days. As long as I continued to work hard, with the family I had, I would never have to worry about homelessness.

Walking through the little corners of funk-blast in that mall, I know that only my fear and my willingness to play Uncle Tom has saved me from what had once seemed to be my predestined Christmas fate, the real fate of all these Green Day Mister Whirlies.

Now I see these homeless people are better than me. In reality, good people are willing to be crucified rather than sell out to a world so brutal and ugly. It hurts my heart deeply to know how much worse it could have been if it had not been for the resources of my family and the slow grind of my work ethic.

❧❧❧❧

Amy and Calvin's apartment is enormous. They have fancy furniture and a parking space under the building. They talk about their neighbors with an air of superiority on the elevator ride up to the sixth floor. I marvel at the old-money hallways. My father, stepmother, and I arrive at their immaculate room with a view. They make a very big deal about using coasters on their coffee table as they serve alcohol to everyone except me.

I note Calvin uses the word "polished" to describe things he deems to be good with the same frequency as my college classmates used the word "dude" years ago to express their used, *what-the-fuck*, Chevy-Camaro-attitude.

As we walk through the Presidio after hearing about their exercise routines, healthy eating habits, and other aspects of superiority, the conversation shifts to my ex-best-friend who is now my stepbrother, Chester.

My mind flashes back to the time when Chester hit on me. It had been three weeks after my parents had separated. I was fifteen and desperately aching for support. He was home from college, and he came over to my house and started talking about a classmate he had a crush on. He talked about the classmate being in various meta-phorical dilemmas, lost in a jungle and bushwhacking back toward civilization.

My mom announced she was leaving the house, and then Chester led me up out of the basement to my room. We were both sitting on my shitty old futon when he revealed the classmate he had a crush on was really me. He tried to kiss me on the hand. I had been somewhat aware Chester was gay, but it hadn't bothered me until he went after my hand.

I was disoriented, as though I had just seen a rattlesnake. Time passed. I moved to a far corner of the house, away from Chester. At some point, my mom came back from her errand. She sat with Chester at the kitchen table. I could hear spits of the conversation. Chester talked about gay marriage.

I still can't understand why I got so upset, but at the time, the pain was unbearable.

Many years later, when I was hanging out with my friend Gary, while our associates were tripping on acid, I realized Chester may have been tripping during the episode. Chester later admitted that he had experimented with LSD three times that semester.

Now, I listen to my father and stepmother tear my poor friend apart. I think to myself that they are talking about him, much as I imagine they have talked about me. He doesn't make enough money; they have to help him. He doesn't manage his relationship with his daughter effectively. She is wounded and sick and he only makes it worse.

With Chester's character lying assassinated in the streets, we all start listening to my father bitch about the taxes on his copious property in the Adirondacks. I wonder if he is doing this for the benefit of Calvin, because it doesn't sound like him.

When we get to the base of the Golden Gate Bridge, where a soldier stands guard with a rifle, I start a conversation with my stepmother, who is supportive and tells me of her own struggles to stay employed at private school.

My stepmother used to be my favorite social studies teacher. She had also been my mother's best friend.

I find myself reflecting with clarity on my last year of private school. From my perch in the hospital, I assessed that it wasn't my intellect that earned me all those As from my stepmom, much as it wasn't my intellect that had caused teachers who despised my father, the administrator, to give me Bs. In and out of the hospital, I had determined that school was nothing but a political joke. Of course, as my passions turned to writing, the really good efforts, like my paper on Tibetan Buddhism with forty odd references, were invisible. I had a female classmate who took credit for the work I had done with the Service Committee. Then there was the two-page satire assignment. I wrote a fifteen-page story and earned a meager B. I was accused of being suicidal in my college essay. Though I continued to work diligently through college and thereafter, no one even cared to read me. The occasional compliment from college professors had only made me rage.

At night, we walk into Chinatown. I suggest to Calvin and Amy that we should get together again while they are in the area. They ignore me and move up ahead. My stepmother laughs and knowingly says, "You know, they are doing other things at this time."

I honor that they have the cultural capital to insult me, and that I do not have the power to fight back.

At the restaurant, Calvin and Amy continue to express their dominance by memorizing every entree and communicating with the waitress as if they are especially suited to deal with our needs.

In leaving the restaurant, Calvin comes up to me and says, "I think you should just accept a cushy job," as though he has researched my situation thoroughly and is pleased to impart his wisdom upon me.

He moves away before I can say anything.

Before I leave the party for the subway, my father lingers with me a moment to say good-bye. A homeless man Calvin has just ignored comes up to me and asks for money. I pull change out of my pocket and point out to the man that a number of the coins are dollars and transit fares.

☽☽☽

Two days later, my father arrives at the deli to pick me up after work for our next visit. Len is also paying me a visit. He is playing the idiot me he used to play. He says in a bizarre and twisted voice that his ears are full of wax and he needs to pour hot oil up them and clear them out. It reminds me that the bizarre cross-eyed doctor who had recently done the check-up on me had, in fact, cleaned my ears out. He says he takes medication but doesn't tell anyone about it. "It's my little secret," he whispers in his contorted way. The statement sends a smooth criminal twinge up my spine.

Yet, when my dad walks in, I am tickled. I have established an ability to get hired outside this hellhole. I watch my father and Len to see how they respond to each other.

Len pauses his ranting, a little surprised for a moment, but does not stop messing with me. A few minutes later, he pitches his bullying tone toward my father.

My father and I are silent as we walk together to the BART. On the train, as the sun gleams off the grassy hills behind the distant buildings of Concord, my father says loudly, "Gee, I wonder how they run the sewage plants in a territory like this."

I recognize this as a genuine fascination of my father's. I recall going to sewage plants and interviewing the workers for my intensive leaning projects to make him proud. I sit there on the train and think that one thing I know for certain is that my father is more interested in sewage plants than I am.

I feel bad for being so wrong about him.

I think how strange it must seem to a man who loves sewage and the environment that his son has developed this strange fascination with the distribution of drugs across the land of the free, so much so that he blamed his own father for it.

CHAPTER 27

A FEW WEEKS prior to Christmas the shrink had finally understood me enough to change the seductive: "Clyde, don't you ever feel horny?" to the more benign "Clyde, are you ready to get out there?"

I have accepted her referral to a singles group. Thus launched, I find myself at a church compound on a hill in Lafayette.

I'm in the room for the thirty to forty year olds and sit next to one of the two women who immediately interest me. The woman is an optometrist who works with kids at a clinic affiliated with UCSF, where she also teaches. In spite of her apparent income, she lives in a rent-controlled area of San Francisco. After the program is over, she invites me to go food shopping at *Trader Joe's*. I follow her through aisles of food I can't imagine being able to afford.

She talks about her childhood growing up in Walnut Creek and says she hates the strip malls that surround the area around which I live. She's tells me she loves the architecture of the newly built library in Orinda.

Back at the church compound a few weeks after Christmas, I am on the lookout for the optometrist. The other woman I was attracted to walks right up to me.

I stutter away any hopes of being suave, trying to respond appropriately.

The optometrist enters and I feel like I am in kindergarten. She comes over and sits next to me, as if she is ready to get in a catfight.

The optometrist and I end up at a special seminar that features a Jewish Holocaust survivor turned corporate success and a German ex-Nazi Youth turned academic. The men started up a friendship and co-wrote a post 9/11 book reflecting on lessons learned from their experiences.

I listen to the lecture, having just barely abandoned the theory that Osama Bin Laden is a mythical representation of my father.

I hear the Jewish man talk angrily about how crimes of greed do not compare to atrocities of murder and death like the ones promoted by Hitler and Osama Bin Laden.

I think about how I have seen firsthand how crimes of greed lead to slavery, genocide, gangsterism, and incarceration in the ghettos, prisons, and mental health institutions that are invisible to these center-of-town folk.

At the same time, I acknowledge the Jewish man has suffered a lot more than I have.

Romance is in the air and the optometrist is moved by the lecture. She appears to be potentially Jewish and maybe even Republican. She waits her turn to talk to the Jewish man. I watch the two of them smile and converse for five minutes.

I step up to the Jewish man when it is finally my turn and I tell him about how moved I am by his statement about crimes of greed.

He gets defensive.

I am amazed by the depth with which he has picked up on my energy.

I remember I have barely said anything and cut him off.

I tell him he shouldn't feel guilty for surviving an atrocity.

I think about myself as I say this and am not sure I really believe what I am saying.

There are complex emotions. There are tears. He shakes my smelly deli hand (I have come directly from work.)

I release my hand first and feel bad about his tears.

I think about how we are both greedy charlatans to be alive and talking to each other. I think of the man that nearly beat me up in the hospital and how he is probably a jobless slave in the mental health system in Montana. I think about how I am here with my car, my dog, and my job, having succumbed to the crime of bloody family inheritance, free to humiliate a Holocaust survivor. I remind myself that if I had been a real black teenager like Tyrone, instead of a Vanilla Ice wannabe, I'd probably be dead for errors that I made.

Suddenly the extreme arrogance of my privilege and my actions at the Norton hits me like a sledge.

I am no longer the epitome of good; I am just a man on a dumbass date.

I am sorry for what the Jewish man went, though—oh so sorry.

♪♪♪

A few days later, I have an interview at a company that runs housing and work programs for underserved developmentally disabled clients. The place is located in beautiful Walnut Creek but is gray with old dilapidated buildings. The human resource manager seems unpretentious, explaining that the job involves management of unlicensed houses, staffed by employees who make nine dollars an hour. Though the position will do nothing to get me hours toward my license, I have a sense this is a safe place for me and other edge-of-town social deviants to hide out and earn a living.

It isn't until the next weekend when, after a movie, I am sitting at a cafe drinking a diet Coke that I get to ask the optometrist what she had said to the Jewish man.

"I told him what I just told you about how traumatic it had been to be traveling in Hungary when I learned the towers had been hit."

I think about the Jewish man's courteous responses and I compliment her for her corn-ball courage. Then I tell her what I do for a living and a little about my last job at the Norton.

The next thing I know, I am in Orinda appreciating the architecture of the library and talking about books and swapping spit at a private place she finds in the back of the parking lot. I have to admit, it all feels a little corny to me.

At work, Mario tells me he thinks I am finally ready to supervise.

But by the time Mario's supervisor comes in to meet with me about the promotion, instead of accepting the position I am putting in my two-week notice. Mario's supervisor says they should have promoted me sooner, that they think I am a really good worker.

I say I think I am ready to go back to social work.

"What, you don't think what we do is social work?" says Mario's supervisor.

I feel guilty about the ironies of this statement. The workers at the deli have been my social workers.

Mario and his supervisor agree to let me work for them on Saturdays, during which I can wear the beeper that my new job requires.

I know better than to burn bridges with this organization. The extra money I earn on the weekend will be a vital part of my survival.

Around this time, I receive my mother's annual Christmas card. Usually, it has been a simple picture with a signature on it, but this year I have received a whole write-up. I am not sure if this is a new practice or if she just hasn't bothered to show it to me previously. The letter references my sister's marriage and pregnancy, then moves on to her first home and ongoing PhD study. Then the card talks about my mom's travels. At the end of the letter there is one line dedicated to me: "Clyde Dee is living in California and feeling better."

I am struck by my invisibility.

What is really notable about this slight, as opposed to the thousands of others I have received over the years, is that it occurs to me that my mom is simply doing to me what I have been doing to her all along. I haven't pointed out any of the good things she's done for me.

༄ ༄ ༄

I make my way up to the building on the top of the hill, which used to be one of the dormitories before the Lanterman Act freed the developmentally disabled from institutionalization in the late sixties. Navigating the concrete slabs that dominate the yard, I walk behind the assistant boss, who shares an office in the main building with the boss, an Ethiopian woman named Noelle, who has not yet arrived at work.

The assistant boss is overweight and acne scarred, but appears to be competent. Though focused, she pauses occasionally and lightens with a smile, as if she has to remind herself to allow time to let the gossip seep in. Throughout the day, the assistant boss teases me a little about my urgent need to get busy. I end up digging into a number of tasks, setting up appointments and contacting future resources.

Later in the afternoon, the assistant boss finally gets around to taking me to the houses I will be supervising. On the way, the two of us stop in to see Noelle.

The assistant boss submits to Noelle's booming voice with its devilish tendency to make fun of others. One of the clients, named Tom, stops by and I watch Noelle play with him with delight.

"He only loves me because I am powerful, but he is just so cute, I can't help it," Noelle says. She uses sign language to tell him that she will take him driving later and he hugs and kisses her. When he leaves she tells us some of her favorite Tom stories.

Three of our houses are located off the same road in Concord and the suburban scenery will become part of an everyday blur.

The first house contains two clients who have been buddies since they were locked up together over thirty years ago. They are taken care of by an older white woman who had once been active in harboring El Salvadoran refugees during the Sanctuary Movement. She works another eight-hour job before she arrives at the house at around three for a four-hour stint.

I respect this woman largely because she appears to take immediate offense to me. She clearly will resent any kind of intervention that comes from a fractured system that squanders its limited resources on supervisors.

After two more stops that are likewise intriguing sociological glimpses of the American class structure, the assistant boss leaves me off at the main campus, telling me that the worker at the final house is solid. I meet the worker, who is white and middle class, and unlike any of the other line workers in the organization, gets paid $13 an hour for his services. Nobody is supposed to know this, yet everyone does. I suspect he is the CEO's son or a family friend.

He opens up his conversation by talking to me about being raised in Lafayette under the tutelage of nannies, as if this will put me at ease. He is my age and has been working this job over ten years while going to school to get a degree in graphic design. He enjoys all kinds of outdoor hobbies, like surfing and skiing.

I meet the three men who stay in this house. I am talking to the house's African-American client, whom I know from reading his chart has a low IQ and carries a diagnosis of autism and antisocial personality disorder. This "anti-social" man shows me all of his Stevie Wonder LPs to befriend me. He follows me out of the room and acts very oppressed by the upper-class white man.

The white man raises his voice, and in a critical and controlling tone calls out the autistic man's name.

Suddenly, I don't trust the worker at all. I question the label of anti-social, figuring it is put there to cover the white man's racist, controlling ass.

At the same time, I know I am not able to address such an injustice and keep my job. I need to use my house skills and feel extraordinarily guilty.

A day or so later, I am running an errand for the house that is located on the campus. It is before our clients (or partners) come home from work for the day and I let myself into the house. Suddenly, I have a moment of panic. I sense my power over these peoples' lives, as though I would abuse. I almost fall over. The fear of being labeled a pedophile comes streaming over my body like a gale wind. The world is spinning. I feel that this might be the rich white man's abusive spirit I am sensing. I feel like this is a flashback to my psychosis. Luckily, no one is around. I remind myself what I've told the shrink, that, in fact, I can trust myself.

A day or so later, I am walking in the yard toward my office and I hear a harsh metallic voice calling my name. I realize I am alone and *hearing a voice.*

I remind myself that I am making enough money to survive, that nobody has to know about what I've experienced. It's just a voice. It can't stop me from doing my job.

Maybe *the voice* is only calling my name because I have beaten it. Maybe I will never have to deal with this voice ever again, as long as I am safely working.

♪♪♪♪

The optometrist and I make candles at her apartment in San Francisco. On our way out to purchase supplies to make candles, we stop in at the clinic where she works.

I feel like a con man coming from out of a crack in the sewer when I see how fancy and formal her responsibilities are. I meet one of her students and he does reflexive kiss-ass skills with envy in his elevated eyes as he looks me over.

When we are done with the candles, the optometrist disappears momentarily and then comes after me in a way that makes me notice she has taken her brassiere off. I enjoy the feel of the moment a little while before trying to act like it is extremely hard to restrain my passion.

Then I tell her about genital warts.

During an appointment in which I was getting warts frozen off my hands, I had the doctor check a small bump on my scrotum. To my shock, it was a wart. I had certainly had larger bumps scare me in the past, but they had been irrelevant.

"That's why I always ask before I leap," she says.

I hear this, noting that she didn't ask.

After meeting the optometrist for a movie the next week on Saturday night, I get the standard kiss but do not get the invite back to her apartment.

The next morning, she calls to ask if I can meet her for coffee. I figure she's had one of those restless nights she's always talking about; she's depressed because she is not married. This is the story of her life.

Over coffee and diet Coke, she states she is ready to buy a house in Orinda and start a family and she has everything that she needs to do this.

I can see where she's going with this but I am preoccupied with thoughts about the weekend staff member at one of my houses. Noelle has been threatening to fire him based on lateness, and an egregious list of complaints that include a potential history of smoking pot in front of the clients.

When I met with the offender, he'd introduced himself as grieving because of the deaths of his friends and relatives. He is African-American and my age and size. Based on his comment and my experience with "psychosis," I immediately understood. He went on and laughed at me when he'd heard I'd interviewed at Hunter's Point and said that's where all his people are located. A little while after we parted, my beep buzzed. It read, 9-1-1.

I am still reflecting. The optometrist's words pierce my thoughts.

"You have a good degree and should be using it."

I explain to her that though I might not be right where she is at the moment, I enjoy her company.

I pause and she is quiet.

Before I know what I am doing, I tell her about my interaction with the African-American staff member. I explain I had been schooled in this kind of Mafia stuff in my own way at the Norton.

"Mafia stuff?" she asks. "I would hope you would have nothing to do with Mafia stuff."

"Of course, I want nothing to do with Mafia stuff," I say defensively. "But that's not always something one can help."

"Well, give me an example of a time you couldn't avoid having anything to do with Mafia stuff."

When I am finished giving an example of an innocuous something that happened at the deli, the Optometrist gets a confused look on her face.

She says, "I don't think that that sounds like Mafia."

The next weekend, the optometrist and I go on a hike with

Calvin and Amy. She appears to instantly feel very comfortable with them.

Early on in the hike, I learn Calvin does research on managed care. I share with him my experience working under managed care on the front lines in Seattle.

He says that, contrary to my experience, mental health care is better and more efficient when managed care steps in. It reduces government waste.

I tell him that's interesting.

At a later point in the hike, I attempt to fall behind and chum it up with him as he finishes up with a phone call.

I figure I'll ignore the class divide and let the ladies talk.

Calvin ignores the fact that I have waited for him and walks right past me, breaking a twig angrily with his shoe.

I find my eyes focusing on cow patties as I try to minimize the disrespect and continue to treat Calvin decently.

By the end of the hike, the optometrist is looking at me as though I am the cockroach coming out of the sewer. The body language is so overt I can't help but wonder what Amy has said to her when they were alone.

A week later I receive a letter from the optometrist in the mail stating she doesn't feel that I have what she needs and she doesn't want to *ever* see me again.

ﻬﻬﻬ

"That's fair," insists the shrink, when I finally open up to her. "And I don't think you can blame Calvin for what has happened in this relationship. I think her opinion changed because you brought up the Mafia issue."

I acknowledge the kernel of truth in what the shrink has said, concealing salty spite.

The shrink continues. "And I don't think there is any government or criminal conspiracy behind your inability to get work all this time. I just think when you go to these interviews you look like a freak and a crazy person. I think that's why you haven't been hired."

I sit before her, calmly breathing with patience that only a history of incarceration can create.

Some time passes and I am forced to reply.

I tell her about the sniffing hikers on "Mission" Peak with Barry the "Bond" hiker who showed up with the Australian shepherd and the Brittany spaniel and how she had started out our next session sniffing in the same manner "by coincidence."

The shrink laughs obnoxiously, "Did you really think I was indicating that I sniff cocaine? I get allergies that time of year. I was not sniffing cocaine at the time."

I understand the shrink's obnoxious ways enough to know that she is genuine when she says this.

And I can see that some of what I've experienced is more than just a worldly conspiracy.

❧❧❧❧

At some point during my tenure at the Walnut Creek social service agency, my heavily criticized ex-best-friend/stepbrother Chester comes to town for a visit with his daughter, Ruby. Calvin and Amy are the hosts.

The day starts at a burrito joint. I watch Chester graciously accept burritos, sensing massive humility. He talks about his low-wage factory job, excluding the detail that it involves fixing monitors for sex offenders.

Chester then alludes to his knowledge that I, too, had a hard time that year.

I immediately sense he's heard about my past two years in much the same way I've heard about his. I recall how my father and stepmother also talked about Ruby's history of being sexually abused by an acquaintance of Chester.

Bathed in Chester's knowing look, I feel bonded to him again. I feel forgiveness. I feel so sorry about the homophobia that existed within me at age fifteen.

On the ride to the zoo, Ruby, who is about ten years old, takes a very clear liking to me. It starts with questions about Maxine, who is at home in my apartment. Ruby tells me stories about her dog, Odie. Though I have felt slightly skittish around children since Fresno, I feel no discomfort around Ruby.

As the day wears on, Ruby grows attached to me. At the petting zoo, I watch her get fearful of the goats and rams in much the same way I did at her age. At an ant exhibit, she begins relating to the ants and I can't help but dip into my child therapy skills to enter her world.

Then, as I leave Ruby's side to go to the restroom, Calvin comes suspiciously up behind me and appears to be determined to take the urinal right next to me when this is totally unnecessary for any other reason than to take a look at my penis.

I figure he is just doing a safety check for his relative and I do not show anger in spite of the taste of salt. Instead, I visibly flick the final drops of urine from my tiny, and flaccid (limp) penis, taking my time.

Before I leave, Ruby grabs hold of me, crying, not wanting to let me go. I am perplexed by the connection that has grown up so quickly between this little girl and me.

Four years later, I will hear Ruby has started hearing voices and seeing mysterious visions and, by then, I will understand.

CHAPTER **28**

I ADJUST TO life out of crisis during the months that follow. With my lease finally up, I am able to find an apartment significantly closer to the Bay. Of course, the complex does not bother to do a background check on me. Other places I've looked at use bad references from the complex in Fresno to inflate the proposed rent.

I am well informed what lies ahead as I am, alone, moving myself back into a strange darkness. My aunt arrives three hours late. To cope with my associated feelings, I imagine writing a Raymond Carver-like short story—a tale fueled by the wisdom of madness in which a main character is moving back to street life, unbeknownst to an out-of-touch family member.

When my aunt arrives and refuses to help me carry anything, I resort to throwing my futon out the sliding glass doors so that it lands in a puff of dust and dog hair on the manicured green lawn one story below.

Instead of raging, I am able to appreciate the help that my aunt has in fact given me, instructing me which box to take first and effectively concealing a hole that had been burned in the rug when my cat knocked over a lamp. In the end, I somehow end up getting a full refund on my security deposit.

In the past, a stressful move, made out of what had decompensated into a suburban drug den and a late girlfriend, had led to raging vehicular behavior.

Antithetical to the stigmatized concept of schizophrenia, I reflect that I have become more emotionally tolerant from madness. Working through it has helped me learn resilience.

꩜꩜꩜

One of my coworkers, Janet, is wonderful with the clients one night when we take them to a local dance. At the dance, faces brighten in response to her enthusiasm. Janet used to work for a private investigator. She has survived in this California economy by working sixty hours a week. When I compare her big-boned humanity to that of the optometrist I shake my head at my foolishness.

My efforts to match her in spirit fall flat. A wallflower pang creeps over me. A young woman whose face is largely concealed by shades pursues me all over the dance floor and I end up running away from her. I end up hiding in the bushes outside the elementary school.

But I am not being a snob here. Somehow, this young developmentally disabled person has more junior high guts than I have, and I can barely understand her courage.

On another occasion, Janet gets angry with me when I snicker at a comment she makes during a conversation about sex. "Don't you masturbate?" she says. I feel my face turn red, and I think of my warts. My response seems to validate her point, and Noelle and my female coworkers all laugh.

After the dance, however, Janet is abruptly forced to leave work on disability due to a back problem.

At work, coworkers have a lot of time to do nothing but gossip; I prefer to ignore this and stay steadily focused on creating my next task. I often feel embarrassed and worry my thoughts will freeze. I frequently ask Noelle defensive questions about my performance. She makes it clear she considers me one of her insecure employees and encourages me to not put myself down.

Once, during a community CPR training, I get called on by the instructor and am unable to speak. I eventually blurt out an overly complex half-answer.

Another man at the training, who clearly has some kind of nervous disorder, says he trusts that I am smart, even though I can't speak.

This would have been a relief except that Noelle and my coworkers often talk about this man behind his back because of his nerves. He typically responds by histrionically raging.

One day, Noelle comments on a coworker's unsuccessful attempts to make friends with others. Then, she suggests that maybe I'd like to spend my weekend with her. The whole staff erupts in laughter.

I feel that although I am working loads of extra hours and am being meticulous in following the rules, I am just hanging on by my fingernails.

When the privileged white worker abruptly leaves, having graduated and now ready to embark on a career, I cover the extra shifts. With all the pressure, I make minor writing errors administering medications; I conscientiously report them to Noelle, per protocol, and she responds by giving me a written warning.

Then, one morning before I get fired, I show up to work three minutes late in the medicated stupor that eight milligrams of Trilafon regularly leaves me in, and find that all my duties have already been completed by a large African-American man who has the whole household humming with a paternal energy. He explains he has already worked things out with Noelle and he is the answer to all my problems. He will cover the all the shifts perfectly and without complaint.

This man's name is Mr. Dennis and he becomes the closest thing I have to a friend during this time.

When I visit the house on campus in the evenings, Mr. Dennis tells me stories about coming up on the streets of Richmond. He'd managed to escape to the bosom of the Job Corps, which threw him into a rural culture and enabled him to find the balance he needed to get a college football scholarship. Then he got into the military as an Airborne Ranger, which landed him in Central America—Nicaragua and El Salvador—wearing black uniforms and firing bullets into crowds of people. As a result, he calls himself a mercenary. "They love to give you those stripes," he said, "and they love to take them away."

Mr. Dennis seems shocked that I don't know what he considers to be very basic information about the Cosa Nostra, the Italian Mafia. He teaches me.

"Certain arms of our military are focused on being the meanest and most brutal in the world," says Mr. Dennis. "And they are focused on intimidating the enemy. Sure, some of our enemies resort to beheading people graphically, but we do the same type of things and try to do them harder and more viciously."

I remember the police in black riot gear kicking and beating a protester in front of me in Seattle.

Mr. Dennis also shares details of his past black-market dealings, which involve American pornography in Asia.

"No matter where you go or what you do in this life, most people end up choosing to live in the same type of area where they grow up," he says. "If you were raised in the ghetto, like me, you will naturally find yourself gravitating toward that kind of life, even if you can see ways to get yourself out."

I see in myself a parallel process.

Mr. Dennis sees where I am at and shares hope for my future.

"You worked hard for your master's degree. You put yourself through school. You should go for a better job—that's what it's all about for you. And don't feel *guilty*."

He also reflects on his own views on life in a philosophical manner. "This job is easy for me. It's all about being a father, a role that a lot of black men don't get to play. It's as easy as raising kids, and I don't mind the long hours. When I work eighty hours I make more money than you do—don't worry about me, I keep myself comfortable."

In public at the school, Mr. Dennis sends me covert threatening messages.

When I share one of them with the shrink, she says, "Now, that man really sounds dangerous. I don't think you should tolerate that. I think you should distance yourself from him."

The shrink's comment does compel me to come back at Mr. Dennis with a little boundary.

He laughs uncontrollably for a spell, but he stops pulling that stuff on me.

Noelle, perhaps jealous that I am getting close to Mr. Dennis, instructs me to confront him about the large portions he is serving our clients. She is specifically focused on the grease and oil he uses and pushes me to add this in my critique. This is something I just won't do. I know it is a culturally loaded criticism.

Even though I avoid bringing up the fats and oils, Mr. Dennis gets angry. Then, Noelle shows up during our conversation and says she would love to eat Mr. Dennis's food, especially the bacon—she just loves bacon.

After Noelle's intervention, Mr. Dennis looks at me with very sharp eyes. There will be no reconciling with him.

Later, I leave forty dollars in cash for the weekend staff person to use to take the clients out. When the forty dollars goes missing, Noelle accuses me of the theft.

I don't react strongly to the accusation, even though I am a letter away from losing my job, because by this time I am starting to figure Noelle out.

Noelle manipulates low-wage earners into making up shifts for people who call out on the weekends. Every week there is a crisis and an extra shift is needed. If the shift cannot be filled, the supervisor on-call has to cover the twelve-hour shift without pay. The way I see it, Noelle keeps everyone on the edge of losing their jobs so she can step in and ask the threatened workers to cover the shifts.

Perhaps sensing my disapproval of this management style, Noelle occasionally leaves me to cover my own shifts even though I keep myself thanklessly busy while others do not. But I have enough self-awareness to know that it would be unfair to blame discontent I feel on the job on Noelle's management style.

After six months, I have earned enough leave to visit my family on the East Coast.

My father picks me up at the airport and drops me off at my mother's place, much as he did two and a half years before. Again, he is peaceful and supportive, and this time I am awake enough to appreciate it.

A few days later, I take a bike ride with him through the old roads in the Pine Barrens that I have memorized through night hiking in earlier years. I get into conversations about his experiences teaching and his *noncompetitive* admiration for my Grandfather McCain's psychological writings.

Unbeknownst to my father, I have ruminated about Grandpa McCain a great deal during psychosis. When my father discloses to me that my grandfather had made his money from supremely wise trading of stock, not from all the books he'd published, I feel some of my suspicions are confirmed.

My grandfather's sponsorship of Timothy Leary at Yale and the fact that my grandfather had done work for the CIA flash in my mind. I think about how many young kids have gone through what I went through permanently as a result of my grandfather's potential misuse of power. I wonder if anyone else might ever see this journey of mine to be family karma rather than genetics.

My grandfather's sister was lobotomized by his family, and she had to move to an institution and become a family secret. Yes, my grandfather had done everything he could to help me in a humble way that I could truly love. Yes, my grandfather was decorated as a great man, but I pray that god will bless my great aunt too! I feel her sacrifice was part of his fame.

⁘⁘⁘

A number of my friends come to pay their respects including my old friend Gary. I learn that he and his girlfriend came out to Seattle to save me. When they hadn't found me in Seattle they had moved to Portland, where they had lived for six months before moving to Texas for another six months. They returned home to Philadelphia just in time to receive my angry phone call from Fresno. When I learn of this extended road trip, I feel so bad for all I put him through, but also relieved that, despite a distant look of pain, he has forgiven me. Gary is still there for me. In fact, I can see that Gary knows how to be there for me far better than I know how to be there for him.

Still, several of my friends do not come to see me, having given up on me due to my diagnosis.

CHAPTER **29**

WHEN I RETURN to California, a medication clinic I interviewed with agrees to give me a three-month trial period before an affirmative hire. I decide to take on the risk without revealing the fragility of my economic situation.

At the new job, a man named Mario will be my manager. Mario manages the people who work for him in a responsible manner. He is also in law school and business school at the same time. He calls his BMW "The Senator." Always whistling with energy, he somehow functions at work even when he has been up half the night studying.

I met Mario when I referred one of the clients at my last job to his medication clinic. I have a strong sense that I impressed him and that he is behind my hire.

I rely on Mario and another employee, named Louise, to learn the ropes of the first half of my job, which involves basic paperwork and light clinical interactions.

Louise plans to start her master's degree in counseling psychology in the upcoming year. I can see she has questions about the work she does and I am able to use my experience and education to support her. Both of us maintain impeccable statistics in terms of billing hours. Neither of us stops for lunch and we both stay late.

In the middle of my first week I head to the Richmond satellite office for the weekly day of supervision. The agency is about a mile from the BART. During the walk, I notice my nerves are up. Adjusting to all the new changes with the job is stressful. Although I have been used to sixty-hour weeks, additional routines of ironing shirts and ties and removing dog hairs from my clothes make me feel drained.

In the first meeting of the day, I carefully take inventory. My supervisor instantly seems to have sour eyes toward me.

Additionally, she vents her opinions viciously. "The local hospital in Martinez won't keep delusional people, even when they sleep with knives in their bed!" she complains. "It's ridiculous; how can we do our jobs!"

As a professional, I've always observed county hospitals to be ineffectual and traumatizing places, even before my experience in Montana. Visiting them has often been shocking.

Suddenly, the supervisor turns to me and asks challenging questions about California laws.

When I explain I've never practiced in California before, her eyes widen. When she learns I have functioned as a "case manager" in the past, she looks even more appalled.

The supervisor spends the two-hour group supervision working with the other therapist who works with the company and ignores me entirely. When I am finally alone with her, she says I am clearly not on the same level as her other intern.

I can feel my face get red, and my heart beats hard. I can barely breathe.

"If you are going to work under my license, you are going to have to start extremely slow, at the pace that I see fit," she says.

Back to work in San Leandro, I occasionally break down and whisper my fears to Louise in the final hours of an intense day. "I depend on this job in order to eat," I say. Louise learns to soothe me, saying she is sure that I have enough support from Mario to make the cut.

"I think you can do it," says the shrink to my surprise. "I also think you shouldn't have accepted the position without a guaranteed hire."

This resonates as perhaps the first indication that my imposed relationship with the shrink might actually help.

The shrink continues: "But tell me what is going on with your eyes. You can't seem to talk to me without taking off your glasses and gouging at your eyes with your fists?"

I notice my fists in my eyes and I think of the J.D. Salinger character, Seymour Glass, and how tired I am of *seeing more of the glass* of class mystification and racial dominance in the eyes of all the chronically normal folk like the supervisor. I reflect on how, for years, so many people have just pushed me out of their circle and off the lifeboat because of the hump in my posture or the trauma in my eyes. Classism, sexism, and racism have hurt me so profoundly.

"I think we have a real psychodynamic process going here," the shrink continues. "I think this supervisor you work with is really not managing you very well. Remember, Clyde, I supervise supervisors. I think you need to go back to positive affirmations 101 and write down positive things about yourself and remind yourself that you are not shit.

"This criticism that this supervisor and you are putting on your performance is exactly what I just called it, shit. It is like you are like a character out of a John Irving novel that just sees shit everywhere he goes. Everything in the world is not shit. Remember, what is going on with you is really like *reverse narcissism*; you're not so bad. Really you are kind, smart, intelligent, *sexy*, generous, caring, and good at what you do. But I can't do your work for you. You have to do this work yourself, so write some affirmations in those journals you write."

My psychiatrist suggests adding antidepressants to my medications. I accept his suggestions—Wellbutrin and Effexor. I have been on both in the past, but I have never tried the combination before.

I take the pills, and I work my ass off.

On the way to work, I start lurching upright out of the stupor of sleep at every stop on BART to make sure I make my transfer and get off at San Leandro. However, despite the fatigue, I see improvements. I am better able to accept myself and build a sense of self at work.

The psychiatrist adjusts the Effexor, the drug he believes is causing the excess sedation.

ꙮꙮꙮ

At the end of each week, Mario and his side-kick, Paco, down pitchers of Margaritas before driving me to a BART station. After that they hit the town at an Asian karaoke bar. I always decline to go to karaoke because I have to get home to take care of my dog.

Occasionally, I drop little hints about my situation that are loosely based on reality. One day I discuss my failure in Fresno with Mario.

"Why did you choose Fresno?" he asks.

I tell him it is where my car broke down; I sold it for an apartment.

"Ho!" Mario yodels. "You are the real deal!"

Mario's response seems artificial, as if he knows I am lying but I don't care. I then feel obliged to tell that for three months I have lived out of my car, running away from thugs in Seattle.

Mario does not flinch in his support of me. I learn he has a property he owns and rents out back in Sacramento, but I do not feel jealous. And having him know a version of the truth about my blue blood poverty is comforting.

One day, when he drives me to BART, I tell him about my willingness to dedicate my life to the organization if they hire me.

"That's good," he says with that certain tone that tells me he is just doing his job, that he himself wouldn't devote himself to this company we work with. He says, "I could get you a job over at Summit Adult Day Program." He has worked there in the past. "I saw the way you had that developmentally disabled kid wrapped around your finger," says Mario. "I like your drive. Things work out for people who are good. You are good, I can see that."

Fighting for acceptance at every corner, I tag along to something I know I will loathe, an extravagant dinner paid for by the drug company, Pfizer.

Taking an elevator, we all arrive at a posh restaurant where I sit next to massive windows that overlook the square. Three or four doctors I don't know are present, acting like brash American tourists, clearly only concerned about whether my presence is going to contribute to their buzz. Mario and his boss Tammy are happy to oblige them.

Before my very eyes I can see how corrupt doctors overprescribe the medications I have been slave to for oh-so-many years for profit. I am so sure now that I was wrong to put my trust in them prior to my psychosis.

Once the doctors are shitfaced, the drug reps rattle off complex science that only doctors can understand.

I pray that no one can see the judgment in my eyes.

◢◢◢

My personal life during this time is full of rejections. I take a woman I meet at the singles group on a hike with Amy and Calvin for a first date.

During the hike, the conversation meanders into politics and the war. I can't help but make streetwise comments about movies I've seen and democracy in the Philippines.

When these go unobserved, I retort in my mind that at least clients in a mental institution would have picked up on what I was saying. Oppression is clearly not something everybody can understand.

When that relationship fails at the third date, I feel tragically flawed.

Another date doesn't go well. The woman says she could never trust anyone, "who would bring a Foucault book along on a date."

I start to go to Quaker meeting in Berkeley. I spend many weekends initiating contact with a humble, unemployed Oberlin graduate.

Finally, when I earn the opportunity to hike with her at Tilden Park, she starts off by telling me about a refugee she is connected with.

I think about my experiences and feel that in a sense I have endured a refugee status. I open up.

I talk and she seems to respond.

I review the details of what I went through: alerting the press, uncovering a possible murder, receiving threats from a connected man, trying to flee the country. I have to skip over the incarceration. I have to skip over the secret service agent and the police search of my apartment, the tampering with my mail, getting followed by cop cars. I talk in generalities. I long for a sense of acknowledgement. I am tired of pretending these realities are just delusions.

After an hour she interrupts me by blurting that she is not at all having a good time. "I mean, I guess it is good you trust me," she says, perhaps responding to redness that overtakes my flesh.

I think about how it is chic if you are Quaker to have a refugee friend, but not to accept that someone from your own family or hometown could have experienced real social persecution.

On the other hand, I have to acknowledge that I am using bad manners. Refugees I've known don't go into details. In this way I can acknowledge that I am a bit of a fool.

❧❧❧

Preparing for my last meeting with the supervisor before she renders her decision as to whether I will be hired, I am asked to step in and complete a psychosocial assessment of a new client. Putting my questions about the future aside, I sit down with a skinny, sensitive Latino man with a mustache who appears to be the kind of person who has been bullied as a child. When I ask him the standard questions as to whether he was ever homicidal, he says he wants to kill a drug dealer who is picking on him.

I am aware I have to assess this. I ask him for the name of the drug dealer. I ask if he owns a gun. I ask him if he is serious about shooting a drug dealer or just selling wuff tickets or testing my street knowledge. His answers to these questions indicate he is not a real threat; he is just blowing off steam.

Though I am on time to my last supervision session, my supervisor is not. She comes through her door spitting fire. I have really screwed everything up *now*. She asks leading questions. She wants to know how I knew this man wasn't serious about his homicidal threats. She does not allow me to tell my story but instead forces me to answer accusations as if I am a witness at a deposition.

I point out that dealers on the street have power over a man like that, that he knows he can't act on his impulses because of retaliation; he clearly demonstrated to me he knew that. He was just mouthing off. Anyone who knows the streets would know that!

"Oh my god," says the supervisor. "Don't you realize that it doesn't matter if you don't approve of drug dealers, that you still have a responsibility here!"

I ask the supervisor why, if I am so wrong about this man, has the doctor also reached the same conclusion that I have?

"You wait and see," the supervisor says. "That doctor is angry and feels you were negligent. You should have warned the doctor in person and documented your reasoning. This is a big mistake you made here."

The supervisor then disappears and returns with the angry doctor. The doctor explains that I had to assess for plan and intent. I explain that I know this and have done this thoroughly and come to the same conclusion she had. She then shows me the writing on the assessment. I can see that I left letters off the end of the words I'd written. Though it is clear that the assessment has been done, I have not provided details.

༄ ༄ ༄

The next Wednesday, I sit in an office with a top administrator and the supervisor, who starts the session by proudly announcing that she refuses to supervise me.

I feel the familiar lump in my throat, but this time I am prepared. I say that, although I am being accused of incompetence, I really have a good feel for what I am doing.

The supervisor laughs. "Did you really think you were going to just come in here and change my mind like this?"

I burst into hard and bitter tears.

The administrator steps in and supportively says, "Clyde, you don't want to work with a person you disagree with in this manner. You'll find another internship."

This causes me to go off my script and recall how the supervisor criticized me for not taking time to read about this population before I came to work with them. I tell her I don't know what books she read, but that I have ten years working, sweating, and breathing with these people and she doesn't know what she is talking about.

The supervisor asks me to please lower my voice.

I continue to point out times when she was flat out wrong and blamed me for not seeing things in her way. I have very clear examples. I continue, however, to cry uncontrollably throughout my defense.

When the administrator has heard enough, he politely excuses himself.

Once alone with me, the supervisor immediately tries to kick me out of her office.

I am crying profusely and say I am not leaving. I tell her it seems she had made a decision about me the minute I had a panic attack in front of her three months before.

She responds by saying she's never seen an intern have a meltdown like that in front of her; what was that about?

I tell her I had been going hungry, without food. I needed this job like my flesh had needed blood and it is a lot of pressure to be under.

The supervisor walks out of the room, indignant.

꩜꩜꩜

I return home late that evening after commiserating with Mario and Tammy at a bar to find my apartment broken into. My backpack has been pulled out of my closet and is sitting by my bed. Things are missing this time: my pennies are gone, my studded belt and the CD player my mom has purchased for my birthday, along with my trusty old disc two of Bruce Springsteen's album *Tracks*.

The break-in is a reminder of the shallowness of my critical support network. There is still no one I can think of to call who would believe it really happened.

I know better than to call the police. It's late at night and this will only put me in danger of hospitalization at this vulnerable time.

I think of the key my dog walker has and take my current misfortune as a spiritual message; in fact, perhaps I have not been generous enough to the innocent girl who walks my dog. Sure, $120 a month is all I can afford, but still, I am being a little cheap. The girl's father is unemployed and always hanging around. Maybe it was he, not Mafia networks or government conspirators who broke in.

When I wake up the next day I am a few steps from the streets. I quickly learn I am not eligible for enough unemployment to make it worth applying. I contact Jack Lueggio's Company in Walnut Creek to let them know about my situation. They are more than happy to work with upper management to get me a gig floating between three or four local stores. I also contact the internship in San Leandro, where I was accepted for work the year before when I was floridly psychotic, and initiate the process of landing a position there. This will include training with doctoral students at ten dollars per therapeutic hour.

As I get my first resumes out, the police call and make an appointment to look at my apartment. They have caught a local meth addict with my key and checks I hadn't even noticed were missing.

After a shift at the deli, the police act as if they understood the position I am in and don't give me a hard time about not phoning the incident in. After fingerprinting my apartment, the cops make me come along and confront the family of my dog walker. I play the part of feeling betrayed but I defend the family when they admit the father has been sheltering the meth addict.

Though a part of me feels angry, more of me feels bad for any man who has to take a fall in this complex land of prison and hypocrisy.

CHAPTER **30**

WITHIN A WEEK, I start shuttling between gigs at various satellites of the Lueggio chain stores. I am rapidly rejected at my first two interviews.

I interview at a homeless shelter in Marin for a position that pays fifteen dollars an hour. I arrive and review the organization's reading material and perceive a familiar mentality in one of their pamphlets, "Yes, homeless people do exist in Marin and they have feelings just like you and me," it reads.

The tone reminds me of the librarian back in kindergarten who had first educated me about dyslexia and schizophrenia. Those pamphlets had presented a fundamentally damaged mind. Now, it is as if these conditions render me inhuman. I think about all the people I've grown up with, most of whom used my misfortune to get ahead; I realize that I am a potential challenge to their superiority complexes. The fact that I've become a pity to them in that organization's brochure is not the librarian's or my poor mother's fault. The reality of social oppression is bigger than that. Perhaps what I go through might challenge my culture's place in the community. Perhaps it may force some to see themselves better, their own delusions. To all that "chronically normal" crowd, I could accomplish the same things that they could with hard work.

Within three weeks, I have two job offers and am waiting to hear back from a job Mario referred me to at the Richmond Partial Care Program. I am heartened by the fact that I am cleared to start meeting with children at an internship and have been permanently assigned to a Lueggio store with peers I feel very comfortable with.

Then, suddenly, my life is set. I get the nod at the Richmond Partial Care after a very lukewarm fifteen-minute interview. I will keep the job at Lueggio's to maintain my income, and the internship for child and family hours.

ﻭﻭﻭﻭ

On Christmas, I get together with Henry, one of my new coworkers at Lueggio's. We go hiking in Redwood Park because neither of us has anywhere else to be. Later, he joins me at my aunt and uncle's, where Henry charms my aunt to the point where she wants to help him with his "acting career" by pulling strings she has as a patron of the Shakespeare Festival.

I merely smirk and admire how Henry works with my support system as if he were running a street hustle.

Eventually, I open up to him about my friend Joe back in Philadelphia, saying he is affiliated with the IRA instead of some nefarious Cosa Nostra.

Henry scolds me for letting anyone know I have such a friend, saying that as a counselor I have to be very careful about what I say in the community. Then he shares with me his experience getting beaten up by a man from the IRA for messing up some drug deal he had tried to pull back in England.

"Clyde, do you believe that the government sends spies into mental hospitals?" he asks.

"No," I respond and mean it. I think of the Quasimodo man back in Montana.

"Well," says Henry, "I believe they do. I believe the government hires big Jamaican men to come and fuck me up the ass!"

A few months later, Henry is homeless and staying with friends.

When he asks me if he can stay with me even though my apartment is a far commute for him, I tell him that he'd have to keep his job and pay me three hundred dollars a month and help me with the dog. I note the controlling nature of this offer, but I need some boundaries so as not to ruin my own recovery.

"Never trust a person who doesn't trust himself enough to drink," Henry says in reply to my offer.

Two days later, he purposely gets himself fired from Lueggio's so he can collect unemployment and he moves to LA to pursue his acting career. Though at one point I hear he is back in town, I never see him again.

꙳꙳꙳

Before long, my days at the Richmond Partial Care Program are increased. I continue to deny persistent anxiety, remembering positive affirmations I've written about myself. For each group, I prepare lists of robotic questions. I base the questions on mundane mental health topics, trying to teach health to people who I pretend are mentally worse off than myself. Though I believe internally that I am doing a poor job, I am able to maintain the requirements of the job.

By the time my schedule allots me a half-day off every other week, I make special arrangements to get two days off in a row to move into the Richmond Hills.

The next year two years are like the movie *Groundhog Day*, until I get hired full-time at the Richmond Partial Care program. Over and over again, I walk Maxine before the working day starts. As I walk, stress and anxiety pour out of my gaping pores and my heart beats madly to a blurted Tourette's-like mantra: "keep it together, keep it together, fuck it, keep fuckity-fuck-fuck shit—aw just fuck it."

Becoming a legitimate licensed therapist means everything. But each day is long, and there appears to be no end in sight, no way to get off the merry-go-round.

꙳꙳꙳

When I finally get a second part-time hire at a voluntary inpatient unit, I leave the shrink's care. Before the last session, I take inventory of the relationship.

I remember fondly how she loaned me some books on narrative therapy and even encouraged me to take a workshop with the co-founder of the movement, David Epston, who came into town from Australia to teach a class. Sure, the course had cost three hundred dollars but the shrink proved to be right. The experience inspired me, because Dave actually listened to a minute segment of my story and asked with genuine concern if I was okay.

The shrink's narrative therapy has helped me realize that I am imprisoned by a self-fulfilling prophecy that can be overcome. After all, the shrink doesn't agree with me when I continue to beat up on myself for being an ineffective group therapist. She encourages the fake-it-till-you-make-it robot reality. And as I find my self-esteem improving, I am aware of my cognitive distortions and starting to listen to the very astute people whom I am paid to help. I am starting to perform better. I owe the people in Richmond so much for supporting me!

And while I am still far from perfect, I am getting better at being able to be in the moment again.

In the last session she expresses she is not being a "greedy capitalist," she is just genuinely concerned. She thinks we have more work to do. I am still unstable.

She reminds me that the job at the deli will always be there for me to fall back on. She also says that "in reality" my family is there to provide financial support. She says I never have to worry about being homeless. She says that, in reality, she has been there with me through all the hard times.

I choose to take it in stride that she continues to impose her reality on mine. In doing so, she reinforces a host of social myths that have dogged me for most of my life: that men do not get eating disorders or feel sexually victimized; that one shouldn't validate a delusion because it might reinforce the delusional system; that because psychosis is not real, it is not really traumatic; that treatment should re-parent or rebuild the subject; that those with educational prestige are better experts; that drugs are only legitimized and localized in black and Latino ghettos because of "antisocial" individuals; that there is freedom in this country to protest.

I listen as she suggests I shoot for a salary of one hundred thousand dollars a year in the Bay Area. She says I need to be more "successful" than my "silver spoon" father, who had the leisure of changing his career and going down to a minimal income at age forty-five. Though I continue to disagree with these judgments, I appreciate that they do demonstrate some real understanding of my unique class status.

Additionally, in the last session, she asks if it is true that my mom is really a nudist with Dick Wigglesworth. I tell her with a little intensity that it is.

"Why do you bring that up now?" I ask.

"Oh, I don't know," says the shrink. "She just doesn't seem like *the type.*"

I no longer judge my mom for this. Judging things only make them worse!

When I leave the office that day there is a little bounce in my step. It doesn't matter if I am depressed or paranoid any more. If I play by the rules, I can live a good life

Intuitively, I know the shrink is not as bad as I have often have made her to be. She represents to me every institution that made money off me and failed to see who I really am. From 1983 to the present, therapy has never been about teaching me to accept or even see myself. It has always involved other people keeping me under their thumb, contained by power-expertise. My predominant memories of all the therapists I have worked with have been pain and hurt and that is not the shrink's fault.

Ultimately, I can forgive the role of the shrink. Maybe it doesn't realize that it is participating in extortion against our culture of "psychosis," or what I will come to call Special Messages.

Meanwhile, a doctor has started to function as the prescribing psychiatrist at the internship at the Foster Care Agency. During his earlier Friday trainings he has talked about the problems in psychiatry and the stigma of mental illness in a way that has earned him trust from me. While he has favored the "more educated" opinions of my peers, I am sometimes comfortable enough to stick up for myself.

I have gotten the opportunity to run more and more family sessions and my caseload has grown to a steady and reliable ten.

I start work with a teenage mother who was institutionalized as a child. The doctor says she is abusive toward him, the system, and probably to her child. He is highly critical of her in front of the team. I can relate to her view of the profession, to her view of institutions.

The doctor addresses me in one meeting, saying that he knows that institutions are stable and helpful, so why don't I?

Streetwise interpretations of South Jersey institutions I worked at flash in my mind; I have watched principles misuse restraint to taunt weaker kids and gain respect from the drug savvy. I recall nonprofit slush funds that go to odd research programs. I recall salaries of aides that absolutely did require augmentation through the much-mumbled illegal business.

I now view these SED kinds of communities as feeders for the incarceration industry because of my own lived experience.

I do not explain any such nuances, but I do exhibit a knowing smile in submitting to his expertise.

Meanwhile, the teenage mother has been on antidepressants that have helped her in the past but the doctor refuses to prescribe them until he is sure she really needs them. He is going to wait until the psychological testing is completed.

When the testing of my client takes over six months to complete and the mother becomes exasperated with the wait and threatens to sue the doctor, one of the other interns gives me the doctor's phone number and suggests that I call. On the phone call I point out that I have functioned as the intermediary and have heard the woman's frustration, and that from my perspective she has a point.

By this time I have realized (via witnessing his regal thankless behavior when I give him special treatment at the Lueggio Deli,) that he doesn't really fit the open-minded persona I initially imagined.

After I leave the message, the program director calls me aside and tells me the doctor is offended. I diplomatically apologize to him the next time I see him and say the phone call was a mistake. Nevertheless, with a cocky smile and a wave of the hand, he bids me farewell.

It is the last time I will be permitted to see him.

I have been cleared to maintain my caseload for the next year until I have the child-and-family hours necessary for the license. A day after I offer my apology, the program director tells me I am rude because I assume I can call doctors by their first names instead of by their surname.

I point out that the other interns do the same thing.

She explains that is different because they are doctoral students

I think about how, if I am let go, my loyal clients would be available for next year's students. I can accept this. But here, the director, who is known to fall asleep during all of her sessions and then blame it on projective identification, is not taking this tack.

Her sentences are prepared and forced. As if she were a participant in a Stanley Milligram social psychology experiment, she enforces the doctor's authority.

She asks if I am in therapy.

I tell her that I have been but cannot afford it now, particularly with the schedule that I am forced to keep for my economic stability.

She says I am badly in need of psychoanalysis.

When I perhaps look hurt by this statement and point out that I am a successful professional at two other jobs in the community, she adds that maybe it isn't all me, maybe it is the social class I was born into.

I let them remove me from the internship. I still don't have the money or support to fight this. Another intern who is treated poorly does have the resources to put up a fight, however, and the program director eventually loses her position.

But I am still okay without the role of the shrink. I am starting to accept myself.

I get a new internship that strings me along for four years in an insulated upper-class community. It gives me a lot of time to grow.

※ ※ ※ ※

Several months later, when an unrelenting schedule gives me an unpaid break, I make my next trip back east.

I have one last critic to make peace with.

I move with my sister through the house that our mom bought her. I observe how, with the help of my father's labor, the basement has been converted into a number of small rooms where immigrants can stay for low rents. The rooms are only somewhat habitable, dark, and windowless.

I notice the new washer and dryer and the dishwasher that all cost money; I know my sister only makes thirty grand a year. I figure it is possible she is getting help from our parents that is unreported to me.

I am overwhelmed with mixed feelings as I compare my sister's life to my own. She, the head of the household, is paying one hundred dollars in rent and occupying upstairs rooms. She, working fifteen hours a week, has power and control.

My mind drifts back to the confines of the closet-of-a-room for which I pay six hundred dollars a month. The owner of the community house, who says she bought the house on "credit cards," (which I have learned means that her parents bought it for her) helps herself to my food and clothing and leaves her dog under my care for months on end while she vacations without asking. Far worse, I share space with roommates who do not have mental health problems—roommates like my landlady who diagnose and treat their kids without acknowledging their own abusive tendencies. Although I am rarely home, I often feel like one of those abused children at the house.

With these realities swirling, my sister suddenly asks me to check in on my nephew, who is bathing in the bathroom.

I enter and find the little cherub sitting in a child's tub.

Fear pulses through my appendages. I am barely able to stand, as if I am balancing on a high wire. I can see my hands in the periphery of my vision. I focus on my hands to balance and feel a painful rush in my head like a gush of wind.

I focus my vision on the reality of bathroom tile. I retreat from the bathroom and ask my sister to go in and check on her son.

I wasn't tempted in the least to abuse my nephew. I hadn't disassociated, but what I had been through was very intense.

My sister notices that I am upset because when she returns she kindly says, "It is okay, Clyde."

But I judge myself for what I put my innocent nephew through. I notice my young nephew avoids me the rest of the evening. I do not know what my eyes looked like to him; even though I had just stood there, I was: begging for aspirin in the hospital; cleaning out the little girl's bathroom in Fresno; watching a special broadcast warning on TV; getting my privates scrubbed by KaCee at the deli; flicking my limp penis in front of Calvin. The world was accusing *me* of being the pedophile!

I think about how the majority of child abuse occurs before the age of three. I am haunted by what it must be like for an innocent child to look at a man having a flashback. I wonder if my face and eyes show anger, aggression, or violence. It makes me think of my grandfather, who starved like a wolf in the Great Depression. I think of the old lumberjack George McKinley who used to rant at me.

❧❧❧

In realizing that I have no control over how my nephew feels, I gain much more empathy for my parents and all I have put them through. A child, a victim, a have-not, a racial minority, an incarcerated guppy has the liberty to perceive life's complications any way he or she chooses.

Perhaps the level of abuse I perceive isn't reality!

I have documented many hurts in the name of recovery, but I am very aware that abuses can be more overt and intentional. The fact that my parents have good intentions and resources and worked tirelessly to maintain the private school community that educated me is what has saved me from my greatest fears: homelessness and protective custody in a prison.

In my years at the Richmond Partial Care program I have seen the suffering of individuals who are better than me, who have dealt with lockdown realities. Individuals who do not have privileges, who may not always contain their behavior when they are overwhelmed.

As the critic in me continues to soften, I am increasingly able to see oppressors in a better light. I have victimized them with my sensitivity as much as they have victimized me. Sometimes oppressors do not always choose their role in society; they must take what they are given. I can forgive them now. People kill each other in America and stories remain buried, covet and unseen. Cultural delusions and the stigma of mental illness have conspired to leave me so isolated!

ノノノノ

When I get back to California, it doesn't take long for me to hook up with a charming English woman. Before long I am swimming with her in the pool that I have never used before at the house in the Richmond Hills. I am admiring her in her bathing suit, and looking up to the sky and telling myself that recovery is in fact real.

A few years ago, I was a sick, untouchable person. Now once again I am a piece of desirable flesh—or at least a meal ticket worthy of love!

CHAPTER **31**

IT WAS A shit to end all shits. It has filled the room with stink and clogged the bowl beneath waterlogged toilet paper. The milky brown water is rising up toward the lip of the commode.

I am standing over the downstairs toilet at my mom's house, pounding with a plunger, cursing myself for the last flush.

I remind myself that I've been in this situation before and the water has never spilled.

But this time it does.

Six years have passed. My wife of a year and a half and I arrived at my mom's Haddonfield house late last night. My sister and her two sons are staying with my mother as well, because my sister has just published a sociology book. We are all getting together to support her at her book launching party.

Earlier in the morning, Dick Wigglesworth demanded his bacon in an uncharacteristically irritated way. My mother, who was wrestling over the stovetop to host everyone, accepted this behavior; but when my biological father, Frank, called, my mom took out her frustration on him, yelling that she wanted him to be more specific with his plans.

My sister walked in and heard this and told mom off for her behavior. Our father, notorious for spending hours making up unwanted schedules for family visits, had scaled back his plans. Really, neither my sister nor I wanted him to get yelled at for not being specific enough. We both had appreciated growth.

I withdrew from the tension in the room by joining my nephews in a ridiculous game of chase. Per my pattern, I, the madman, was the one who resisted joining in with the general madness.

Now, however, with shit water drenching my socks, and a contained call for help going unanswered, I call out again—this time with a slight edge in my voice.

I throw off the top off the toilet and hold up the water bobber as I continue pumping the plunger.

A minute or two later, mom interrupts my pumping. "What do you want, Clyde?"

I politely ask for a heavy-duty plunger.

When I was growing up, family plungers had always been heavy duty!

I hear my eight-year-old nephew in the background screeching, "Oh my god! There's *shit* all over the floor!"

He had been wondering what was taking me so long, sticking objects under the door in a playful manner. Now that shit water is running through the crack in the door, he knows.

My eight carrot shits are an incredibly sloppy, lengthy process at this time in my life. Since I have switched to Abilify, my appetite has been up. I have taken to eating fifteen pounds of carrots per week to contain it and have gained upward of twenty-five pounds. Psychotropic medication affects many bodily processes!

At a bi-yearly visit to a Kaiser psychiatrist, who is oh-so-much-better than the last one I dealt with, I decided not to risk going off the medication. Instead, I continue the battle of resisting food, much as I did when I was a seventeen year-old anorexic.

From the other side of the door, my mom issues instructions. I have already done everything she suggests and ask again for a better plunger.

Suddenly, the door swings open. Dick Wigglesworth says the plunger always works for him. His shirt is off and he is in his tighty-whities. I watch his bare octogenarian thighs stride right into the shit puddles. God bless him. He pumps the bowl *twice* until he is out of breath and then he declares I am correct—this plunger simply is not doing the trick.

My mom reports they have no better plunger and offers to go and buy one.

I gratefully accept her offer.

She ignores me and comes into the room behind me with a mop, trying to make a dent in the shit puddles. The cold water on my feet mixes with the ghastly feel in my head of what will turn out to be bronchitis.

Finally, I join the family madness. Like my sister did that morning, I yell at my mom. I tell her to get me a proper plunger!

My mom is out the back door and heading toward the car when I hear my ever-supportive wife's voice.

"Pooopsie, Is there anything I can do to help?"

I ask my wife to go with my mom.

꜄꜄꜄

I met my wife a little less than five years before, after a very rocky year-and-a-half relationship with an English woman. Emotions and reason mixed, and we essentially became joined at the hip in a complementary relationship.

Her parents are first generation German immigrants who left traumatic war memories behind, met each other in Canada, and moved to Marin with nothing but carpentry skills and a work ethic. The year I was born, my wife's father started up a family business that flourished and was just closing down when I met her.

On our third date, as my wife-to-be was telling me about her licensed, Marin MFT therapist's response to my diagnosis, I was struck by intuition.

My wife was being treated for OCD and codependency; I, well versed in the MFT standard-of-care and stigma-logic, finished her sentence in an empathetic manner.

Her therapist had in fact urged her to break up with me

She started sobbing at my accuracy and said she wouldn't listen.

While the financial success and stability of my in-laws would have offended the unfettered schizotypal personality who marched at the WTO protest, "psychosis" has equipped me with the ability to accept and accommodate. While my heart still aches with disparities in the world, I have been able to learn a great deal about being a balanced survivor from them. They left horrific personal traumas behind.

Prior to the marriage, I saved enough money for a down payment on a suburban home outside of Richmond, but I was flexible when my in-laws suggested that my wife contribute 30 percent to the property so that the two of us could afford to fix the old place up. My wife augments her rental property income with her own gardening business. She humbly works with her hands and uses the rest of her time to take care of her properties, and me.

I think about these things, and the vast changes in my life, while I am pumping the plunger.

My sister has ushered the kids outside and into their vehicle. They are off to visit with her ex-husband, the father of my nephews, in Trenton.

Later in the evening when the eight-year-old comes back, we will process the event as a family.

He will admit he was afraid the shit would never get cleaned up off the floor of his grandmother's house.

The three-year-old, who on our last visit eagerly learned to pick up dog shit, will address the incident with curiosity, wanting to know how it was possible.

I will reply that the problem came about because my poop is too big. I will know this is true because I initially flushed before using toilet paper.

"You boys remember why I told you not to use so much toilet paper," my sister will say, ignoring me. "Because that's what happens when you use too much toilet paper."

It's true that as a child, I had gotten worms from my father's fold and wipe system, while it occurs to me that she still champions it. In this subtle manner, I often feel cast as unfit for the world's shit in family visit.

❧❧❧

I am still straddling the can. I pump and pump with a fervor that is hard to achieve. Like I do every day at work, I put everything I have into it because I know at the end of the day I will be able to retreat to my wife, our home, our dog, and our cat. I do things that some staff won't, like sitting with the clients, pissing in the leaking urinal, and shitting in the toilet that so often gets feces smeared all over it. I do these things so as not to forget where I've been. I feel lucky, not entitled, to live outside this world when I leave.

Just before the expiration of the fifteen minutes that it takes for my mother and wife to return, the blockage in the toilet breaks and the water goes down. I busy myself with cleanup.

❧❧❧

It is a year of abnormal amounts of snow throughout the east. My wife, my mother, and I go out snowshoeing along the Delaware. Hawking up phlegm as we proceed along the trail, I think about how, after finally obtaining my MFT, how after getting trained to run Mary Ellen Copeland's Wellness Recovery Action Planning (WRAP) groups I have begun using self-disclosure with clients. I think about how I have started a group focused on "psychosis" to help those who are institutionalized or whose minds are overwhelmed by special messages, voices, poverty, drugs, genocide, and gangsterism to find a balanced way out. As the three of us navigate the strait between the estuary and the river, I become overwhelmed with the fear of exposure and the ongoing danger of discrimination at work.

I think about how serendipitous oranges, apples, lemons, and bananas show up at work on the unit and follow me on my personal routines. I think about ongoing name coincidences and spy innuendos and how I now respond to them with humor. I have collected quite a plethora of situations since I have stopped being a robot. Now I am no longer enslaved to their meaning.

The next day I accompany my nephews and my sister out sledding.

I speak to my sister between runs down the sledding hill. I appreciate the sacrifices she's made to shed light on the national delusion with regards to immigration policy. Her focus, the way immigration law affects Latino textile workers, is something I understand better after reading her work. She really is working hard to expose the same shit *Cesar Chavez* was a generation before, while raising a family as a single mom.

She asks me about my own writing efforts and starts what will be a general campaign to support me.

It occurs to me that feeling silenced so far back is what motivates me to keep pushing forward. It has taken me many years, but I acknowledge myself in spite of a sense of invisibility. I look at my sister and I am grateful that, even though she is a character in my book, that she supports me.

I continue to sled with my nephews for hours until the younger of the two needs to retreat with his mom. I stay with my elder nephew, appreciating his remarkable athleticism as he attempts to balance, standing up on his flexible flyer sled as if it were a snowboard.

I share stories with him about the outdoors in spite of the nagging phlegm in my system. I stay until he finally can take no more of the cold.

I remember the flashback I had in front of him six years before. I pray it won't be the life event that makes or breaks him.

Hours later we are racing, late, toward the train station in Trenton in my sister's car. I am amazed by all my sister has to do to maintain her academic status. The whole car, containing my wife, sister, and nephews, is focused, stressed, straining, and striving toward our destination, Columbia University in New York where my sister is due to have her book launch party.

My sister needs to arrive at the party an hour early to prepare for her presentation. She wants the elder of my nephews to come with her for emotional support. He wants to stay behind with his brother and travel with his aunt and uncle.

I offer him my IPOD to play with.

He accepts.

I am struck by a memory: as a child my parents made me stay back with my sister at the Quaker Conference instead of joining with my peers, because, they said, my sister cried for me. I recall the gift I received for my sacrifice: a pair of cleats I inappropriately wore everywhere I went.

When I grew to be picked on and depressed, I recall resenting this sacrifice and blaming it for my misfortune.

I worry over my role in the decision process.

Now, after dropping my nephew and sister off at the station and starting my walk to the train station carrying my younger nephew, I plan with my wife to buy my older nephew a snowboard for his birthday.

I will buy him a snowboard and pray for balance in his life. Later it will be a skateboard. As an uncle who lives on a different coast, these small gifts, my prayers, and accepting responsibility for the way my own shitty blunders might affect his life, are all I can contribute.

ノノノノ

At the train station, my wife and I and our youngest nephew reunite with both sets of parents and stepparents, the whole lot of us standing on the train platform in the cold wind. My little nephew says he is cold and everyone pitches in trying to block the wind from the little kid's face. He laughs at how stupid the whole lot of us are. He is such an ingenious comic at the age of four. He can sense the high level of false politeness: the edge of resentment in mom's voice as she complies with my stepmother; the cooperative smile of my stepfather who declared yesterday that he hated my father; the wrongful read of my resentful forehead crinkle by my father, who throws his glaring eyeballs toward me. It's all great material for a budding young comic.

On the train, my nephew sits between my wife and me. I talk

about how I am sure there will be a wine and cheese social after the book review. I note the likelihood that one of the cheeses will be Brie, because all academics like Brie cheese.

My mom and stepmom are in a very serious conversation about an academic who made front-page news recently for shooting up the faculty that denied her tenure—it is a story that touches both of them, each of them having recently retired from teaching careers.

By the time we are out in the New York streets it is snowing and I am well into a forty-five minute argument with my nephew.

I argue that my wife would obliterate any attempt he could possibly make to destroy her.

He calls himself "the man who plays by his own rules" or just "the man" for short. He talks about his friends who will join him in obliterating her so that she will no longer be able to tell me how to live my life.

I explain that we'd both better submit to her harsh supernatural powers.

He gets into graphic and violent detail.

I counter by upping the ante in terms of my wife's violent capacities.

I am amazed with my nephew's creative abilities. He's got great ninja skills.

I can only assume that everyone else is annoyed with me; even my wife has disengaged from this conversation. Nevertheless, I continue because I truly believe my nephew could be a famous comedian, or perhaps a rap musician. Even if he follows through with his developing ambitions to be lawyer, I figure supporting his ninja skills will help.

When my father and stepmother break off and say they will meet up at the event, my wife and I follow behind my mom, who gets lost and ends up being pelted by what has become freezing rain. It seems as if she has stopped about five people to ask for directions, but we blindly follow her to yet again re-cross the street. I, for my part, am too exhausted from holding my nephew to get involved.

FIGHTING FOR FREEDOM IN AMERICA ☙

Once we arrive at the Sociology Department we are relieved to shed our wet clothing and locate my sister. The boys take places on a couch next to their grandma and I find a place in the back of the room.

When the professors start pontificating about the merits of my sister's writing on textile workers, the boys get antsy. I take the youngest one to the bathroom in the middle of the program and let him poop a tiny little turd that doesn't require a lot of paperwork.

I am present when my sister finally gets a chance to speak. She points to me and says I have come all the way from California to support her. She has mentioned my name in her acknowledgements as well.

Though she did put some personal things in her book in a way that greatly enhanced it, she did not make reference to my "schizophrenia" burden. I still do not approve of that word or what it means to most people and admire how my sister is able to expose delusions without dragging her family through the mud.

I vow that I won't publish.

The boys continue to interrupt her and jump at her side while she talks.

She handles it well and I feel happy she is getting the recognition she deserves.

When my sister is finished, the chair announces that, thanks to some wasteful charitable foundation, there will be a wine and cheese social that everyone is invited to join. While others chat and interact with each other, I hover around the table targeting the diet Coke, the carrots, and, out of respect for my sister, the Brie cheese.

An Asian professor, who appears to be about as uncomfortable in this setting as I am, comes up and whispers in my ear that she used to be a textile worker. She adds with an air of contempt that she has never admitted that in her work because she feared it would have prevented her from getting tenure.

I think both about the irony of the fact that she has trusted me with this information, and the fact that in order to get recognition in

309 ☙

America, many people have to hide the truth. Cultural delusions are so dumbass!

ﻜﻜﻜﻜ

The next day, my sister goes back to Illinois and I walk with mom for an hour or so before heading over to my father's place. Because my cold is getting worse and time ends up being limited, the three of us have opted for a long walk instead of another snowshoe. There is silence as we walk through the neighborhoods of Haddenfield, my mom's home.

In the living room earlier that day, I came across what I believed might have been mom and Dick Wigglesworth's stash of marijuana located in, of all things, a ceramic frog. I flashed back on how I used to believe that frogs were a Mafia symbol and the irony made me chuckle.

Now I work hard to accept Haddenfield without acting existentially irked, the way I'd acted during college years. People jogging past on the street know my mom, Casey Wigglesworth. They stop and say hello. This town is where she feels comfortable.

And at this very moment people are being shot dead in the ghetto and in the Campo. Task forces weed through homes, and it is all good and safe in Haddenfield.

As such, I find myself observing a paradox of memories in my interactions with my mom over the past few years.

On one visit years ago, before I met my wife, mom had said: "You never played sports seriously, the way your sister did."

I'd had to remind myself that I'd been called up to play varsity as a freshman on the soccer team, made captain of the baseball team as a sophomore, and had done endless running and lifting to stay in shape for these activities. These facts, I figure, like many others, have been relegated to family secrets.

My mind fast-forwards to my mom's paradoxical manner of fussing over providing me with financial support when I had been using my savings to purchase the house. The task had been to get a gift from my parents to look good to the mortgage broker and lower the interest rate. My future in-laws had immediately written me a portion of the check to ease the burden on my parents so the purchase could be made, but I still needed a significant contribution from my two parents. Noting my mom's support of my sister, I asked her first, promising to pay her back within a year.

I look up as I walk, recalling these Haddenfield backstreets I used to bike as a kid. Then I think of how the request had horribly offended my mom.

I suggested, instead, that I might get the contribution from my father, reminding her that the check had to appear as a lump sum. I reminded her that a check of repayment would be coming immediately as soon as the bank loan was secured. She chose finally to pay a larger portion; I could get the rest from my father, but it had to be paid back in a year.

Then she sent me the wrong amount and the deal was delayed by a day.

We ignored the associated drama.

My wife made a homemade thank-you card for her, but when she came to the house for the first time, a day before the wedding, she did not make any comments or request a tour.

As I think over these past realities I can see that the quickest route to freedom exists in acceptance—acceptance and honoring my mom for her sacrifices.

Somehow, prior to fighting for freedom, I had felt flagrantly victimized by such behavior. Now, with emotional skills and the support of my wife I am able to marvel at all my mother has done for me throughout my lifetime.

I look out at the town's polluted lake, at a pack of ducks running away from me; the duck closest to me shits! I recall how, as my wife and I had readied ourselves to go snowshoeing with my mother a few days earlier, I'd waddled along behind her, chiding myself for the monstrous shit that I had made. My mom had told me to stop apologizing, that it was a plumbing problem and a plunger problem, that it was not my fault.

I had been grateful for this support.

I reflect back on so many events. Throughout them my mom had demonstrated an ability to adapt and grow; without that, I would never have recovered.

I think back to the night my wife and I arrived; my mother had actually left towels out for us, and sheets so we could make the bed.

"One time, one of my friends yelled at me for not leaving things out," she'd admitted. "I was grateful because I was not raised to be a gracious host. I never realized that it upset people. My parents were always too busy and we had to take care of ourselves. That was part of my problem with your father: he was raised to be hosted and expected me to know what to do."

I think about this and about how ultimately she didn't abandon me. In a way, when we had our emotional cutoff, I was equally responsible for abandoning her.

A block before we return to the house, mom breaks the silence by blurting out that she has to tell me something: my stepfather has Alzheimer's. Now there is no time to talk about it without neglecting my father. Suddenly, it makes sense why my stepfather is getting so angry and becoming so thoughtlessly demanding. My wife has noticed his memory problems.

Our next walk will be full of discussion: her fears about Dick getting violent with guns he insists on owning; her sense of duty to hide the reality of his condition from others because of the glaring stigma the problem carries; her regrets that neither of her children are local to help out.

＊＊＊＊

I drive. Flashes out the window change from Haddenfield to other suburban towns and now are primarily rural Lumberton. We arrive.

My father's mansion is really a simplistic treasure when it is not a hell of a wreck. When he first bought it with ten thousand dollars of his sister's money, it looked like a one-room schoolhouse. He'd taken me inside and told me he was going to move this wall this way two inches and that wall that way three quarters of an inch. He would put a bathroom in this closet, and an addition out the back. Once he had it looking nice with a wood stove that functioned as its primary heater, he designed it to run off solar heat. The first solar house in all of South Jersey, it has been featured in numerous articles that my grandmother proudly sent along to me.

And now we all sit in the living room before the stove, talking. The four of us plan to take a walk in a local park that is new. I wonder what the snow will be like as the talk keeps flowing, and we all demur a bit. My father has built a chest of drawers where he keeps chopped wood he uses to stoke the fire. As we all admire his work, he disappears outside and refills the drawers. He is pushing seventy, just as I am pushing forty. His stomach is going in and mine is going out. When I recently purchased pants that were the same waist size as his, it was an act of acceptance for me.

At the park, my father curses the property rights and wasted money that has made the entrance to the park longer than it needs to be, a waste of energy that NIMBYs impose upon the state. He still drives fifty-five miles an hour and has huge bumper stickers on the back of his vehicles that read "Slow Down, Global Warming."

I recall speeding through the seventy-hour weeks that earned me my graduate degree, how I'd thought that it wasn't fair for him to judge others and passive aggressively impose his will on people like me who had to work for a living.

Now, however, I can see I have developed some of the same self-serving unpopular perspectives, calling all my neighbors racists for protesting the fact that the city wants to build a middle school in our local park. My neighbors are concerned that Richmond kids will be going to school in their "safer" neighborhood, mixing with their privileged offspring. I, the contrarian, am hoping that our neighborhood will become more integrated so I can feel less hostile about life's disparities.

In spite of my growth and awareness, my father and I have struggled through a host of difficult interactions over the past six years.

There had been the stone cold silence on a kayak in Richardson Bay, until my wife's brother arrived in his own kayak from across the bay to join our party, at which point my father started making energized efforts to communicate with him. I let my hurt feelings roll.

On my next trip back east, my father seemed to ignore me and cater to my friend, Gary, who was joining me on a trip to Tupper Lake. The two of them drank beer and chummed it up, and I'd felt excluded. When I suggested a canoe ride, my father talked about himself for ten minutes and then a silence followed. I had not known what to say. When the two of us reached the end of the lake, an uncharacteristic wind struck the lake and we were forced to cooperate with one another to paddle back against nature's elements. That was as good as it got.

The edge between my father and me continued on my wedding night. He had asked me to organize a party at the last minute for his relatives and then there was criticism that my wife was not present. I had been part of planning everything and, suddenly, found myself alone and imposed upon. Then, he took control of his part of the evening, insisting on giving our relatives the ability to make unwanted toasts and telling one of his characteristic stories: depicting me as untalented and ungifted, but courageous. Of course, my only request for the wedding evening—that my father not make a pariah of my aunt, whose support was most instrumental in my recovery—did not go well, as a cursing contest occurred between them.

Suddenly, as if she can sense my mental buzz, my stepmother says, "You know, you should really talk to your father on this visit. He is going through a rough political patch in his work with the Quakers and he could really use your help."

Without missing a pace I turn around and walk back to my father, get behind him, and start asking him questions. It is the first time I have tried this in a while.

It's not until the next day, when the four of us travel out to the Pine Barrens and get on our respective skis and snowshoes, that my dad and I are more successful with our connect.

With my wife and stepmother leading the way, I think about how grateful I am to be feeling so sick. I think about how, if I weren't so goddam sick, I would be anxious to exercise my body and it would be oh so much harder to be patient enough to get the real scoop. Indeed, it has been the selfishness in my own reckless running that has kept me from understanding my father, as his has kept him from seeing me.

The four of us eventually end our trip, with my father saying he feels energized, like he wants to get out and exercise more often. Not bad for a man of nearly seventy.

Back at my father's house, the four of us sit down for lunch before my wife and I head back to my mother's house.

While my stepmother is getting lunch ready and I am lingering to help her, I tell her how I feel about individuals like me and my stepbrother's daughter, Ruby, her granddaughter: to suffer as a result of the horrific stigma is the first part of the tragedy, but then to overcome it and be told that you never really had schizophrenia is another tragedy. I now feel this is stigma in its highest form, because it robs people like me and Ruby of a culture and identity that we ultimately need. It forces us into secretive lives. It perpetuates cultural delusions.

I look at a picture of Ruby. Anyone can tell by the twinkle in her eye that she's gotten through the hard patch. All reports indicate this.

"What's so horrible about schizophrenia," I think out loud, "if it one day becomes a respected culture, Ruby and I will be seen as having special abilities instead of disabilities. And we will be able to better learn to use them to contribute meaningfully to society."

Throughout the meal, I sense intense hostility coming from my stepmother, who usually appreciates my perspective. I imagine that she has mental illness in her family and that I've likely hit a nerve.

In the future, my stepmother will reveal to my wife that her mother had been committed to a mental institution.

My stepmother eventually shoots into the silence. She complains about my absence when my father was going through prostate cancer. There was no one around except their friends to support them.

Now I can see that when I did not come home for what turned

out to be a near-fatal operation, my calls had not been enough. It is true; I was caught up in sixteen-hour getting-licensed days. It is true that taking last-minute time out of my schedule as a single therapist with a massive caseload would not have been easy. But, I could have been more thoughtful. Hence, the silence and the snubs: retaliation messages, not paranoia, as my initial therapist, Donna, would have called it.

I recall how, when I was "psychotic," I had expected my mind to be read as well.

I am so grateful that my mom visited me in Montana! I am so grateful my dad volunteered to come help me clean my apartment in Antioch!

♪♪♪

When, in a few years, I make a move to an administration job, I will find my father to be my most conscientious supporter. He will report that, in addition to being an active participant in raising me, he worked sixteen-hour days to assert his version of justice in the private school community.

Though, unlike my father, I will only tolerate long administrative, cutthroat hours for two years, I use the experience to gain a better understanding of him. I see how being so focused on work has made him a little short on temper. As a child I had blamed it on alcohol. I come to see that his own conflicts with his up-from-the-Great-Depression father led him to be intensely competitive, like many individuals of his generation.

And so I will gain back the security and support of the things that I was most "delusional" about during my struggles—namely, my immediate nuclear family. Like most people, I eventually come to an acceptance and appreciation of them.

I pray that, ultimately, in spite of the hard memories my story may stir, my family will feel honored by my efforts.

I pray one day my life will be fully out of the cellar, visible in spite of the stigma of schizophrenia.

∿∿∿

During an editing session, an old family story will come to mind.

I will remember how I had, at age nine, tried to eat a mothball, requiring poison control to be called.

I will be miffed that, in spite of my acute memory, I can't remember a thing about the mothball. I will ponder how sensitive I was to disassociate at the WTO and at other points in my journey. Then, suddenly I will get a memory of being lulled and coerced into an unsupervised bath in the Adirondacks with a slightly older female friend.

And finally, I remember the hand disappearing beneath the suds.

I will come to imagine that through this memory, not only catastrophic events, but also odd mixes of embarrassments, may add to my shame. I will finally understand how moving targets come about: people like Joy from the Todd Solandz movie that I showed Kathy in Seattle.

Finally I will be able to speculate that trauma associated with a small aspect of my life, sex, contributed to ongoing social vulnerability: to the tickle of hot piss in the hair from Tupper Lake realtors' sons; to the "gravel grungy" that the rich white boy campers gave me.

It's true, it will occur to me that it is possible that the elder female friend had picked up on something vulnerable about me before she led me into that bath. I will also think about the possiblity that I am just recalling a false memory.

I will think this kind of natural incident may not distress everyone the way it may have upset me. Perhaps there is something more.

When I will get around to sharing this memory with my mother, she will tell me that I am getting confused that, in fact, a youthful babysitter had been caught molesting me when I was very little.

When I will have this reality confirmed to me, I will have the greatest sense of relief. It will help me understand a piece of my pain.

And so I am finally able to see that my rage toward others— toward

Joel at the deli, for example—was unfair. It wasn't the player-kids' fault. Maybe Joel was just trying to grow out of being one of those kids at the Fresno daycare who taunted the outcast, Kyle.

Indeed, talking to my father about sexual trauma that occurred within our growing-up circle of support will bring back still other memories. I will recover memories that--be they false; be they dreams; or be they real experiences-- have meaning to me in terms of adding to my sense of sexual trauma.

And so I will come to better understand why I have come to reject my culture, my family, and my country so strongly. Indeed, the hypervigilance that I have toward my mom and others is not really fair to them. I have used my own wounds to turn around and potentially wound them. Indeed, being so selfish as to write about them in *Fighting for Freedom in America* may make it hard for some who are close to me. I can only pray that they will see that I needed to do this to recover. I can also acknowledge that it could have been far worse as it is for many.

Recovery from mental health challenges for me is about being unrelenting, like water that bubbles up like a spring and flows over boulders of stigma.

It is not a mentality that has room for vengeance. It kills the center-of-town-folk with kindness.

Recovery and healing come when we can maintain faith that the world will change when the higher powers are ready.

True revolution and transformation in my insulated mind is the oppressed improving their own lives and those of their oppressors— not with guns, gangs, nuclear weapons, and terrorism, but by the slow exposure of covert injustice, by using a window of opportunity to drill into the vast iceberg of cultural delusions, to gain inclusion and then to educate.

For me, recovery from "paranoia" is a peaceful process of accepting the world as it is and healing in spite of what "they" might do to me. It comes from a spiritual connection that is too often distorted by bullies into symptoms of pathology. It is about ultimate survival. It is about smiling in the face of sadism, owning your own truth, having faith at all costs that things will be all right. It is about being effective in the world. It is about the freedom to learn from mistakes without punishment. It is about building new communities of support that you can join on your journey to the sea.

ﭼﭼﭼﭼ

Back in California a few mornings later, my wife and I get up early and head to a local park out on the bay where we usually engage in an hour and a half jog. Today we bring Maxine, whom we have picked up from a friend's house. We plan to walk instead of jog due to my bronchitis, which is clearing up fueled by a Z-Pack.

My wife and I walk the gravel roads that weave between eucalyptus groves and bay views and fields of tall grass. I see the sandy shores where the bay meets the sand. On the point, fishers are stationed on a pier, enduring plenty of wind and drizzle. On the beach, the sunbeams break free from the clouds and stream down.

I process all the hurts that have occurred between myself and my family and the society in which we all live. I talk and talk and talk and my loyal wife encourages me. I stop frequently to apologize. In the past this behavior has driven others away. Usually, my wife claims it distracts her from the pain of the run. Today she just smiles and kisses me and validates me.

In many ways, the conspiracy against me is over. The Norton was a small ghetto microcosm in a city that sought to creatively regulate a very important element of our American society, the drug trade. It was passed onto new management. I hadn't understood my role in the Norton and now I assess some of my "pre-psychosis" behavior as being ignorant and disrespectful.

The experience of having my rights taken away from me has taught me to accept the inevitable existence of crime, greed, and capitalism. Acceptance of such elements of reality helped me learn to manage trauma emotions, emotions that led to years of unstable relationships and social exclusion.

I now feel comfort in the idea that what I went through was something like the ordeal that many protective custody prisoners endure in order to get out of a gang.

Not until I learned to demonstrate an ability to control my fear and keep quiet about the world I know, was I granted passage into the free world.

What remains a crying shame is that people who don't learn the necessary street skills in a timely fashion end up in ditches along with those that catch the stray bullets.

At the same time, I still often find myself thinking about what would have happened had I not developed an ability to learn from "psychosis." Many millions toil for decades in a system that offers no way out. That this is as good as it gets is the unreality that torments me with survivor's guilt.

Now, medicated and with an MFT license and a career in mental health, I recognize I was lucky to have received so much lousy treatment. Now I am privileged to create and deliver a concept of recovery that grows out of those experiences; but still, the Mad find themselves confined to prisons, hospitals, and concentration camps, and dogged by homelessness.

When I think of the toils of my clients, I remember the Mexican shaman in El Campo Verde. The old man and I sensed in each other a common ground, a sense I also get from the people I work with in Richmond. The more I benefit from this sense of camaraderie, the more I think that if this world is going to survive through the apocalyptic era of global warming that my father has feared for decades, it is going to have to start rewarding a different kind of knowledge. It is going to have to stop banishing those who offer it to the outskirts. We will have to remove the gags from those who are now deemed powerless, oppressed, and unfit, let them up into the light, and learn from them.

The Mad, once celebrated spiritually in sacred texts, are now denigrated in American society. People who care about them often refuse to connect with them for fear they will reinforce a "delusional system." I long to teach people ways to actually go down the rabbit hole. It can be fun. Learning how to manage the gifts of "psychosis" can lead to better functioning, in my opinion.

In many third-world cultures, the mad recover at higher rates and lead productive lives without the benefits of modern medication and treatment. And, even now, with recovery concepts starting to hit the fan, there are still no therapy treatments that have been developed specifically for psychosis.

I will take the beautiful wife and the beautiful house, but I will never forget. As a madman, I gave and gave to the rich who did nothing but complain. Still a steadfast madman, I dress up every day to fight the idea that a mad person needs to be bullied into endless submission.

I will never forget the injustice that continues to consign the mad to the streets, the back wards, the prisons, the jails, the ghettos, and the board and care homes. I will never forget how many of us are still fighting for freedom in America.

CPSIA information can be obtained
at www.ICGtesting.com
Printed in the USA
FSOW01n0830091115
13125FS